All the Weight of Our Dreams

On Living Racialized Autism

edited by
Lydia X. Z. Brown
E. Ashkenazy
Morénike Giwa Onaiwu

DragonBee Press
An Imprint of the Autism Women's Network

Published in the United States of America by
DragonBee Press
An Imprint of the Autism Women's Network
5100 Van Dorn Street, Suite 6633
Lincoln, Nebraska 68506
www.autismwomensnetwork.org

First Printing, 2017

ISBN 978-0-9975045-0-7 (paper)
ISBN 987-0-9975045-1-4 (electronic)

All the Weight of Our Dreams: On Living Racialized Autism /
edited by Lydia X. Z. Brown, E. Ashkenazy, and Morénike Giwa
Onaiwu
www.autismandrace.com

Ordering Information:
Quantity sales. Special discounts are available on quantity purchases by schools, colleges and universities, nonprofit organizations, associations, corporations, and others. For details, please contact the publisher at the address above.

All the Weight of Our Dreams

On Living Racialized Autism

Table of Contents

PART THREE: Intersected Realities

PART FOUR: Our Personal Is Political

PART FIVE: Cultural Work and Movement Building

PART SIX: Autistry

Dedication

For Abdirahman Abdi, Abubakar Tariq Nadama, Adrian Jones, Adrian Parmana, Ahziya Drew Osceola, Ajit Singh-Mahal, Alexis "Lexie" Agyepong-Glover, Antonio Jarrod Brooks, Antwone Nicholson, Asher Abdussalam Bashir, Avonte Oquendo, Basma Rafay, Brandon Thomas Williams, Cassandra Taine Killpack, Chad N. Jackson, Charnice Milton, Christina Marie "Nellie" Sneary, Christopher J. Melton, Cordero Anthony Webber Jr., Daniel Aswad, Daniel Corby, Deondray "Dooley" Ashe, Davontae Marcel Williams, Erianna Beltran, Faryaal Rashid Akhter, Gabriel Britt, Giovanni "Gio" Alexander Bass-Kopystenski, Gulpreet Kumari, Hana Alemu Befekadu (Hana Grace-Rose Williams), Heaven Octavia Woods, Jawara Henry, Jaelen Elijah Edge, James "Hymie" Many White Horses, James Thompson, Jasmine Nicole Bowman, Je'Nhyla Sharmaine T'Ara Simms, Jhoel Jesus Gaspar (Noria), Jonah Jackson, Joshua Jacob Mendoza, Julian Roary Jr., Kaiya Kalora Kapahu, Kazue Kawazura, Kazuko Saito, Kenneth Holmes, Lakesha Keyon Victor, Lavender Banks, LaVonnya Gardner, Lilian Leilani Gill, Malik Deshaun Drummond, Marcus Hill, Melissa Taylor Stoddard, Mieya Daniel, Minnet Cecelia Bowman, Mohamed Usman Chaudhry, On-yu Choy, Paul Nash Childs III, Raashanai J. Coley, Randle Carlton Barrow, Robert Antonio Guinyard Jr., Ronald Madison, Saharah Weatherspoon, Scarlett Chen, [Unknown] Seo, Seth Sueppel, Silverio González, Stephon Edward Watts, Steven Eugene Washington, Sze-ming Chan, Taariq Cross,

i

Tamiyah Audain, Terrance Cottrell Jr., Terrell Stepney, Teyshawn Daryl Young, Tia Ann Jones, Tiffany Pinckney, Timothy Boss, Thomas Wiggins, Tony Khor, Vincent Phan, Yusei Ikeda, Zain Syed Akhter, [Unknown] Zhang,

our fallen but never forgotten, whose stories in all their complexities must be retold in the face of racism and ableism that would stamp them out.

For Alexis Toliver, Amy K. Alward, Amy Frechette, Amythest Schaber, Andre McCollins, Angela Weddle, Anita Cameron, Arnaldo Eliud Rios-Soto, Ashe Nidam, Benjamin McGann, Bill Wong, Bo Broadnax, Brandon Bragg, Bree Ransom, Brian Thompson, Bridget Liang, Cara Meeks, Charles "Charlie" Fisher, Chris Akubuilo, Christopher Fornesa, Christopher Gonzalez, Cyrée Jarelle Johnson, D'Andre Williams, Darnell Land, Dawn-joy Leong, Derrick Land, Donald Washington, Eric Michael Garcia, Erin Brandeberry, Faruk Ali, Gillian Wilson, Heather Thomas, Hector Manuel Ramirez, Heina Dadabhoy, Huan Vuong, Ianthe M. Belisle-Dempsey, Jackie Pilgrim, Javonte "Jay" Gorham, John Howard, Kayla Baylor, Kayleb Moon-Robinson, Kiran Zubair, KJ, Kylie Marie Brooks, Lamar Hardwick, Leah Grantham, Leah Lakshmi Piepzna-Samarasinha, Leanne Libas, Leitha Wiley-Mydske, Lisa J. Ellwood, Lola Phoenix, Malcolm Harris-Gowdie, Mallory Cruz, Manuel Díaz, Manish Hudar, Marcus Abrams, Marques Carr, Maxwell Barrows, Melody Latimer, Michael Buckholtz, Michón Neal, Mickey Jay Samantha / Mickey Valentine, Miriam Dell'Antonio, Mónica Vidal Gutiérrez, Mustafa Nuri Çevik, Naoki Higashida, Nicholas Hemachandra, Nina Malaya, Olivia Montoya, Omoróse Añyá, Patricia Elaine Chandler, Phil

Martin, Reginald Cornelius "Neli" Latson, Reggie Williams, Reyma McCoy McDeid, Richard-Michael Horsley, Riley H., Rodney Jackson "RJ" Peete, Sabrina Zarco, Sahir Prashar, Sandy Yim, Sara María Acevedo, Seraph Isaac Jones, Silver Huang, Sofia Bonilla, Stephen Wiltshire, Steven Kuroiwa, Sunny Cefaratti, Talila A. Lewis (TL), Tario Anderson, Tito Rajarshi Mukhopadhyay, Tracy Garza, Troy Canales, Tzuriel, Xeres Villanueva, and so many around us and with us,

our friends, our comrades, our extended family—among many, many more—who survive, who resist, who disrupt, who *keep living* and *whose lives matter*.

Acknowledgements

Immense gratitude to Finn Gardiner for the cover design, Melanie Yergeau for the great bulk of the formatting, Shain M. Neumeier and Claire Barber-Stetson for assisting with editing, Amanda Gaul Worboys for handling legal and financial issues, Lori Berkowitz for web development support, Tracy Garza for final formatting technical support, Sharon daVanport for other logistical and moral support, and the rest of the Autism Women's Network board of directors: Corina, Heather, and Mara. We couldn't have made this happen without you!

Our generous supporters (many of whom chose to donate anonymously), whose grants and donations made this project possible:

The Autistic Self Advocacy Network · The Establishment · The Ohio Developmental Disabilities Council

Aaron Herman · Ailee Feber · Aimi Hamraie · Alex Conall · Alice Wong · Alison Kafer · Allan Hollander · Allegra Stout · Allison Fontaine · Amber Aschwanden · Amy Sequenzia · Ana Stanescu · Andrea Miller-Nesbitt · Andrea L. Shettle · Andrew Dell'Antonio · Anne Foreman · Ari Campbell · B. Lacki · Benjamin Lamey · Bethan Thomas · Bethany C. · Bob Yamtich · Britta Potter · C. Giulia · Carolyn Ogburn · Caitlin Wood · Cereus S. · Cheryl Green · Clare S. · Clay · Colin Kennedy Donovan ·

Corey A. Sauer · Cory Silverberg · Cristina Deptula · Daniel Au Valencia · Darlene Pineda · Dave Babbitt · David Cusack Johnson · Deb Duncan · Diana Crow · Diane Coleman · Djibril al-Ayad · Douglas Moran · E. Kimball · Eli · Eliza B. · Elizabeth Bartmess · Elizabeth J. Grace · Emily P. Ballou · Emily Sansom · Emily Titon · Emily A. Tredger · Emma Shouse · Emmalia Harrington · Erika Leaf · Erin Human · Erin Lewy · Erin Olander · Eve Neumann · Evelyn Israel · Everett Maus · Fran Odette · Gabriel Arkles · Hannah Dickens · Hannah Stern · Heather Powers Albanesi · Heather Ure · Ilana Watson · J. Bischof · J. Doe · Jack · Jack Robin Wright · Jacquelyn Hoseth · Jane Meyerding · Jane Strauss · Jennifer Allen · Jennifer Partin · Jess Wilson · Jesse Weinstein · Jessica Cowing · Jessica Hatch · Johanna Bischof · Jordan Glass · Joy Balaban Koenig · Julia Jones · Julia Watts Belser · K. Boatright · Karen M. Hillman · Karen Nakamura · Karl A. Krueger · Kate Kosturski · Kath Baker · Katie Miller · Katie Murphy · Kelli · Kerry Chin · Ki'tay D. Davidson · Korena Paul · Kris-Ann · Kristy Young · Lan Van · Lauren Reichel · Lei Wiley-Mydske · Leroy F. Moore Jr. · Li K. · Lori Berkowitz · Lucas Scheelk · M. K. Steffens · Maddy Ruvolo · Marie Lauzon · Marsha Rose Katz · Melanie Yergeau · Michael Dane · Michelle Lauck · Professor Morton Ann Gernsbacher · Natalie Asha Biggs · nekobakaz · Nick Murphy · Nick Walker · Or Glicklich · Peter F. Gerhardt · Priscilla Wanderley · Rayna Rapp · Rebecca Ferguson · Regan Brashear · Renee Speh · Rhonda J. Greenhaw · Riley Calais · Robin Mandell · Robin Penn · Robin Stephens · Robyn Volker · Samuel Barbash-Riley · Sandy Kinnamon · Sarah Hunter · Sarah Kurchak · Sarah Ross Pripas-Kapit · Sarah Teresa Gibbons · Savannah Logsdon-Breakstone · Shain M. Neumeier · Shannon Des Roches Rosa · Sharon daVanport · Shauna L. Phoon · Sheila Gibson Stoodley · Sherree Merenstein Drezner · Susan Marks · Steve Silberman · Steven Gould · Steven Thompson · Tara Uliasz · Terry Gibson · Thea Hutchison · Thomas Owren · Tobi McEvenue · Tung Shen Chew · Valerie Antolak · Ylanne So · Yoshiko Dart

Cover Art

Lydia X. Z. Brown

I drew the cover art in Fall 2015 using black pen and PrismaColor illustrator markers on drawing paper. The color palette is blue with teals and greens. The image depicts three smiling people: (left to right) Morénike Giwa Onaiwu, a Black woman wearing a blue patterned shirt; Lydia X. Z. Brown, an East Asian person wearing a teal collared shirt and black blazer; and F. Ashkenazy, a multiracial woman wearing a green patterned shirt and beaded necklace with an owl on it; all of us smiling together. Words above our faces in slightly stylized block letters say, "Intersectional Neurodivergence Now!"

A Note on Process

Lydia X. Z. Brown

In compiling and preparing this collection for publication, we chose to use an editing process that emphasized substance over style. Oftentimes, editing that focuses too much on "proper" spelling, grammar, punctuation, and other aspects of language only reinforces white, wealthy, educated "norms" of language and communication while devaluing and erasing language usages of racialized, poor and working-class, and un- or informally educated people.

Recognizing the violence of imposing such expectations on what constitutes "publishable" material, I asked our editors (three people of color and two white people) to follow these guidelines when reviewing and providing feedback instead:

1. Spelling should only matter when referring to proper names (organizations, places, people). The other exception to this policy is where a misspelling constitutes a change in meaning (i.e. "As part of ***pubic*** policy" as opposed to "As part of ***public*** policy").

2. We ask editors not to focus on grammar, style, voice, punctuation, capitalization, or spelling, because we want to encourage and highlight

all forms of communication, speech, and writing. We are aware that forced conformity to arbitrary standards of "better" language usage has a violent and oppressive history, especially targeting poor people, those for whom English is not a first language, cognitively disabled people, and uneducated people (which is often related to class, race, and disability).

3. We ask that editors instead work with authors to help them refine, expand, and deepen their ideas. In other words, focus on substance and content, not on form, structure, or linguistic rules.

4. As an example, a good and useful comment might look like, "What do you mean in this sentence? It sounds like you could be saying either (a) X or (b) Y. If you meant X, maybe you could change the language to say [suggestion]. But if you meant Y, maybe you could change the language to say [other suggestion]." An unhelpful comment could look like "This is unclear" (instead, tell the person what is unclear) or like "Fix all the commas" (instead, you can ask the person if their usage is intentional).

We provide our guidelines here for both transparency and accountability, as well as to provide context for our process that we hope will be beneficial in your reading.

Preface: Autistics of Color: We Exist... We Matter.

Morénike Giwa Onaiwu

For months it has saddened me that when people learn of our anthology on autism and race/ethnicity, some of their most common responses are confusion and/or bewilderment. Despite a plethora of statistics that document glaring and undeniable disparities that exist between white people and people of color with regard to diagnosis rates, access to critical resources/supports, outcome measures, societal perception, etc, people (white people in particular) frequently wonder, "An anthology about autism and race...why?" And several have remarked something to the effect of: "Autism is autism, right? Does race really make a difference?"

These aren't KKK members asking these questions. These aren't Confederate flag supporters asking these questions. These aren't White supremacists/hate group leaders asking these questions. These are everyday people. Educated people. Upstanding people. People who consider themselves to be progressive and supportive about these matters. They might work with autistic people; they might have an autistic sibling, partner, or child. They frown down upon overt racial discrimination and might have even sported a "Yes, We Can!" Obama sticker on their vehicle years ago when that was *the thing* to do.

They are our friends. Our colleagues. Our neighbors. They genuinely care for us and for people like us. They want the best for us. And yet their perspectives are so obscured by their own intrinsic privilege with regard to race and ability that they don't understand. Can't understand.

It should be noted, however, that it is **not** only white people who ask (or think, even if they don't ask) this. It is also something that people of color are unclear about—even some people of color who are autistic. In fact, sometimes especially among people of color who are autistic; many of us have a lot of unlearning to do. Ableism and racism have become deeply ingrained into the collective mindset of humankind. There are so many complex, unspoken, and often contradictory rules about behavior, identity, culture, and society for us to try to comprehend, exacerbated by the reality that since few of the messages we receive about our neurology or our ethnicity is positive, some, perhaps many, of us internalize those unflattering messages.

We—the autistics of color—are seldom acknowledged. Our faces, bodies, and voices are conspicuously absent from not only literature and media, but also from much of the discourse surrounding race **and** that of autism as well. And when we do appear, we are rarely depicted favorably. We are painted as defective, flawed, undesirable, *different*. To be pitied. Not only are we non-white, but we are also disabled too? Uh oh. (Or wahala—o!)

When people finally deign to discuss us, it is often to underscore troubling data about autism, most notably the tremendous *cost/burden* to society autistics are. Typically invisible, we seem to be only dragged into the spotlight as examples when others need to use us to make a point, and even then we are merely reduced to tales of woe and dismal anecdotes. Afterward, we—our plight, our issues, our needs—return to the realm of the ignored, collecting dust until we are needed to serve as unwilling tokens for someone else's cause yet again.

This might sound calloused, but it is the simple truth. We—those of us who exist at the intersection of disability and race—aren't treated as if we are "real." Little concern is paid to the innumerable factors present in our lives that impact how we view ourselves and the world, to how we ourselves are viewed by the world, to our strengths, to our needs. This is a grave injustice. Our lives and experiences cannot be splintered or subdivided into neat little categories; race over here, disability over there. We whose lives are greatly impacted by *both* racial and disability matters deserve to be more than tokens one day and non-existent the next.

There was nothing like this anthology in existence for people like me when I was growing up, and that is a shame. I would have cherished something like it because it would have made me feel less alone. Less strange, less weird. Less concerned by the fact that I never fit in.

It's true. I never fit in, anywhere. I was always "different." Never "normal." This is something I was acutely aware of as young as early childhood.

Some differences were obvious, such as how my chocolatey skin, full lips, flared nose, and thick coily hair differed from that of my predominately white classmates. Or the fact that my relatives were spread across three different continents and spoke several languages other than English. Or how my West African last name, which was two syllables and four letters long, apparently defied proper pronunciation by my (white) teachers, but my classmates' Western names didn't (including names like McConaughey, Kowalczyk, Oppenheimer, and Schwarzkopf, which I personally found to be harder to pronounce even if they were "white" names).

But other differences weren't as obvious. I remember helplessly trying to explain to a biracial cousin why I didn't "have it easier" than her merely because I was monoracial. We were both in middle school at the time, and she was frustrated with the endless microaggressions she faced from both people of color and white people about her mixed background. Her concerns were legitimate, as she was never considered "black enough" or "white enough" for some people who unfairly wanted to make her "choose" one over the other. But her assumption that I was "luckier" than she because I looked "black" and she didn't couldn't be more wrong. My experiences were different than hers, but they weren't easier. In some ways they might have even been more difficult.

Because of their racially ambiguous appearance, people weren't as taken aback if my cousin and her siblings didn't understand something in the way that they nearly always were when I didn't understand. However, in my case, because of my dark skin, because of my ethnic features, because I "looked the part," I was *supposed to* automatically understand and be fluent in all these random aspects of life attributed to black American culture. I was expected to speak in a certain way, dress a certain way, listen to a certain type of music, eat certain foods, date certain types of people. If I didn't do these things something was wrong with ME; I wasn't being "black" even though there is no singular way to "be" black.

I wasn't considered "black" enough for my black American peers; despite our similarities in physical appearance, I had a "funny" name, my family's customs, food, language, religion, and dress weren't the same as theirs, and I was viewed as "too white" in my speech and my mannerisms. But the white world didn't exactly welcome me with open arms either; I was clearly an outsider in that world as well. I was "too Americanized" to be accepted by many in the African community, yet because of my lack of familiarity with certain key aspects of American culture due to my West African heritage, to Americans I wasn't "American" enough.

And then on top of all of that I was a hyperlexic twice-exceptional autistic AND I was a girl; the way I spoke, interacted, moved, and processed things was so very different, which added an additional layer of separation like an invisible barricade. I was a minority group within a minority group within a minority group within a minority group! There was no place that I belonged, no place where I could find someone who understood me. Even those who accepted me, cared for me, loved me still did not understand me. Having something of my very own, like the anthology, by people and for people who were like me…just as different…would have been inexplicably meaningful.

Moving beyond my youth into adulthood, decades later there was still nothing like this anthology for people like me when my kids were diagnosed as autistic as toddlers—and that was only five years ago. Nor was there anything like this anthology for for people like me when I too was diagnosed just a few years ago, as an adult. According to popular opinion, autistic people didn't/don't look like me; autistic people didn't/don't sound like me. Autism = (white male-presenting) toddler wearing a Thomas the Train t-shirt; autism = (white male-presenting) quirky teen gamer; autism = (white male-presenting) geeky computer programmer; autism = (white male-presenting) adult rocking and staring off into space…a ready scapegoat for all of their caregiver's life disappointments; autism = Temple Grandin, puzzle pieces, ABA therapy, and Autism Speaks.

But now people will know better. They will know *us*, because we are right here, speaking. Speaking through our poems; speaking through our drawings; speaking through our essays; speaking through our art. We are here. We exist, and we matter. And we invite you…frankly, I *implore* you…to take the time to read this anthology. Take the time to share in our lives, our thoughts, our experiences.

Take the time for us to explain to you **all the weight of our dreams**.

All
(the whole, entire, total amount, quantity, or extent of;
every member or part of; the whole number or sum of)

"We who exist anyway
Our selves proof of a revolutionary survival power.
We who must keep breathing and breaking bleeding recreating.
Revelation."
(Lee Lyubov, "Revelation")

"I'm Black. I'm a woman. I'm the child of immigrants. I'm a
mother. I'm autistic. And I know there are more people like me
somewhere. Try not to be afraid; you're probably not as alone as
you think you are."
(Dee Phair, "Unpacking the Diagnostic TARDIS")

"We protect the places that protect us, and we are the shelter of
places that shelter us. We stand over our mothers' bodies and
sin....My children will be wrapped in the love my body has taught
me."
(Jen Meunier (Ghizabaeassigaekwe), "we autistics, we
villages, we humanoids")

The
(used with a qualifying word or phrase to indicate a
particular item as distinct from others; a definite article)

"Just as I cannot separate my disabled experiences from my
racialized identity and experiences, I cannot recognize ableism
without recognizing how it is affected by racism, or recognize

*racism without recognizing how it is affected by ableism. I
frequently center my work on disability justice, but the struggle for
racial justice is my struggle too. I, too, am racialized."*
(Lydia X. Z. Brown, "I, too, am racialized")

Weight
(the amount or quantity of mass or heaviness; the force
that gravitation exerts upon an object; a heavy load or
burden; the significance or value of an object)

*"I came to this place of assimilation through the sheer will to
survive, the sheer will to thrive, the sheer will to be considered
alive, a life worth living. I sacrificed my happiness and my health
to be the person you see today, the one who can look you in the eye,
the one who can walk without a severely non-sequitur gait."* [5]
(Pretty Eyes Ellis, "Blood, Sweat & Tears: On
Assimilation")

*"I couldn't save them from their families, couldn't heal their coping
mechanisms… I loved them, they loved me, & it breaks my heart
that so few other people saw what I saw."*
(Kassiane A. Asasumasu, "Things about working with
'emotionally disturbed' children that will break your
heart")

*"But I can say with certainty that it's not mental illness or autism
or an interest in violence or being bullied or social awkwardness or
violent role playing or violent video games or violent creative
writing that lead to mass murder….Ironically, those same
assumptions are used to justify real violence against people like me,
and often by the people who in theory are supposed to protect us."*
(Lydia X. Z. Brown, "I am autistic, and I am obsessed with
violence.)

"…I do not want another kid loathed because the media decided to pin the blame on their brain…. I do not want another child being isolated…I do not want another child to have nightmares like I did…This has got to stop."
(Kassiane A. Asasumasu, "Things about working with 'emotionally disturbed' children that will break your heart.")

"Yeah, I notice.
I notice that I'm different from other blacks because I'm autistic.
I notice that I'm different from other autistics because I'm black.
You Think I Don't Notice?"
(COBRA - Confessions of a Black Rhapsodic Aspie)

"…Violence against us happens all the time, both by other people in the community and by government forces."
(Lydia X. Z. Brown, "I am autistic, and I am obsessed with violence.)

"Once you experience anxiety to the depth that I do, then you know it will stay with you; it doesn't hide away, or leave temporarily— it's there for a lifetime."
(Keara Farnan, "A Struggle Within Itself")

"Autistic students need to be given more positive visibility, more of a voice….the intragroup diversity within this population ought to be included…"
(Joseph "Joey" Juarez, "Understanding the Challenges Facing Autistic Students in Higher Education")

"I grew up learning that Passing was Necessary. I grew up hating that I had to try to Pass."

(Jane Strauss, "Passing—and Passing")

"If my children are autistic or mentally ill or both, I don't want them to grow up in a world where their humanity is questioned every single day, or where police brutality based on their disability status could end their lives."
(Lydia X. Z. Brown, "I am autistic, and I am obsessed with violence.)

Of
(indicating connection, association, possession, or specific identity; pertaining to)

"Today I remembered from your graves and bones
that I am kin to you,
and you were loved, and therefore
I, too, am worthy of love."
(Kaijaii Gomez Wick, "Viva La Lebensunwertes Leben")

Our
(items those which belong to us; indicating we have possession of one or more objects)

"You are order, you are chaos, you are electric words
like stim and echolalia,
words that hum and buzz
and loll around on the tongue...You are me, and I am you."
(Kaijaii Gomez Wick, "Love Letter To My Autism")

"My love for my community is my shield and my strength...I am standing for love...
This is for those who I will know in the future. Who I love without having met yet. For those I know now,

and love with such ferocity there are not words for it."
(Kassiane A. Asasumasu, "Litany Against Fear/Litany for Love")

"Neurodiversity is part of a new scope of sight that needs to reach even deeper than social models of disability which retain the white colonial privilege of that delusion. Autistics of colour are among those who fall first and hardest to the violence against us that punctuates that delusion, and so our voices need to be heard across the movements that are rising today…"
(Jen Meunier (Gzhibaeassigaekwe), "we autistics, we villages, we humanoids")

Dreams
(a succession of images, thoughts, or emotions passing through the mind during sleep; aspirations; goals; aims; hopes)

"Learning to cope. Learning to stand. Learning to embrace oneself. Learning to live….Being human. Being accepted. Being loved. Being free…A growing community. Hope. Change. Faith. Surrounded by the love and support that strengthens us."
(Morénike Giwa Onaiwu, "Autism Defined")

"I worked hard to rebel against the labels placed on me, to be authentic. I am not a walking stereotype. Nor am I defined by diagnosis. I do not fit into the boxes others try to put me in. I am me. I am no longer an outsider."
(Stephan B., "My Experience")

"I am also happy to be comfortable being me, with all my quirks and routines."
(Jennifer Msumba, "All Kinds of Different")

xx

"I'm not a 'freak'—there are lots of other people who are different in the same ways. I don't have to keep trying to meet societal expectations and pass as 'normal,' because there is nothing wrong with how I am. I can't always speak, but that doesn't mean I will be silenced. I am free to take off the invisibility cloak."
(Shane Bentley, "The Silencing Invisibility Cloak")

"I want to believe in peace. I want to believe we can unlearn violence & affirm our interdependency. I dream of a community of lovers, who navigate pain, joy, laughter and grief together, collectively & with care; experiencing endless beauty. I think I am dreaming of a modern day heaven, or perhaps I am dreaming of the good we were meant to be."
(Ki'tay Davidson, "Why I Quit Philanthropy")

All the Weight of Our Dreams: On Living Racialized Autism.

What does autism have to do with race? It seems simple, but it is extremely complicated. I urge you to read this anthology and explore this in depth as you dive into the hearts of the authors. They are yellow, brown, red, black, and multi-hued; they are young and old; they share their purpose, their passion, and their pain. But before you embark upon this journey, I have a "spoiler."

On every page, in every account, from every contributor you will find one profound, universal theme threaded silently and artfully throughout the entire anthology. Again and again, you will find that the answer to the aforementioned question, now unspoken, "What does autism have to do with race?" is a gentle, but resounding, *"Everything."*

Foreword: On Autism and Race

E. Ashkenazy

White. Japanese. Mongolian. Black. Cherokee. Indonesian. Multiracial. American. Autistic. Married. Parent of an autistic child. Deaf. Bilingual. Jewish. Female. Welcome to my world.

As a person of color, I face a multitude of personal and collective challenges as I strive to define my unique experiences and to have my voice heard. The autistic community also shares this truth. The experiences of people of color, and of autistic people, are distinct, yet as a whole we demand respect. It is our right to determine how we wish to identify ourselves, both within our communities and within society.

This essay begins with a discussion on race and identity, which is in and of itself worthy of rich detailed dialogue, before I merge it with the equally diverse and multifaceted world of autism.

The human brain is wired to sort and classify what we take in via our senses. Though our brains are eager to work efficiently, it is a precious courtesy awarded when a conscientious person recognizes, understands, and appreciates the intricacies and details that define an individual.

I am a multiracial person who experiences disability. Within that simple statement lives a complex experience that only I can define.

One of my favorite aspects of being multiracial is my ability to easily blend into the various cultures I've encountered. In my travels around the world, for example, I have often been pleasantly mistaken as a native and it's a lovely feeling of acceptance and belonging. In Israel, I was Israeli. In Palestine, I was Palestinian. In Italy, I was Italian. And in Mexico, I was Mexican.

When I lived in New York City, my hairdresser was Puerto Rican. Though I am not of Puerto Rican descent, when I entered the doors of my hairdresser's shop, I was suddenly Puerto Rican. I looked like others in the community; therefore I was trusted and treated as such. I admit I basked in that luxury and always walked out with the best hair on the block.

A dear friend of mine is Vietnamese. When we're together, I tend to be pleasantly labeled as also being Vietnamese. The same thing happens when I'm with a friend of mine who is Filipina. I am transported to all of these great worlds and experiences simply because I effortlessly blend in with other people of color. This is the most beautiful part of being mixed, as sometimes there simply are no barriers to break. Instead, there are smiles, knowing nods, and gestures of acceptance.

When I look into the eyes of others who are of mixed race, I see all sorts of things: shared heritage, shared stories, shared joy, and shared pain. I can catch all of this from a simple glimpse. Whole experiences can be deeply shared just by looking another person like me in the eyes, even for a moment. Sometimes this other person and I might stop to chat and exchange backgrounds and experiences. Other times there's only time for a quick nod of acknowledgment, or perhaps an unspoken, "Hey, how nice it is to see another on my path. Stay strong." This is the beauty of being mixed.

My father was born in America. He identifies as white though he is a small percentage of both Japanese and Mongolian descent. My father is proud of his strong French heritage, which comes from his father's side. His family maintains their culture and traditions over here in America, as they keep in close contact with family members who still reside in France.

My mother is black, white, Cherokee, and Indonesian. She was born in Texas in the late 1940s and identifies as black. My mother acknowledges and appreciates her multiracial background, as her mother—my grandmother—often shared stories about her own father, who happened to be white and German. My grandmother also spoke of her mother's Cherokee ancestry.

Job opportunities and high ambitions moved my parents to many places across the east and west coasts. Our homes were filled with art that reflected our cultural backgrounds and identities. My parents proudly discussed our heritage, as well as who were as a family. I applaud their progressive approach, as the option to choose how I wish to identify played a huge role in helping me to feel comfortable in my skin as a person of mixed heritage.

I would like to take a moment to recommend Mixed Nation at www.mixednation.com. (Check them out on Facebook too!) This organization promotes a multicultural movement that embraces biracial and multiracial individuals. Celebrating diversity and cultural harmony, Mixed Nation seeks to empower, inspire, and embrace people from all walks of life, from all corners of the world.

Despite how I was raised and how I identify myself, people often assume things about me, and/or label me, based on either innocent or intentional biases and prejudices. For example, I have experienced insistence from others to choose just one race. This is unfortunate, as placing me in this position creates barriers and attempts to nullify both my voice and my identity. I sometimes find myself in positions where I am educating people that it is my right to embrace the identity that I feel best describes me: multiracial.

I feel honored and privileged to be able to lay claim to a number of ethnicities and cultures that are unique and vastly different from each other. It's as if I have the treasured keys to each of the cities I can trace my heritage to. But when I am mislabeled, whittled down, or subjected to another person's convenience and/or opinion, I feel that I am stripped of my crown, robes, and title of Her Royal Multiracial Highness, cursed and left to die by exposure.

Dr. Chester Pierce, Emeritus Professor of Education and Psychiatry at Harvard Medical School, coined the term microaggressions in the 70s. Professor Derald Sue at Columbia University has re-popularized this term, giving it the meaning of everyday exchanges that send denigrating messages to certain individuals because of their group membership. Social scientists have defined microaggressions as the new face of racism.

The Microaggressions project on Tumblr (www.microaggressions.com) has done some fantastic work to explore and share this concept and its impact on minorities, people of color, and other marginalized groups and individuals. In their words, the Microaggressions project is a response to "It's not a big deal" because "It" is a big deal. This project shares Professor Derald Wing Sue's expanded definition of microaggressions:

"…brief and commonplace daily verbal, behavioral, or environmental indignities, whether intentional or unintentional, that communicate hostile, derogatory, or negative racial slights and insults toward people of color."

Educating others about microaggressions is not about shaming. It's about showing how ignorance—even if it's innocent—creates uncomfortable, painful, and even hostile environments and places in society for people of color.

Examples of microaggressions include questions and statements like, "What *are* you?" "You don't act like most blacks." "Where are you *really* from?" "You're not very smart for an Asian person." "No, with those light eyes, skin, and hair, you're definitely white."

Arthur Chu, who explained that microaggressions exist because of *macro*aggressions, shared one of my favorite quotes about microaggressions on Tumblr. *Macro*aggression = shooting a kid. Microaggression = acting like it's no big deal he was shot.

My DNA report from 23andme.com reveals that the largest percentage of my genetic makeup is just about 60 percent Caucasian European ancestry. My other percentages are split between West African, Cherokee, Indonesian, Japanese, and Mongolian ancestries. I enjoy being a part of a good number of vastly different ethnicities and cultures. That noted, I am far from immune to microaggressions. Here are a few examples of microaggressions that have been directed toward me:

"Yeah with that dark thick wild curly hair, I definitely knew you were black."

But my hair is not thick or frizzy. Matter of fact, my hair looks pretty much the same as the naturally curly hair of most white or Asian people. And even if my hair fully fit the terms used to describe it, the sentence above is a loaded offensive microaggression.

"I see a little bit of Japanese or whatever, but with your coloring you look to be much more Indonesian or islander."

Yet Asian people of all backgrounds, whether they're from the north, south, east, or west come in various shades. Why is it so unbelievable that I could be part Japanese and Mongolian, especially given that I am multiracial and part black?

Not all commentary about my race is sudden. Sometimes, from trusted acquaintances and friends, I eventually hear microaggressions along the lines of:

"So anyway, as an African-American woman, what do you think about [insert the latest race-related instance that the media is currently covering]?"

Though I am familiar with issues that black Americans face, I was not raised in a predominantly black community. Therefore my thoughts on these ever so necessary subjects and discussions would be more accurately coming from the perspective of a *multiracial* individual who happens to be part black. I do not share the same lived experience as the specific community members being referenced in the said event. Matter of fact, assuming that one person can serve as *the* voice or face of an entire community is an assumption that has jumped straight from the hotbed of microaggressions.

"It's really cool to have a black friend! My world is just way too white!"

This well-intended microaggression serves to yet again whittle me down to *one* experience and *one* race.

"Wow, your baby's hair is almost as much of a 'fro' as your oldest son's hair."

Though they are multiracial, my three sons often easily pass as white. My oldest son does have coarse hair, yet my middle son and toddler have fine hair. The sentence above is a microaggression because it assumes that my children automatically have 'fros' no matter what their actual hair type.

All of the responses above were uttered by people I consider close friends or close acquaintances. This tells me that microaggressions can be born from the most innocent places in our hearts. But it is innocent ignorance that oftentimes tends to be the most difficult and uncomfortable to undo or set right.

I would like to share two more examples of recent experiences that I have had.

I have a dear relative who is white. When I mentioned that I am currently working on an autism and race project, she asked, "Why do you need to talk about that? What does race have to do with autism?"

Though her tone was positive and her heart genuine, waves of white privilege emanated from her. Here is a woman who I love so much who provides abundant fuel for my soul. Yet here is also a woman who goes about her life, traveling wherever she wants to in the world, doing whatever she wants to do, and all without having to think about race. That is, unless race is brought to her attention by a media outlet, or by a movie, or by a family member who happens to be a person of color.

Though race might not be an issue in one person's life, it does not mean that it doesn't either dominate or play a large role in another's. A more conscientious way of asking about the autism and race project (that would have steered clear of microaggression territory) might have been phrased, "Tell me more about autism and race. What are some common themes that arise?"

Actress Lupita Nyong'o, experienced public backlash when—in addition to her Kenyan heritage—she also claimed Mexico as a part of her nationality and culture. Though public outcries stated otherwise, it is certainly within her right to do so, as she was born in Mexico and speaks Spanish (in addition to English, Luo, and Swahili). Luo tradition calls for a child to be named after the events of the day, so Lupita's parents gave her a Spanish name, as they were residing in Mexico when she was born.

Why shouldn't Lupita be able to identify as Mexican-Kenyan or Afro-Latina, or frankly, whatever she best feels describes her identity? If Lupita were born in the United States, I am sure she would claim American status as an important part of her nationality and culture. Claiming a heritage and culture is not only about color. It's about lived experience, attachment, feelings, tradition, home, and love. One of the most helpful public comments I came across on the topic was simply put: folks just need to let folks be.

Lupita's experience reminds us that there's more to a person than what they look like to us, as the true essence of a person's identity and experience reaches far beyond skin color.

In the spirit of joining the national conversation on race and identity, I'd like to stress that if someone who is biracial, mixed with black and white, identifies as black, then they are black. If someone who is biracial, and mixed with black and Asian, identifies as Asian, then they are Asian. If someone who is multiracial identifies as multiracial, then they are multiracial.

As far as terminology and words that are commonly used by governing institutions and the public to categorize and describe people of color, it's important to know that not all black people embrace the term African-American and prefer instead to identify as "Black". Writer Maisha Z. Johnson explains, "My identity isn't as simple as saying that my blood is African and my nationality is American. It can't be contained by the national borders drawn by colonialism and imperialism."

So how do we begin a discussion about autism and race? How are the two related in significant ways? What do family members, caregivers, doctors, diagnosticians, service providers, therapists, and community members need to take into account?

We bring race into the great conversation about autism because autistic people of color are oftentimes having a vastly different life experience in comparison to their white peers.

Though many autistic people of color live in loving supportive homes, despite having the support of their families, they don't always have the support and understanding of their communities. How can we positively target different ethnic groups and cultures with powerful information that shapes how autism is both viewed and approached? What can we do to ensure that the information we put out serves to educate and enlighten others about autism and the importance of community support for those living with and experiencing autism?

It is human nature to want to be accepted. We all crave this feeling of belonging or of being a part of a group filled with individuals who love and accept us. It's primal: we have a higher chance of survival if we're part of a group that will support or take care of us if needed.

But what happens when we pick up on social conditioning in our early years that clearly implies or states that we don't belong? What happens when we see other people laughing together, bonding, or having a great time and we're stuck wondering why we're not welcome? What added effect does this have on autistic people of color? And what happens when autistic people of color feel unwelcome within their own cultures or families?

For example, let's say that an autistic person of color is being raised in a community and culture that generally tends to view disability as a weakness and embarrassment. This situation is very different from that of an autistic person growing up in a community where seeking a diagnosis and related services are viewed as necessary and proactive.

Let's say than another autistic person of color is a part of a culture that upholds strict expectations of how community members should behave both at home and in the community. This person will likely face more than just autism-related challenges. They might be expected to interpret, understand, and adhere to community roles and expectations that are usually subliminally picked up on in infancy and childhood. This situation can prove difficult for a number of autistic persons regardless of race or ethnicity.

Further examples of common themes an autistic person of color might be experiencing include:

- Struggling with cultural expectations on top of general expectations from parents, significant others, family, and/or friends.

- Living with feelings of being an embarrassment to both family and community members.

- Living with frequent harsh backlash when a parent, family member, friend, or a community member calls them out for stepping out of line, or for once again doing whatever it is that the community tends to frown upon or shame.

- Feeling out of place not only within the world or society in general, but within their own ethnic group as well.

- Struggling with culturally based power dynamics and/or hierarchical structures, both formal and informal. These dynamics can vary from overt brute strength to super-subtle unspoken agreements, communications, and interactions that would be practically undetectable without meticulous long term study of a cultural group's day-to-day living.

I'd like to peel away a few more layers of this giant onion by exploring a small number of firsthand stories. When I travel to give presentations, it is not uncommon for people of color to approach me afterward to share their experiences. I have heard a good number of positive touching stories, yet I have also heard countless heartbreaking stories.

One woman shared with me the struggles she faces in playing a large role in raising her niece who is autistic. They are black and she mentioned that they live in a neighborhood that's a tough area. With tears in her eyes, she explained her fears for her niece, as she feels that her niece might be targeted and cussed out and/or beat up by those in the community who do not understand or accept autism or autistic behaviors. She related how women in her specific community are expected to act a certain way and that those who don't "make the cut" become targets. There is also great mistrust of police officers, so it's not a simple option of being able to report bullying and abuse issues to law enforcement officials. Matter of fact, she shared that the police do not come to her neighborhood, and that even if they did, she would worry about them turning on her niece. Things could get ugly and downright tragic within seconds.

Another person of color I spoke with mentioned that life had been a great struggle for her and that she is oftentimes only a step away from suicide. She shared how ashamed she is of being autistic and spoke of how she feels like an outcast in her family, which is Chinese. She explained that in her culture, disability of any kind can bring shame on a family and is often a taboo topic. Her parents have been unable to accept her. In turn, this young woman has trouble accepting herself. She grew up walking on eggshells and was often heavily punished for not being socially aware of cultural customs, and for not performing at top levels in school. Her siblings graduated from medical school with top marks and honors, yet she is drawn to art, a passion her parents consider to be foolish and unexceptional. Regrettably, she didn't receive any disability-related testing or accommodations until she was in college. Luckily, at her current university she became involved with a group founded by and for individuals on the autism spectrum. She has slowly been learning to accept herself, yet the effects of her childhood, in her own words, will forever be a black cloud over her.

Another story comes from a father who lives in a rural area with his family. His son is biracial and autistic. He spoke of their countless experiences with racism, and of trying to make things better between both cultures from both sides of their family. What struck me most about this father was the pure love that exuded from him as he spoke of his son. Together, this father and son had faced a good share of difficulties, yet their upbeat attitudes, resilience, and refusal to let the bad outweigh the good made me think about how lucky these two were to have each other.

One of the most memorable stories that remains close to my heart involves an autistic teenager. She poured her heart out to me telling me that her family members who live in another state have never fully accepted her. When she visits in the summer, her cousins make fun of her and point out all of the things that she does that they view as "white". The very things her cousins are mocking are the things she's had to teach herself in order to survive and fit in within the predominantly white schools she's attended. Her cousins don't realize how much teasing she faces at school for being autistic and for being a person of color. In turn, this teen feels alone and isolated. She shared that her parents do not comfort her or try to understand what she is going through. Her mother's advice is often to ignore people who make fun of her, or to give them a piece of her mind. Yet this young girl feels that there's nothing she can do because she a) has little self esteem and b) is unable to defend herself with words when put on the spot. This teen confessed to me that she planned her suicide though she never went through with it. I think of this girl often, as she has the most striking friendly eyes that make you want to reach out and give her a hug. I hope things begin to work out for her over time and take a turn for the better. I am most certainly rooting for her, and I know that if I can see what's worth loving in her, then there are others out there who feel the same. But even more importantly, this girl must learn to love herself, which is no easy feat for someone who feels alone, unloved, and insignificant.

So what can we do as parents, family members, friends, service providers, and community members? What are some initial steps that we can take to bring these issues to the forefront so that we can address them?

Here are some ideas:

- Listen to and welcome the stories and insights that autistic people of color have to share with us.

- Provide a safe space and platform for autistic people of color and make it a point to hear their voices with sincerity.

- Be the change. It takes only one person, and then another, and another, and so on to clear away old thought patterns and ignorance and to provide fertile grounds for new approaches and ways of thinking.

- Monitor assumptions and realize that an approach that works for one person might not work for another.

- Invite autistic people of color to speak at universities, symposiums, conferences, and community gatherings that bring the very people together who can enact significant change.

- Brainstorm your own creative ideas and then run them by autistic people of color.

My thoughts and experiences form only my opinion and I do not claim to speak for all. My intentions are simply to point out that our lived experiences, family, culture, and home lives influence who we are and who we identify as much more than what we look like on the outside.

Social responsibility and conscientiousness involves asking people how they identify versus assuming. Social responsibility involves getting to know people on an individual basis versus lumping people into a general category or group. When we slow down and think about what we're assuming, saying, and doing, we just might offend a lot less people and become empowered to nurture enlightened respectful conversation and to embrace the future of a truly mixed nation that truly includes autistic people of color.

Introduction: Notes from the Field (Not the Ivory Tower)

Lydia X. Z. Brown

We have the right to exist as we are without fear of violence.

This should not be a revolutionary statement, but here I am, less than twenty-four hours after one of the deadliest mass shootings in the modern history of the country where I live, struggling to parse what I know, what I feel. As an autistic, disabled, queer, and genderqueer person of color, here I sit knowing people at the same or somewhat related intersections have been targeted in such a public way. Waiting for my comrades, my friends, me to face similar violence or its also violent repercussions. Knowing that too many people who claim to speak for people with disabilities, for queer and trans people, for Muslims, for (Afro) Latinx, Black, and Brown people will avoid acknowledging the complexities of intersected lives.

In the wake of the shooting last year at a regional center in San Bernardino, California where people with developmental disabilities receive supportive services, commentators asked in disbelief how anyone could target the disabled. They spoke as though violence against bodies deemed abnormal, defective, disruptive is somehow not already normal. This kind of ableism – the assumption that disabled people are automatically innocent angels untouched by and unaware of the real world – quickly gave way to declarations of the shooters' terrorist intentions. After all, they were Brown and had Arabic and Muslim-coded names.

In this same country, I witnessed a white man's shooting spree in Newtown, Connecticut where public obsession with the mass murderer's neurology still missed the likely trauma inflicted on him in childhood in an Applied Behavior Analysis (ABA) classroom for autistic children – the same classroom he went to during his shooting rampage. (Trauma never excuses deliberate, calculated violence at such disproportionate scale, but when this happened, only fellow autistic survivors of ABA got the possible connection.) I witnessed another white man's shooting spree in Isla Vista, California and the aftermath where his explicit statements that he hated women and people of color were ignored in favor of the designation that he was "mentally ill." I witnessed yet another white man's shooting spree in Charleston, South Carolina inside a Black church and the aftermath where his explicit statements that he hated Black people and wanted to start a race war were ignored, again, while he was called "mentally ill."

White supremacy – the prevailing value system behind structural racism – has to distance whiteness from violence. Nothing about strong manhood and hating women (patriarchy, misogyny, toxic masculinity). Nothing about patriotism or protecting so-called democracy (or empire) where really, only some have any political power at all and others are literally colonized. Nothing about anti-Black racism. Nothing about anti-LGBTQ hate and bigotry (queerantagonism or transantagonism or transmisogyny). White man murders Black people because he wants to start a race war; it's not racism but mental illness. White man murders women (and some men) because he is angry about not being dated; it's not misogyny but mental illness. Brown person murders anyone (but especially more than one person); it has to be "radical Islamic terrorism" (and maybe a touch of mental illness). The Pulse nightclub shooting in Orlando is the deadliest mass shooting in U.S. history, they say, conveniently forgetting, for instance, the genocidal violence of Wounded Knee in 1890, where U.S. soldiers gunned down anywhere from 150 to 300 Lakota people after repeatedly stealing land.

Today, I find myself again in an emotional slump, needing help reacting to something. Horror, fear, sadness, anger, devastation – these are the appropriate and expected emotions. They creep on me, but from a distance, as though I am already too numb to let myself feel the rawness in my soul. Now one of the deadliest mass shootings in U.S. history (a history rife with them from both individual and state actors) has targeted queer and trans Black and Brown people, celebrating, dancing, living on Pride weekend. And the blame has been laid once more on Muslims and psychiatrically disabled people. I fear for the safety of my comrades who can't be stifled into only one "difference slot" but whose lives and experiences will be sidelined and conveniently erased. I am angry about the impending perversity of targeting queer and trans people who are Muslims, people of color, and disabled in the name of responding to anti-LGBTQIAP violence.

They say autistic people lack empathy. I am living proof that often, we have the opposite problem. While too many of us are overwhelmed by extreme hyper-empathy, I'm struggling to reconcile my existence with a world that wants to stamp it out – a world with no empathy for people like me. I am told I can be successful and accepted if I hide my autism, or if I buy into the model minority myth designed for east asians like me, or if I stop presenting openly as queer and genderqueer. I witness another mass shooting – really, a blip in the violent history of my country – and I know the arguments about "those people" are coming. This week, the U.S. Congress will consider passing a law that would make it easier to forcibly institutionalize people like me or subject us to coercive treatment in the name of public safety. These coming months, as you read this anthology, the two people vying for the U.S. presidency will repeatedly shift the blame on people who happen to be Muslim and people who happen to have a mental disability as the problems that need to be fixed.

This collection is not easy or light reading. Autistic people of color come from different spaces and communities. We are on our own journeys of healing and self-discovery. We live with our own traumas, connected and similar as they may be. We know, however, that we need this collection more urgently than ever – we need the voices of autistic people who are also Black, Brown, Indigenous, and People of Color, who are also Muslim, who are also queer and

4

trans, who also have psych disabilities. We need to be present with each other, and to the extent it is possible for each of us, in combating the systemic violence that will target us in the wake of this latest mass shooting. We're already creating space of our own – from the revolutionary artwork of Sabrina Zarco to the groundbreaking activism of Kylie Marie Brooks, from Jennifer Msumba's work to end institutional abuse to Kaijaii Gomez Wick's searing poetry, from all of us, for all of us.

Race and disability may be in large part made-up social constructs – or ways of understanding people and society – but they indelibly mark the lives of people of color and disabled people, and especially disabled people of color. Racial and disability categories can both be quite slippery, with the specific characteristics and types of people put in one category or kept from another shifting by time period or cultural context. But we have to name racial and disability oppression, as well as the particular oppressions created when they overlap, if we want to get at the fundamental social reasons that autistic people of color face such disproportionate violence everywhere from rhetoric (how people talk about and around us) to schools and the streets.

Mainline autism and autistic organizations exist largely without us or with few of us autistics of color. That's not surprising in a constellation of disability spaces where Black disabled activists Leroy Moore and Emmitt Thrower were unable to gain full funding for their documentary on police violence against disabled people of color, or where almost all major works on neurodiversity and autistic politics have been produced in large part by white autistic people with few contributions from us, or where the Tuskegee syphilis experiments on poor Black men are rarely connected with the Fernald radiation experiments on children deemed developmentally disabled. Where too many of us share the unsettling experience of often being the only person of color in a roomful of disabled advocates or the only openly disabled person in a roomful of activists of color, expected to be everyone's well-behaved token and personal educator. Where those of us living at the crossroads of multiple marginalized identities and experiences have to create our own groups, as I did with the Washington Metro Disabled Students Collective in meatspace or a relatively new online group called Sick, Disabled, and Mad Asians on Facebook.

We need this collection because much autistic community activism, especially in the U.S., has focused on closing the Judge Rotenberg Center (JRC), an institution notorious for using painful electric shock as a behavioral modification, but in the many essays and action alerts, almost no one mentions that the vast majority of residents at the JRC are students of color (mostly Black and Brown) at over 75%. We need this collection because historical and contemporary eugenics have always tied together the fates of people of color and people with disabilities, from sterilizations in mental institutions to sterilizations in prisons. We need this collection because childhood (as defined by legal minor status), guardianship, conservatorship, incarceration, and civil commitment all depend on the interconnectedness of ageism, ableism, racism, and classism. Custody (the defining marker of childhood, guardianship, and incarceration alike), you see, means care and control.

We need this collection because racial justice is a disability justice issue, and because disability justice is a racial justice issue. We need this collection because the idea that we're all the same because we're autistic is just bullshit. Because too many people out there need the reminder that we're real. That others are out there just like them. That we can cut through white-centric autistic narratives and narratives of people of color who are expected not to be disabled in any way. That we are enough. That even when we're struggling with the self-hatred and the self-doubt and the years of trauma marked literally and metaphorically on our bodies/minds, we can and we must be here for one another. We must practice the lessons of self-care I have learned through the work of my queer and trans Black comrades who first wrote of its importance in maintaining the healing energy necessary for our souls to avoid giving ourselves up for the sake of the movement. As my comrade, Ki'tay D. Davidson reminded us, we are worth more than our production. Don't believe the ableist, racist, capitalist myth that we are only worth the number on our paychecks, or the letters after our names, or the number of actions or events we've been to as organizers and movement people. We are worthy. We are valuable. We have the right to exist as we are without fear of violence.

Our dedication names some of the many autistic and similarly disabled people of color we have lost to violence by family members, by treatment and services providers, and by police. I want to name those taken from us because their stories are often untold or else suppressed when those closest to them attempt to tell those stories. For

7

some of those killed, their families (of birth, adoption, or choosing) are already speaking their names, but are largely ignored in spaces where they ought to be centered. For others, their names might not be spoken much at all. In many cases, a family member was responsible for the death, leaving us to make a decision that it is important for us to honor the lives they might have led. These lovely people might have been writing poetry and painting landscapes for inclusion in these pages, might have been holding signs at a demonstration against the JRC or Autism Speaks, might have been organizing a new autistic-led retreat, might have been joining us for late-night, badly planned dinners where we struggle to accommodate everyone's sensory issues around different or mixed textures. They might have been part of creating our vibrant communities, but instead, they have been taken from us. We honor their lives, and their absences, and we work to change this world so we can stop this violence.

Our dedication also names some of the many, many others currently working, in whatever way, toward creating a world where we can actually enjoy the right to exist without fear of violence. Some of the relatively few who are openly autistic while also people of color, creating some space for themselves and for the rest of us if only by their visibility in whatever spaces they occupy. Honoring our past will always be important, but our future, and how we can make that future a non-violent, truly just, loving future for each of us – that is critical for our movements. This collection has been two years in the making, hindered by lack of funding (not unlike other projects and campaigns led by disabled people of color) and multiple intorocoting access issues, but we believe it has been well worth the wait. We do this work because we live with the shadows of our collective pasts, but also because we know that a truly just future needs all of us in all our magnificent complexities, in our human vulnerability and weaknesses, in our cultural work, in our very existence as what and who we are.

In solidarity!

Lydia X. Z. Brown
12 June 2016
Washington, District of Columbia, United States – land now occupied, stolen from the Anacostank, Mattapanient, Nacotchtank, Nangemeick, Pamunkey, Piscataway (Conoy), and Tauxehent peoples

PART ONE:

LAYING THE GROUNDWORK

A Letter to People at the Intersection of Autism and Race

Finn Gardiner

Dear readers,

You are not alone. That's right: there's an entire world out there with autistic people who look like you and come from similar cultures. Media representations may portray autistic people as being uniformly white, but that is far from being true; autistic people belong to every racial and ethnic group on earth. You don't have to be a white, upper-middle-class man from a western country in order to be "legitimately autistic."

Many of us pick up toxic, damaging messages growing up in societies that devalue us for our race and our neurotype. It is not your existence that is bad or shameful; rather, it is society's bigotry. We are told that we're intrinsically inferior for our skin, our hair, our names, our accents, our ancestry. We are devalued for the way we interact with the world around us, the way we process information, the way we hold our bodies, and the way we develop.

Growing up as a Black Autistic person, I learned a lot of destructive beliefs through this cultural indoctrination. I was constantly told, either directly or indirectly, that my existence was worth less than that of white people or non-autistic people. These took the form of covert messages, like the myriad times that I noticed that the people on TV and in books and in magazines didn't look very much like me or my family. Or all the coded language—"law and order," "the ghetto," "street culture"—that white people used to imply that any problems within the black community stemmed from intrinsic pathologies, and were not related to the systemic oppression and mistreatment that we had experienced under the regime of white supremacy. There were also overt messages, like being called ethnic slurs to my face by a classmate in Alabama. Learning how to respond to being called the N-word or a "porch monkey" in a social skills class, or listening to a junior white supremacist's fantasies about moving to a country with no black people in it, is a lesson no child should ever learn.

Similarly, clinicians, teachers, and family members would frame my being autistic as a series of deficits and unwanted traits that had to be expunged in order to make me "indistinguishable from peers," because acting openly autistic was a sin against the holy gods of ABA and Ivar Lovaas, and every other methodology that aimed to extinguish autism, rather than to work toward a society that included us. Flapping my hands? Unthinkable. Talking about my special interests? How dare I. Inadvertently making social gaffes? Time to be screamed at for five minutes straight until I'm so filled with shame

12

that the idea of trying to get close to people strikes terror into my heart.

I had to make my hands quiet and my voice demure.

Later on, I encountered the hateful rhetoric directed at autistic people that either insinuated or stated directly that it is better to have terminal cancer than it is to be autistic, or that autism is a silent spectre that creeps up on previously "normal" children and steals them away from their hapless parents, similar to the changeling myths common in Europe before the advent of modern psychology.

Though my examples are specific to those of a Black person growing up in the US and Western Europe, I do think that most of us who are autistic and experience racial prejudice go through similar experiences. Members of dominant communities push us toward the margins and render us as "other," while valuing the narratives of their own kind.

These messages are patently untrue; they're the cumulative effect of hundreds—even thousands—of years' worth of cultural programming. They are the cultural mythologies built up in societies that have engaged in white supremacy, colonialism, imperialism, the exploitation of indigenous people, and systematic prejudice against disability that treats it as though it is a fate worse than death, rather than a natural part of human existence.

Grand juries pay no heed to the wrongful deaths of black people like Eric Garner, Mike Brown, Tamir Rice, and Sandra Bland by the hands of racist police officers. Politicians like Donald Trump, Geert Wilders, Marine Le Pen, and Nigel Farage harangue about how brown people—who often belong to the "wrong" religion—should be deported from western countries. Respected collaborative blogs publish articles that declare, without any vestige of sarcasm, that there are benefits to bullying autistic people.

In *Claiming Disability*, Simi Linton highlights ways in which disabled people's lives are rendered less valuable than non-disabled people, including warehousing people in institutions like the Willowbrook State School in New York, where Geraldo Rivera reported that "one hundred percent of all residents contracted hepatitis within six months of entering the institution," and that "[many] lay on dayroom floors (naked) in their own feces." In Nazi Germany, people with disabilities "threatened the idea of Aryan perfection, constructed around a very narrow band of acceptable behavior, appearance, and genetic makeup" (Linton). Every year on the Day of Mourning, disability activists remember the deaths of disabled people killed by their caregivers. Katie McCarron. London McCabe. Alex Spourdalakis. All of them have had their lives cut short because the people entrusted with their care have adopted the mentality that disability is burdensome, and that it is more merciful to kill them than it is to allow them to live.

These untruths are inscribed on our bodies and imprinted in our minds.

Remember, however, that these images of your race and neurology that society has constructed—and the people who parrot these damaging ideologies unthinkingly— are not a true reflection of your worth as a person. You are valuable for your own sake. *There is nothing wrong with you just for existing.*

I know I benefited from encountering positive messages, both about race and about autism, as I came of age. Through the public advocacy work of people like Mel Baggs, Laura Tisoncik, Kathleen Seidel, Luke Jackson, Kassiane A. Asasumasu, and Denise DeGraf, I came to understand that autism was not something tragic or shameful, and that I could reject the pathology paradigm. *I was born right the first time.* Discovering the concept of intersectionality and anti-oppression, and the insidious nature of anti-blackness via the work of intersectional feminists and womanists like Monica Roberts, and finding community among other queer black men, allowed me to gain a healthier, self-accepting relationship with my blackness.

We in the autistic community should work diligently to resist these damaging messages and place the needs of those of us whose racial identity and autism intersect at the forefront, rather than being treated as a collection of tokens or erased entirely from the discourse. Combating this stigma can take many forms, depending on your comfort level, energy, and interests.

If you're an autistic person who experiences racial prejudice, here are some ways that you can counteract harmful stereotypes and myths. They include (but are definitely not limited to):

- Talking about how the intersection of race and autism affects your life

- Reading books and blogs by authors who talk critically about autism, race, or both: examples include Gradient Lair, Timotheus Gordon's blog, Intersected, and Autistic Hoya, and my own blog, Standing in the Way of Control

- Creating videos about your experiences

- Creating artwork or design that reflects your experiences with autism and race

- Connecting to people with similar experiences to you via social media like Facebook, Twitter, and Tumblr—for example, you could create a hashtag on Twitter, like "autisticpoc," for solidarity and collaboration

- Sharing posts about autism and race to social media

- Writing op-eds or letters to the editor

- Contributing to online or print publications

- Taking selfies with signs you've written about your experiences, and posting them to social media. Use a hashtag like "autisticpoc" so that other people can share similar photos.

All these things, whether they seem big or small, contribute to reducing stigma and increasing visibility. Our voices are important, and we should work to amplify them, rather than allowing the media to continue to peddle an image of autism that is white-centric and does not take into account the ways in which our stories deviate from the common narrative.

While all autistic people need support, understanding, and respect, autistic people of colour have specific needs that can go beyond those that also apply to white people.

Many of us are less likely to have been identified as autistic at a young age, meaning that people go without support and may not understand why they feel different from other people. We are also vulnerable to hate crimes or discrimination that affects us on both fronts. For instance, a young black autistic man, Neli Latson, was imprisoned for four years after being arrested outside his local library in Virginia while he was waiting for it to open.

As Kerima Çevik writes, "This disaster is the intersection of autism, ableism and racism colliding with the school to prison pipeline. See everyone who is poor in Black America prepares their son for that moment. They teach them the social cues and red flags. They tell them to have a way to make that phone call and an understanding that they will be harassed by police at some point. But autism parents are told they need to teach compliance and concrete ideas about police to their autistic children."

Latson found himself being mistreated not only because he was a black man who had the audacity to be in public, but also because he was an autistic man schooled in compliance.

That said, I know that fighting stigma on multiple fronts can be wearying—tell me about it. I've been there. Take care of yourself. Find things that give you joy and relaxation, and revel in them when you need a break from battling the ills of the world. Remember that regardless of what bigots say, you are worthy of existence simply because you're here on this planet today. All people deserve the right to dignity and respect. *Your life matters.* Keep fighting. We'll be here for you.

Citations:

Kerima Çevik, *Intersected*, "Making Neli Latson Matter: The Invisible Intersected Black Members of The Autism Community." 16 November 2014. Retrieved from http://intersecteddisability.blogspot.com/2014/11/making-neli-latson-matter-invisible.html

Simi Linton, *Claiming Disability*. 1998, New York University Press.

URLs for suggested blogs:

Autistic Hoya, by Lydia Brown: autistichoya.com
Autistics Speaking Day: autisticsspeakingday.blogspot.com
Gradient Lair, by Trudy: gradientlair.com
Intersected, by Kerima Çevik: intersecteddisability.blogspot.com
Standing in the Way of Control (my blog): expectedly.org/blog
Timotheus Gordon: timotheusgordon.com

Viva La Lebensunwertes Leben

Kaijaii Gomez Wick

This is an elegy for everyone
who could not chew their food,
or walk, or hunt, or gather,
who was no great inventor or quick thinker,
who was blind and deaf and had
brains falling out of their skull,
and who died of old age, buried with
ribbons of sapphire-studded gold and spears and closed
eyelids.
This is an elegy for everyone who has died
from their diseases, and who lived as long
as they did because someone loved them.
This is an elegy for everyone whose life was
called disgusting, unnatural,
a sky-heavy stone tied to a mother's back instead
of her greatest love.
This is an apology, an embarrassed offering,
my attempt to neither abandon the work
nor take all the credit, a song of gratitude
for living so that I may live.
I am sorry that I do not know all your names
or your gushing gallows humor
or the way you looked in the sunrise.
I bet your pillboxes would have glittered,

your cannulas danced, your hair fanned the pillows
like the blood from your trepanations.
God, I wish I could read your biting essays,
gasp at the pounding of your fist on a podium.
I am sorry that I do not know what fruits
or elixirs or liquors you loved the best, what
blood or fingers or skulls or smoke to offer you,
how to build an altar.
I come to you with this, a teardrop
keyboard-typed elegy,
to say that your life mattered.
To say that if you ever wondered if your
descendants would honor you,
the answer is yes.
To say that if you ever wondered if you could
make everyone of your blood remember
again and again that
the best thing about bigots
is that they lie,
that life is worth it, that even when
you are not productive
or beatific or practical,
you are worth any help you need,
you did. Sometimes when I am going
from one place to another I suddenly have
to breathe a little easier because the wisdom hits
me like sonder and sundry. I remember like
I remember a broken organ and my hair
tenderly braided in the hospital.
And someone braided your hair for you too,
and you were buried
and mourned and missed. I know your children
cried over your corpse for months—we

have seen your skeletons, your cavities
from how your lovers fed you dates
because you could not reach them yourself.
This is an elegy and an apology and a poem
of sobbing, aching gratitude.
Today I remembered from your graves and bones
that I am kin to you,
and you were loved, and therefore
I, too, am worthy of love.
When millenniums pass and they decode
my poems and gaze upon me, buried with letters,
loved in life, they will perhaps cry too,
remembering that there is no useless eater,
no better-off-dead, no joyless life,
and perhaps their elegies will begin as such too,
waterlogged, burned, buried.

PART TWO:

NEURODIVERGENCE IN A NEUROTYPICAL WORLD

Blood, Sweat & Tears: On Assimilation

Pretty Eyes Ellis

I've learned now that when I go on a date, the first thing I need to tell them is that I'm Autistic. It's worse if I wait, even if I think it shouldn't be. Even if I tell myself that upon getting to know me, they will understand. They won't. This world forces me to understand it, but no one will ever put in the effort to understand me.

"You don't seem autistic at all!" She says with a knowing smile, her cup of coffee casually held in her hand, tipping slightly as she nods her head up and down, smugness oozing out of her pores and dripping onto the table, onto her jeans, onto the floor. Her hair is glossy and it jiggles up and down, agreeing with her. Am I supposed to take this as a compliment?

"Thank you, you're right. You know my identity and my life better than I do. Also your statement implies that it is better to *not be* autistic, a statement which must be patently true. Thank you, neurotypical date, you are so kind!"

I die a little inside every time someone says this to me.

23

Who else has said this to me? More people than you would think.

My doctor has that same smug smile. He will indulge my delusions of autism, you see. He is doing me a favor. Unlike my last doctor whom I divulged my little secret to, the one who straight-up denied me care and asked me to leave her office if I didn't want to "grow up."

"But you don't *act* autistic," he says, pushing his glasses down so that he can look over them at me, the classic look of a disappointed father. He is a doctor. He deserves a modicum of my respect, even if he is being a jerk, so this time I answer un-sarcastically:

"You don't know what it took for me to get here, sir."

I came to this place of assimilation through the sheer will to survive, the sheer will to thrive, the sheer will to be considered alive, a life worth living. I sacrificed my happiness and my health to be the person you see today, the one who can look you in the eye, the one who can walk without a severely hampered gait. In order to talk to you at this moment, "like human beings" you might say (others have said), I did hundreds and perhaps thousands of hours of research—to copy you like a cat, to know what to say and what to do in this world where what you say and do is more important than how you think or feel.

When I was 8 years old, I knew I was in trouble. I knew I didn't fit in. How important is fitting in? Ask the bruises and cuts that appeared daily on my frail body. Ask my progress reports at school where the teacher wrote "does well at homework but does not contribute in class;" "needs speech therapy;" "has problems socializing appropriately with children her own age." Ask the elementary schools I got kicked out of. Ask the remedial P.E. class they built just for me, the "normie" children peering out of the window to point and laugh at me learning how to throw and catch a ball.

At the age of 8, I could not tie my own shoes. I could not identify the children who had beat me up in the school yard—I wasn't looking at their faces, how could I know? I could not speak in complete thoughts, if I had to answer more than a yes or a no my mind would just copy-paste from a book I had read or a television show I had seen. I could memorize entire books verbatim.

I studied neurotypical communication like my life depended on it. It did. I thought I did very well.

Somehow it wasn't enough.

When I was 18 I knew I was in trouble again. I've been in trouble a lot in my life; it feels friendly, almost homely there. I had just gotten out of the worst relationship of my life and for the first time sought out professional help on my own. I just didn't understand—why did I keep getting hurt? Why couldn't I understand when people were being cruel to me?

I told the psych that when I was growing up, the teachers thought I was autistic. My hippy parents fought tooth and nail to keep me from getting diagnosed, to keep me out of the system.

It was probably the best thing they ever did for me. They do horrible things to autistics to this day.

As soon as I was diagnosed on the spectrum, my counselor stopped talking to me like an equal and started talking to me like a child. She told me it would be better for me to live in a home, or with my parents. She told me to quit my job and get on disability. She said that people wouldn't stop hurting me unless I had the help I needed.

The help I needed was drugs and a group home.

Let me back up a little. At 18 (going on 19 at the time) I had been living on my own for 4 years. I had been working for 5. Suddenly after my diagnosis, I was told I couldn't take care of myself. That I shouldn't take care of myself. Words like "mental age" were being thrown around, my mother made me check in with her about everything and she bought me toys for my birthdays when she remembered my birthday at all. She talked to me like I was a little girl. She still does.

The group home was one of the most sobering experiences of my life. The most important thing I learned there was this: I may be autistic, and I may be a battered woman, and I may have a slew of other mental health disorders and problems immeasurable, but I do not need to live in a group home. I do not need to live in a home run by Christians where they force you to have meetings every week. I do realize my social worker was trying to help me, my counselor was trying to help me, my psych was trying to help me. I was in a desperate situation,

26

which often calls for desperate measures. But I am stronger than that and my life is worth more than that.

It was time to study again. It was time to assimilate even more. Once again, I hit the books. I made neurotypical friends and copied them in a near slavish manner. I hid my face from the world and put on a mask, a mask that I was afraid to take off even when I was alone in the still of the night, when my hands wanted to dance across the windowpane making shadows in the moonlight, when my body wanted to rock back and forth for no other reason than that it was comforting and predictable, when my lungs wanted to howl and shriek instead of "talk in a civilized manner."

When my friends wanted to cancel or change plans, I hid my anger. I hid the hurt that would last for days, the weight that seemed to want to crush me. I never asked for anyone to accommodate me ever—it was always my fault, I'm the oversensitive one, I'm the one who needed more time, more study, more fixing. I would lay awake every night, picking apart the interactions I had had—an activity I'm told neurotypicals do as well—except I was looking for different things. I was looking for where the autism was bleeding out, searching for places and ways to stuff it back in. Had my eye contact been too much or not enough? How long should I have held that hug for a friend I had known for a while versus a new friend? A friend of a friend? "What is the protocol?" I would whisper to myself over and over again, as if social interaction is a code that you can crack. I would feel ashamed of these thoughts, fully aware that "normal" people don't obsess over these things, "normal" people just know—they have a gene I don't have, they have a brain I don't have, they have a life I don't have.

I have since come to the conclusion that to utter the phrase "But you don't *seem* autistic" or any of its variances is more than just annoying, it is more than just rude, it is more than just ignorant—it is a violent act. It is an act which seeks to do violence upon my body and my soul. And instead of being disgusted by my own autism, I am disgusted that I accepted assimilation, and henceforth will seek to refuse it at every juncture. You will understand me because I will force you to. I will put it in your face and you will eat it as a dish served just as cold as the assimilation which society has shoved down my throat for decades. I will remain silent when I feel like remaining silent. I will dance when I want to dance. I will howl and shriek as the spirit within me moves.

This is a lie, and I know it. I still need to eat and keep a roof over my head. I still must fill out paperwork and say "Yes ma'am" and "No, sir." in that quiet, colonized, civilized tone. I am a person of color and I am small and I am poor and if I want to live then I must know my place. But I am fighting to make this lie a truth.

I am autistic and I am fully aware that I am part of the problem.

Assimilation—a saving grace or a curse? Assimilation—was I a part of something bigger or did I lose myself? Assimilation—through sweat, blood and tears I have come to this place, this place where you have the audacity to erase me still, and society dictates that I thank you for my own erasure.

Autism Defined: A Poem

Morénike Giwa Onaiwu

This is autism.

A world where we are defined as a list of "deficits" and "problems" needing to be overcome.

This is autism.

A world where our killers can be showered with sympathy and compassion for having had to endure a life with us.

This is autism.

Incessant fatigue created by having to navigate societies not designed for us, not respectful of us, not accepting of us.

This is autism.

Being misunderstood. Being judged. Being discriminated against. Being manipulated.

But this is also autism:

Learning to cope. Learning to stand. Learning to embrace oneself. Learning to live.

This is autism.

Originality. Uniqueness. Sensitivity. Detail. Tenacity. Courage. Truth.

This is autism.

Being human. Being accepted. Being loved. Being free.

This is autism.

A growing community. Hope. Change. Faith. Surrounded by the love and support that strengthens us.

This is autism.

The word that allowed me to finally understand my children.

Finally understand my mother. Finally understand myself.

Finally know myself.

This is autism.

Understanding.

This is autism.

Resilience.

This is autism.

Survival.

This is autism.

Purpose.

This is autism.

Future.

This is autism.

Acceptance.

This is autism.

It is me.

It is you.

It is us.

This is autism.

Portable Shame

Emmalia Harrington

To say a fact several thousand times must make it true. It's been drilled into me that being autistic means that I'm terrible at communicating. My screaming "You're hurting me!" and its variations every morning since I grew hair illustrates my troubles in conveying messages.

My mother with her wispy straight Caucasian hair was the authority on how to look after my mixed heritage scalp. The first and inviolable rule was that I could not be trusted to tend my own head, for I will make a mess, snapping strands and leaving nests of snarls in my wake. Screaming profanities and tugging my head until I face the ceiling is the gentler, approved method.

The second rule is that my hair must always be braided. My curly-yet-not-kinky hair is too slippery for cornrows, so it gets a single braid down my neck. Ponytails are the realm of hubris. To let more than a finger's length hang unbound is to cause each strand to lock together, making felt of human hair. The next time the comb would make me wail, mom would lecture me on how loose hair equals pain.

My screams are evidence that I can't be trusted. Sounds come out of my mouth, but I don't mean what they say.

Mom says I only make noise so she can look bad. Proof is dad's angry voice telling mom to listen to me.

Rule number three says that dad is the last resort for doing my hair. Though he comes from a family of hairdressers, and he maintains his wealth of tight curls with little more than a pick. Personal knowledge and experience cannot be trusted, nor his empathy for my plight. The only valid POVs come from the outside.

When he combed my hair, he'd respond to my wails and act with greater care. His words were mild, asking how I felt and if he could do better. I would end with a slightly rigid braid, not the floppy creation mom views as perfection.

More proof of my inability to express myself came after mom's discovery of wonder product one, Infusium. The tangles melted away! My hair was pretty from morning to night! My continued shrieking was contradiction of the truth, not to be taken seriously. Daily pain was now punctuated with bouts of squirting from the spray bottle.

Under Infusium's influence, my hair went bad with strands glued together until I manually broke them apart. Explaining myself to mom didn't work once, nor a thousand times. Mom would say it's my fault my hair turned unyielding in its spray coat, that if it bothered me I should brush it out when the spritzing flurry is over.

Along with hearing autistics can't express themselves, I have the dubious gift of remembering. I can't count the number of years I heard that I'm no good, I can't manage,

I make things worse. I'm not sure how I jumped from incompetent to just like other girls my age. The years of helplessness she drilled into me and my scalp make this a non-option. If I tried to take a comb to myself, mom would rip out the knots that form, reminding me that I can't be trusted to do the job.

Wonder product number two offered me a shot at independence. By relaxing my curls, my hair would grow tame enough that even I could manage them. Once a week in the shower with the shampoo and conditioning kit freed my mornings from pain. The Infusium bottle gathered dust, the comb ran through my hair in seconds, I formed my own braids, but nothing I did was good enough.

My hair wasn't uniformly long. Hanks fell out throughout the day to hang by my face. Shorter strands rose up, forming a cloud. The products must have weakened my hair, but the relaxing kit was not to blame. Me and my ignorance tore my strands into the puffy monstrosity mom and others saw. While socially approved girls went around with sleek hair or deliberately controlled volume, my cloud of curls followed me everywhere, marking my disgrace.

Well into adulthood, I picked up a photo of my six-year-old self. My face grinned at me from the pre-Infusium time of pain. A halo frames my head.

Months passed. Questions popped up willy-nilly, while old memories emerged. Before her wonder spray, mom tried other products to keep my hair down, but my fluffy crown never got the hint. At age nine, I tried to ease her frustration by tucking smaller hanks under the longer, pulled into control strands. During the times I had my hair blown straight or hot combed, stray pieces would slip and float in the air.

After a childhood of hearing I'm incompetent, keeping my hair clean and tangle free is not a thing to be proud of. No amount of brushing, shampoos or braiding will undo my curly haze or chin length hanks. It's never been articulated why they make me a bad person, nor why I'm supposed to have perfect control over inborn traits. As much as I'd like to ask, I doubt my autistic self could get the message across.

Caught in a Box

Fragmented Perfection (Cindy Facteau)

Caught in a Box that was fashioned by me
An escape from reality—a chance to be free
My only companion here seems to be Doubt
It screams from within and it pounds from without.

Obsessions crash in like the tide to the shore
They will not relent—they always want more
Misery beckons with a treat in it's hand
And grandiose thoughts suddenly become far less grand.

"A penny for your thoughts," is what they all say
I'm a dollar fifty short—I gave mine away
Retrospectively thinking, I should have kept some
But shorting oneself is so easily done.

Caught in a box that was fashioned by me
Doing my best to ensure I get free
If Doubt will stay quiet, I might get to think
And bring myself back from my perch on the brink.

A Struggle Within Itself

Keara Farnan

The anxiety that lives inside me never diminishes; it only keeps growing inside my mind—constantly. I feel alone and saddened by the fact that no one around me, not even my friends and family, understand how I feel; it's really upsetting. When I attempt to join a large group of people in conversation, everyone stares at me. They cannot see the pain that I feel inside: they cannot see through all of the fears that keep me from saying hello. I will turn my head from and glance back at them; I can never manage to make full eye contact—not even once. A part of me fears that if I say hello then others will turn around and walk away; most people do not take the time to get to know me—they resent me. It's never a mystery within itself that people entirely avoid me; I cannot run away from those who mock me, only slowly shut them out. It may be my thinking that keeps me from being happier; however, nothing is going to change at this point it time—only worsen.

I am nervous inside and a total wreck and I try and put these demons to rest; it's really quite depressing. A sudden glare or whisper causes me to think that others are speaking behind my back; it really hurts my feelings. It's my anxiety telling me that I may not be good enough: it's my anxiety that possess me. As I am standing before this large group of people, I realize that it's just me who feels possessed by anxiety—only myself. I don't feel like any understand just what it means to suffer from anxiety; it's difficult to describe, let alone manage—depressing. I can try to shut out those who continue to hurt my feelings and talk about me behind my back; yet, somehow the anxiety will continue to follow me. When I play these scenarios over in my mind I begin to go crazy; it's as if no one else can hear me—just my anxiety.

All my life I have struggled to manage my stress level; most people do not understand that it's not something I have control of. Once you experience anxiety to the depth that I do, then you know it will stay with you; it doesn't hide away, or leave temporarily—it's there for a lifetime. When I play my guitar it does help to ease some of the pain; although the anxiety comes rushing back to me, even as I strum the string, or form a "G major chord." My anxiety tells me that I need to play louder, even harder than before; I need to be heard for once. The song I am trying to play is struggling to form its own melody; it doesn't know how to speak for my anxiety. As I slide my fingers down to the third fret of the guitar there is a sudden hope inside of me; it feels as if I have found a song to play. I begin to pick the strings slowly and steadily, the pain diminishes for a few seconds; however, this only works for a moment.

I want to believe that there is more to life than just my anxiety; my anxiety is not my friend, nor is it something I should be dragging behind my back. When I try to hide my feelings of anxiety, I am only running away from my issues. I worry excessively, not on purpose, but because of my anxiety; it's something no one really understands. My anxiety is louder than words; it accompanies me throughout my life—it's in every breath I take. I try to walk away and deny that I suffer from anxiety; however, by doing so I am only hurting myself.

My anxiety is the reason why I cannot say hello as I walk past a large group of people; it's in my soul entirely. As I walk through life I know that the anxiety is always going to be there, right with me. The anxiety I feel inside is larger than I am; it is in the movement of my body and in every breath I take. My anxiety is a disorder within itself; it wants to diminish, but it doesn't know how. Anxiety, it always will be a part of who I am; it is who I am.

The Moon Poem

Taiyo Brown

The moon is in the sky.

The moon is small.

The astronaut flies to the moon.

The astronaut's name is Taiyo.

Taiyo is seven years old.

He flies to the moon.

The moon is big.

His dad pushes the walk button.

He is crossing the street.

His mom is at home sleeping.

There are 20 different stars in the sky.

***

Background information on this poem produced through a dialogue between Taiyo Brown and an editor:

1. Why does the astronaut want to go to the moon? "'Cause he wants to fly."

2. What is it about the moon that is interesting or appealing to him? "'Cause it has no gravity"

3. How does he get to the moon (you say he flies, but does he have a ship, or is he flying with a jetpack or something)? "He flies with a jet pack."

4. What does he do when he's on the moon? "He gets the rocket ship parked on the moon."

5. What does it look, feel, and/or smell like to him? "It smells like salt."

6. Is there anything else important for us to know about the astronaut? "The astronaut flies to space."

7. How did he become an astronaut? "He began flying around space."

8. What does he like or dislike about being an astronaut? "He doesn't like that other astronauts will fly to the moon."

9. Does he mind being so far from his family and Earth? "He's okay being alone."

10. On the flip side, how do his parents feel about his being on the moon or an astronaut, in general? "They feel happy because he will be on the moon having fun."

11. Would you want to say more about the different stars that you mention? What are they, and how are they

different from each other? "Because they have different sounds"

12. Does Taiyo visit these stars, or do his parents see them from Earth? "Taiyo sees them from earth by himself" or "I see them from earth by myself."

13. The stated topic of this volume was about autism and race. Is race a factor in the astronaut's experience? "No."

Bullying and Abuse

Christopher Tucker

I'm sick of the bullying and abuse of people on the autism spectrum so here's a list:

1. If someone says they have an autism spectrum disorder, back off and apologize.

2. Don't call autism an excuse. You don't know what they go through.

3. Try to give them a break. They don't know social situations like you do.

4. There is no cure for autism, it's a part of them.

5. People on the autism spectrum learn social situations. If they make a mistake, let them know and they will not do it again.

6. They can't control autism, so don't tell them to do it.

7. How can something somebody's born with be an excuse?

8. No two autistic people are the same.

9. Finally, be supportive and help them when they need help.

'Autistic' Name Calling: How and why it hurts an Autistic

HarkenSlasher

For starters let me introduce myself, I go by the name of HarkenSlasher (my AKA) and I was born and raised my entire life in The Philippines (sorry for my bad English), a Southeast Asian archipelago situated on the west of the Pacific Ocean. I received my official diagnosis when I was 2 years of age and I have to spend another 2 years in a special education class together with an intensive therapy.

Despite the seemingly odds that people around me thought I can't accomplish, I was able to integrate in a mainstream classroom during my first grade and currently I'm taking a degree on Information Technology in University of City of Manila without all people knowing my diagnosis. But like any autistics, my transition to various stages of my life is a cumbersome one compared to my Neurotypical peers. I can remember my grade school days as the happiest part of my academic life as I was still oblivious with social nuances and I have my younger sister as a classmate who can protect me from the school bullies (Yeah! Kudos to that). In addition, I was led to believe in a delusion that I was cured of my autism by a Catholic Priest (though I was still a pious one) by the grownups around me.

But everything turned upside down as I set my foot on high school by myself. I was ostracized for my obsessions (aquarium fishes at that time), fleeting gazes, awkward gestures, hyperactivity and frequent meltdowns. To make matters worse, my 'tormentors' began calling me names and used my diagnosis as a frequent taunt without knowing the fact that I'm really autistic. Emotionally drained, I started to ask questions until I saw in the internet my condition. "I was autistic indeed." I concluded and felt some relief.

Armed with the concrete justification of my neurology, I was just ready to blurt out my diagnosis but I was appalled with the ignorance and of harshness of people regarding autism that I decided not to "spill the beans" for the meantime.

Recently as I was presenting my thesis proposal about an application that teaches visual skills to autistic kids to my professor, he jests that I should try testing my application to one of my colleague. I hate to say this as I'm in no way a qualified professional to give diagnosis and judge a person if s/he's autistic or not but in some degree I can relate my hidden behaviors to this colleague. Anyway, I just bit the bullet, pretended to giggle and berate him by saying "How rude sir!" in a joking manner.

But behind my grins, I have the sinister motive to knock the sense out of this bigoted person. But then again I just carried on. Seriously though, I was hurt deep inside. I do not want to be known as a laughingstock and my stimming and repetitive behavior summed up as running gag. Furthermore, my professor that also happened to be a gay man should understand the plight of those in other minority group. He should also feel the same pain of being caricatured as a butt of jokes in movies, films, TV, etc.

Sadly this doesn't end here; my other colleagues started making autistic jokes and I can't forget one of them saying that it will miserable if s/he should know that they are autistic. To add insult to the injury, when it is finally our call to defend our thesis, my panelists who although gave the green-light made another remarks, used autism again as a stuff to laugh at.

"Sigh! I give up!" I said exasperated while monologuing with myself.

I infer that the root cause of this incessant 'autistic' name calling is the sheer lack ignorance of autism itself together with the putrid trait to make an initiative to make fun of imperfections, flaws and anything deviating from the norm deep ingrained in the Filipino culture.

As you can see, we Filipinos have the propensity to describe something in a creative yet degrading way. It seemingly became a way of our life that it came to the point from government officials, church leaders, celebrities to young people to use autistic as a slur to add punch to jokes or insults. Also, being called autistic here in our country immediately equates that a particular person has a laughable behavior.

In addition, the situations is also aggravated by the seriously low awareness (let alone acceptance) of Autism in our country. Most of my fellowmen forget that Autism is a spectrum disorder which means it is not a one-size fits all description. We autistics share some core symptoms such as impairments in social development, communication and having repetitive behaviors but it doesn't mean that every autistic is a Rain Man with savant like abilities or a non-verbal one with a mentality of a 5 year old. Just like any individuals with autistic individuals as no exception, we have a variety of traits, personality, gifts, challenges and the like that it's impossible for a person to pigeonhole us into a Caricaturish character. You can encounter us from wide array of places, time and locations such as special education schools, grocery stores to the upper echelons of the corporate world. Unfortunately, in my country people here are prevented from seeing the plethora of different autistics in different spectrums as people here are blinded by their reliance in knowing information in television, media and pop culture.

I admit that although autism was covered in our local news to some extent, it still fails to show any positivity or more importantly other autistics from other spectrums. Instead the mainstay of our television stations in their programs is about the hardships and struggles of a weary mother from raising his autistic child. And for the record this is what I hate most but no local TV station had ever attempted to film news, documentary or something that shows an autistic who speaks for himself/herself (let alone the achievements and merits). It always boils down to the parents who do the talking with their autistic child only in the backseat or not at all when it comes to representation. Because of this, people and especially the Filipino people thought that all of autistics are not intelligent, child and child-like. Consequently we autistics are infantilized in the process.

Ironically, our national Autism Society raised a campaign not to use the 'Autistic' word in a derogatory manner due to its rampant use as mentioned earlier yet they insist that to use a person-first language (which denies me of who I am) to refer to autistic people. Presumably they made this move to avoid the negative connotations with autism to be attached permanently with the person but on the other side; I felt I'm robbed of the liberty to use a word that describes me best and betrayed at the same time by the organization that I trust to celebrate my difference but in contrast chose to treat it like a cancerous growth that must be removed from me.

Then again, I blame this to the narrow minded people (pointing to my fellow countrymen) who thought that name calling someone as 'autistic' will make them funnier and that must be simply dismissed as "just a word". Change must begin now as not only autistic individuals are harmed but also countless individuals who are also affected by this seemingly harmless teasing.

As an Autistic, it is my right to claim the word "autistic" as a word that is a part of my personality and gifts without the negative repercussions associated with it during a long time of ignorance and ableism such as being hopeless, retarded, desperate parents, locked in his/her own world and a lesser human. Moreover, please do not sugarcoat my diagnosis and neurology with terms such as special child, angels or other condescending whatnots

For the mean time though, I'll just try my to best to hide in my Neurotypical shell and brush off this harsh name callings until the day that Autism comes a gift to be celebrated rather as a curse.

Confusing Friendships

Keara Farnan

Walking away from the crowd,
Frustration inside,
I will try to speak,
Though the words;
They never come out right.

When angry, you walk away;
You will not even look at me.
Sky up above—melancholy;
You won't talk to me, or open up.
As I am walking around,
Footsteps loud and clumsy,
I try to recall why

You do the things you do,
No explanation.
I am not going to fight, say it isn't so,
Across, over there I thought that,
Maybe I was understood.

When upset, you look
Red-flushed lines on your face.
When angry, you refuse to speak,
Though it shows
Nothing I knew before.

Walking around, you
Seem unconvinced.
When pacing back and forth,
You seem too unsure of what to do.

Laughing at my jokes,
Recalling memories,
I feel like there's no way
To prove to you that you
Were wrong.

When listening to the words,
Coming out of my mouth,
No direct eye contact.

Driving away in your car,
Other direction you may go,
Leaving fears to rest.
Never saying anything at all,
Just being awkward,
Not looking you in the eyes.
Being coy and acting shy,
Maybe to say that I am afraid
I will mess things up.

Anxious and unsure in the streets
As you get out of your car,
Walking into the house,
Receiving too many—what feels
Like complaints unsaid.
When upset and angry at me,
I am sure that you may feel
At times you would like to walk away.

Uptight with a clenched fist,
Numbness in my hands,
I don't know why
This is such an attempt.
When frustrated,
No words at all.
Looking back,
Memories are unclear.

Understanding the Challenges Facing Autistic Students in Higher Education

Joseph "Joey" Juarez

The increasing rate of autistic students is the highest growing demographics of people with disabilities on college campuses and is expected to continue to rise at a fast pace (Pinder-Amaker, 2013.) Among the groups within the autistic community which are in a particular disadvantage are the Latinx, African American as well as other autistic students of color who do not conform with the heteronormativity of gender and sexual orientation in addition to other socially constructed confines along with how they are mutually constitutive. Once these students arrive to the college scene, gaps of disparity begin to develop between neurotypical and autistic students in college classrooms (Gobbo, 2014). Those disparities will amplify in their college lives if their needs are neglected or not adequately addressed. In general, individuals in the Autism Spectrum face an array of difficulties navigating the complexities of college student life (Well, et al. 2014). A practical approach then, is to begin a constructive dialog across the main campus components, administratively, academically and psychosocial with the vision to improve their college experience and to integrate this population into existing campus spaces or to create their own.

Autistic students navigate college life and encounter difficulty doing so in conjunction with social demographics. One of the goals of transitioning autistic students into college life entails addressing academic, psychosocial, intra-personal, extracurricular, and institutional aspects where students on the autism spectrum are struggling in conjunction with other marginalized identities. Part of the general consensus of current academic literature (Well, et al. 2014) is that autistic students face difficulties with relationships in colleges and that they are particularly likely to go awry. These relationships include interpersonal, housing inside and outside of college affiliation, extracurricular affiliations, administrative personnel, as well as professional interactions with faculty and staff. Autistic students also lack navigational capital: "Navigational capital refers to skills of maneuvering through social institutions." (Yosso, 2005) Autistic students are the fastest growing demographic of people with disabilities on colleges. They are particularly reluctant to disclose their disability which is negatively impactful since they cannot access academic accommodations, thus negatively predicting their academics outcomes. Autistic students are more likely to be misunderstood by authority figures, increasing their risk to be cited and perhaps even dismissed from their university. Their difficulty with relationships is inherent to their less developed social cognition[2], which is the ability to sense social dynamics and adjust accordingly, thus by the nature of their condition it is amplified at the college context.

Coming into a college campus as an autistic student can be an intimidating and in some cases overwhelming life situation. Often misunderstood and in danger to get in trouble by the campus administration, police and their representatives as well as other authority figures is an everyday challenge. As an example, a white male acquaintance of mine who is on the spectrum and was diagnosed this year, confided in me how his behavioral quirks were perceived as sexual advancements in the view of a couple of women. As a result an investigation was opened by the campus authorities that accused him of sexual harassment, an unfortunate result of misperceptions inherent to his daily autistic behaviors that had nothing to do with targeting his accusers. Although most colleges have a department within campus such as OSD (Office for Students with Disabilities) that focuses their effort to aid these students academically, this office does not just dedicate their efforts to autistic students as their efforts focus on students with disabilities broadly that qualify for services. Also, for reasons other than academic, this population struggles with student life. Trying to assert and encounter their own identities and how their disability and developing identities fit in the complex campus life is a major challenge. Having said that, it is also important to consider to what extent autistic students utilize generic services and resources within their college campus and available to all students such as Counseling and Psychological Services, Legal Services, Health Services, etc. Autistic students have underdeveloped self-advocacy skills compared to neurotypical students thus assisting autistic students with self-advocacy at the college level when it is a period where one sets foundations for their future is in much need at college campuses across the board.

As with social demographics generally if we address autism as a monolith we risk enabling only the most privileged members of such to benefit or at least optimally benefit from whatever is available from advocacy. For instance, many social justice movements have historically granted access to the optimal benefits of its advocacy only to its most privileged members including but not limited to the civil rights movement, first wave feminism, LGBT rights movement, disability rights movement including neurodiversity movement, reproductive rights movement, Chicano movement, etc. I highlight this insofar as to point out how when one addresses social demographics in isolation across contexts advocacy further privileges its most privileged members while keeping its less privileged members from experiencing the optimal benefits of advocacy. As the current prevalence of autism is estimated to be one in sixty eight and may grow, one in sixty eight minors are eventually going to become adults. Therefore, higher education generally needs to prepare itself to accommodate these incoming students as not doing so would be presupposing the continuous marginalization of one in sixty eight of our national population. Also, higher education cannot effectively accommodate this population if they address autism as a monolith.

An important aspect within campus life is their police/security personnel's lack of sensitivity towards a population that may act odd or different but without violating any specific laws or rules per se. Some autistic people have non-threatening, harmless rituals that get them in trouble with authorities very easily. I have observed personal experiences during my undergrad years living at the university dorms that were viewed as "housing violations" although they were totally harmless. Looking back now at those incidents I know that if it was not for outside assistance resolving those issues they could have escalated such that I could have been expelled and would have never been able to complete my undergraduate degree and pursue my Master's degree. Therefore, university housing is an outfit within campus that needs improvement on how to deal with autistic students in general. Although those instances were without major consequences, I can see how easy would be for an autistic student living at university dorms to end up in the wrong place at the wrong time. In a way the media is responsible for picturing anyone with a mental disability as violent and dangerous. We see those assumptions that if a person is "mentally ill" they therefore pose great danger and are therefore stigmatized. (Link, B.G., 1987) Thus if we can bring more awareness to the campus security officers and housing personnel more generally there would be less misunderstandings and threatening scenarios for the autistic students we will have in the future. There is a perception that autistic adults are more likely to be psychopaths than neurotypicals when that is not the case at all and there are actually more neurotypical psychopaths than autistic psychopaths (Kapp, S. et. al. UCLA.) Therefore, a comprehensive study of this population is of dire necessity to bring visibility to autistic students and their issues to develop a better understanding of the extent to which autistic students are integrated and accepted within our student life diversity as well as the extent to which they are disintegrated and unaccepted within our student life diversity.

Our college campuses are not as diverse to the extent our campus personnel claim. The more awareness we have of underrepresented (Brown, R. 2000) students on our campus and the more of those students we take into our school the closer we get to have a climate of student life that is accepting across difference for all populations. We can diversify our campus and if this means allocating more resources for students of different identities, then so be it. As Alice Walker states, "The most common way that people give up their power is by thinking they don't have any."

Autistic students need to be given more positive visibility, more of a voice, and as with every population, the intragroup diversity within this population ought to be included if we are to push for optimal change in our student lives. we must take intergroup and intragroup differences, dynamics, and issues into account. We all live systems of inequity so it depends on what aspects we experience privilege and disadvantages and in what contexts. We also must understand how systems of power, privilege and oppression jeopardize students on the autism spectrum in terms of their life experiences and quality of life. Doing so and following through with it would eventually result in a genuinely integrated university rather than one where people of different populations happen to be warehoused in the same place in which it is disjointed. As much as possible let's not wait until an issue that bothers majority or dominant people comes up to address matters of diversity.

It is already challenging enough for students of minority populations to navigate college life but it is especially hard for autistic students given their social cognitive challenges.

Passing Strange

Eliora Smith

The sunlight turns me into an
Olive tree,
Old lands inside me and
Wind in my leaves.
My smile betrays the shadow of my mother's nose,
Ghosts of the dead
Rumbling beneath my skin.
Happy, joyful, free I stim
Like a hurricane,
Uncontrollable and
Uncontrolled.
The Shekinah rages through my branches,
Nothing stopping me from
Jumping, rocking,
Flapping.

People do not see me like this.

Sunlight is
Toobrighttoohairshtoohard,
I smile differently in public and
Do not let them capture it on film.
I am afraid to let the hard permanence of captured light
Reveal the past, the present, and myself.
(I am learning to smile in public. I am learning not to care.
I am learning I am beautiful.)

I think it is better to drown, unnoticed and unheard
Than have them steal my breath and blood and bones.
So I am never
Happyjoyfulfree
Where they can see me.

I stim hard when I am afraid
(I am never not afraid)
Stim hard when the fear becomes
Imminent, urgent,
Hands twisting feet rocking bounce bounce bounce,
Chew pencils to nubs suck quarters to feel
Cool in my mouth, solid.
I am by myself and I have
No name.
Brokenfreaklazyfaker "eccentric"
Boxes built with degrees of disdain.
(I have a word
A box I will keep like a shelter
And hang a mezuzah on its door.
I am not broken, not wrong, not faking
Only "different".
Maybe strange, but now I am no stranger—
I am myself and I am not alone.)

I have learned to live with
Fear. It is constant and so only grows beyond me
When there are doctors deans men with white coats and
rules.
Fear will keep me safe in the end,
Like it kept my great grandmother grandmother mother
safe.
Keep me running, keep me careful.

Fear will keep me quiet, so they don't see.
There is fear in my blood and in my books and on my
walls
A history of hatred taught me how to be afraid
(20 years of head-racing heart-pumping blood-burning
fear and there is nothing left
But exhaustion.)

I shut down when there is too much.
(There is always too much sometimes it piles high enough
To knock me down.)
I am one of the lucky ones.
I am invisible,
And what they cannot see they will let pass.
Silent and broken they do not fear me;
I think they prefer it.
When I am excited I get big and loud, full of gestures and
Words,
And they do not like this.

In school I am:
Weird dresses Jewish comb your hair,
Hush too loud perk up smile,
Let everyone else talk, conceited
Clumsy,
Creepy talks to herself stares too much,
Why are you crying, it was 60 years ago,
Weird.

A collection of words which mean outsider.

There is no group for what I am.
I am not white, I am afraid of them.

(All this can be taken away,
Remember when remember when remember when.)
I sit alone in English class while they read "Night"
Like something once upon a time and far away,
And I listen while they remind me:
I was hated the day I was born.
I am not "normal".
(What does that mean? I cannot divine the magic formula
rule book cheat sheet even enough to know how I am
breaking it.)

Years later I will know there were
A thousand signs
And a thousand fears barely known that make me
Not like them.
I will realize this was always there and I was always me
As I struggle to breathe behind my mask.
But I am invisible
Or else they do not care to look.

Why I Decided to "Come Out" of the Autism Closet

Morénike Giwa Onaiwu

I've always been autistic, but I haven't always known it. I've known that I was different from other people, but that difference didn't have a name that I was aware of. It was just the way I was. Some of the ways that I was different were things that were pretty cool. Like the way I could easily remember and reproduce much of what I'd seen or heard; the way I could figure things out that stumped other people; how deeply I felt about things; my naturally authentic nature.

Other things, though, seemed more challenging for me than other people, like socializing, making myself understood, unpleasant noises and sounds, and dealing with sudden changes. I was a living contradiction: I was reading on a college level in early elementary school but couldn't tie my own shoelaces; I could endure intense pain but the sensation of a tag from a shirt against the back of my neck or water inside my ears generating endless tears; I could converse easily with adults but struggled to make sense of my peers' chatter. And even when comfortable, sometimes I couldn't speak at all, because the words wouldn't come out right or were too hard to find—and I needed my pen and paper to speak for me. Etc, etc. My communication, socialization, sensory experiences, and speed/manner of processing and responding to everything were so very different than everyone's (except my mom).

Being the way I was...it was the only way I knew how to be. For the most part I didn't have a problem with myself, though I did wish things that were so easy for other people weren't so hard for me. So I guess I did somewhat have a problem with myself, but only in comparison to other people; not from within. Because of that, I struggled with accepting myself for years because it seemed that who/what I was must somehow be wrong. Fortunately, eventually I realized I was exactly the person I was supposed to be. Sadly, it took years. But at least it happened. It still didn't have a name, but I didn't know there was a name anyway.

Speaking of names, until adulthood I had scarcely even heard the name of term "autism." I had little concept what it was. I recall a daytime soap opera I watched as a child that featured a character who had an autistic daughter. In most episodes the daughter was hidden away at some expensive "special school." Shockingly, the girl's mother was embezzling funds—to pay for her daughter's tuition. According to the storyline, she felt that she had no other options. The take away message seemed to be that autism was something rare, debilitating, and tragic—and that those unfortunate enough to be afflicted by such a thing required costly care. Other than that, I had little conscious exposure to known autistics nor information about autism. It just didn't come up.

Fast forward many years to motherhood, in which I find that I am blessed with the most amazing children on the planet, two of whom happen to be on the autism spectrum. It was through their diagnoses, subsequent research, and thorough self-evaluation that I began to seek answers about my own neurology. Through them, I first suspected and later confirmed that I was autistic too but simply hadn't been aware. It was extremely eye-opening and powerful for me to finally have this insight about myself. Equipped with this new knowledge, everything began make so much sense to me.

I only wished that I had been able to have this awareness much younger, when I needed it thoroughly. It would have helped me understand how I best operate, learn, handle challenges, socialize, etc. I could have avoided costly mistakes, made different choices, sought strategies to have my needs met in a way that worked for me, and I could have had opportunities to stand up for myself. Armed with this knowledge, I am now able to do those things. But I realized that unfortunately there were many lost opportunities from my past.

I knew I could never get those years back. But now I wanted to try to give others what I hadn't been able to have for myself.

A chance to know, and accept, thyself.

I think it's important to point out that I was already a part of the "autism community" as a parent of autistic children; I didn't have to reveal my own diagnosis to others. And in some ways, both because it often seems that the voices of autistic adults are (sadly) perceived as less relevant than the voices of non-autistic parents/caregivers and because individuals like me are often disdained and/or disregarded by some members of the autism community as "not really autistic/not autistic enough/not like my child," it may seem that there was little to "gain" from coming out as autistic. And a lot to lose. But I still wanted to. For nothing had changed—except everything had changed. I was the same person before and after the discovery...except I wasn't. I was no longer unaware about who I was. All of me. My full, true, perfectly imperfect autistic self.

I more than wanted to come out; I needed to. I wanted anyone out there who remotely identified with me in any way (age, gender, ethnicity, region, etc) to be encouraged by my existence. To know that they were not alone. I wanted autistic kids (like my own, and others) to know that it's okay to grow up to be an autistic adult—like me. I wanted people to know that though I have very real challenges, being autistic has also afforded me many strengths too. That my (nor your) life is not "destroyed" by autism, but it is very much intertwined with it and all of its elements (positive and negative). I wanted autistic adults who were (like myself) late diagnosed to know that there was a community—the autistic community, filled with people like me who have found one another. I also wanted people from various groups often less represented in autism to hopefully feel a sense of kinship with me.

Maybe if I could be willing to share about my life others would be willing to live their (autistic) lives.

So when I came out as autistic, I did it big. That fateful day I participated in a local cross-disability festival that highlighted various films, images, and other content with a focus on disability acceptance. I stood next to a "larger than life" image of myself that was part of a traveling photo exhibit. Next to my image were the following words:

"Morénike is an autistic adult who proudly wears the hats of wife, mother, advocate, and student. She is passionate about social justice, global health, education, adoption, and community empowerment."

I came out as autistic publicly, and I have never regretted beginning to live my authentic life. I am free—to be me. I swung the closet door open that day and stepped out, never to return.

Done Fighting Exhaustion

Ondrea Marisa Robinson

I did what I could do.
I sent letters explaining what I go through.
I expressed about myself having anxiety.
I tried everything to get people to understand me,
But it did not work.
The staff went by with what the doctors said,
Not by what I was feeling and dealing with.
The staff didn't have empathy and put themselves in my shows
What it would like to be exhausted traveling for a long period of time,
To be anxious when dealing with annoying crowds, and to be dealing with autism.
I was denied at a chance four times to get what I needed.
I tried to do what was right like sending letters from other people
Who know me and wrote things on my behalf to try to get what I needed,
But like it was said, the staff working in the office didn't geive me a chance.
So I am done fighting.
Some of you can suggest to me to create a petition,
Appeal a decision, or keep bugging the staff all you want,

But it's not going to change anybody's mind—not the doctors, not the staff, not the naysayers.

The process was exhausting enough, and I'm not being exhausted anymore.

In fact, I'm not being frustrated anymore.

This will be put in God's Hands, and the situation was out of my control.

And I'm certainly not going to take it out of my control,

Because I would be making a mess.

And God would not be pleased with that at all.

I can't force the staff, the doctors, or the naysayers to understand if they choose not to.

Although it is their loss, I'm done.

I just want to be at peace.

Sometimes I wonder if I'm being Masochistic

Jessa Sturgeon

Sometimes I wonder if I'm being masochistic by being a philosophy student, particularly one who focuses on mind and language. Sometimes it feels like the majority of philosophical research on those subjects has at least one part that basically says "I'm pretty sure I heard about an autistic person who can't do that, so autism definitely means unable to do that. Also I have a totally unrelated theory that doing that is what makes us ~human~/~moral~/~insert other value judgement here~."

Even when they don't mention autism by name I can see how they've already decided that that I'm not human and I don't count and I'm probably impossible or delusional. Most research is just so lazy when it comes to autism and so blatantly hurtful and full of hate that I can tangibly ache with how wrong it is and reading the words is so physical and understandable in a way that words usually aren't.

That physical sense of understanding is something I have to have before something can really and truly be useful for anything other than word games.

Word games seem to be the most important skill, though. Or at least externally valued and rewarded the most. I'm very good at them but sometimes I wish I actually understood what I was doing.

I think in so many words. There are always so many words, but most of them I don't even understand even when I do understand them.

Sometimes when people want to be very nice and helpful they try to figure out ways to develop a system for me to communicate that I've become "non-verbal." Because they're so nice and so helpful and I usually care so much about them it's so hard to admit that I can't. I don't how or where to draw a line on something I can't even sense. And then I'd have to admit that I don't even know when I'm "verbal."

I learned to talk by cutting and pasting echolalia together. I still think and talk by cutting and pasting echolalia together. So it really scares me when people ignore or deem meaningless communication that they deem to be echolalia.

I am usually fairly adept at selecting enough different sound bites and remixing them to say things that don't seem entirely tangential or illogical to their intended audience. My understanding is often more syntactic than semantic though. Compared to the "non-verbal vocalizations," "irrelevant tangents," and "meaningless repetitions" of my thoughts and feelings and private communications, those complex word collages feel flat and distant, sometimes beyond my own understanding.

Does moving words around in a fog of confusion that I don't understand at all but others can pull satisfactory meaning from count as more or less verbal than saying words and sounds that mean a lot to me but mean nothing to my audience?

Having so much practice with confusion is exhausting but it can also be useful. Identifying and quoting the words that form connections between patterns I can barely comprehend has been one of my most useful skills. I write most of my papers by filling a document with nothing but quotes and citations and moving them around until I can figure out the right words that fit between them.

I can see and feel the physical holes in the arguments made in most published philosophy about language and mind and certain other subjects. It's not terribly hard to pick up all the words and rearrange them so the holes are gone though. Sometimes they're missing some necessary vocabulary, but generally most of their words are fine. It's just how they have and haven't been connected with each other that needs fixing.

I generally feel more like an editor than a writer, even when I do what is called writing. Writers have to think and create and produce original words.

I've always been very good at organizing seemingly disparate objects into meaningful and aesthetically pleasing whole patterns. Stuff like "arranging" toys instead of "playing" with them.

What's the difference between rearranging words and novel thought? Is there even one? I've often been kept awake all night by the fear that I would be expelled from school for plagiarism. I never plagiarized. Did I? I never tried to at least.

I've had to study and write about Descartes a lot. *Cogito ergo sum* is seared in my brain as the most confusing and least understandable way I've ever seen words connected. "I think therefore I am" is a statement so outside of my understanding of anything. I understand questions more than statements usually and there are two in particular that I can understand a lot even though I can never understand any of my answers to them. Do I think? Am I?

Things about working with "Emotionally disturbed" children that will break your heart.

Kassiane A. Asasumasu

This is a response to the awful, pooooor aduuuuuuults Cracked article about working with "troubled children". I worked in a classroom for kindergarten -4th graders with an educational classification of Behavior Disorder/Emotionally Disturbed. I loved them all, each and every one. Most of them had been through more by age 7 than anyone should be ever. This post is dedicated to them. I hope they are all safe & healing now.

Many adults who work in schools, particularly in special education settings, aren't there for the reason I was there. I was there because of a love of children, even (especially) difficult children. I was there because I remembered struggling and I wanted to be the adult who wasn't around when I was a student. I tried. But the system is set up to fail. Here are the things about teaching my "emotionally disturbed" students that ultimately broke my heart.

1. Their difficulties don't arise out of nowhere.

Tho majority of my students had spent some time in foster care—meaning they had been removed from their families of origin. Others had early onset mental illnesses. Some had both of these factors going on.

White children who are dealing with enough at home that they get removed from their parents in this part of the country? They are dealing with multiple kinds of abuse. So we had 8 year olds who were having flashbacks to being molested. I had a kindergartener who saw her mom get stabbed. A student whose stepdad took his medication for funsies, making the boy's medication levels completely unpredictable. Even the students who had never been removed were dealing with not optimal home environments. The parents just didn't have the coping skills, & things an adult gets away with? Gets you classified "emotionally disturbed" if you copy it at school.

What this meant in practicality was that we were often trying to undo what happened over the weekend, or we were trying to help a student who always felt in danger to learn and to practice emotional regulation skills they may have never seen modeled before. That's setting some students up to fail—if they've never seen emotional regulation, and they neurologically don't have a frustration tolerance, learning & "behaving" is tasking their resources to the brink.

2. Other adults are unempathetic assholes
The systems set up in these classrooms tend to run on "points" or "tokens" and they lose tokens for Behaviors. Some may call it "failing to earn" but to the students, it's losing. Keep in mind that these are fairly young people,

and they often are at a distinct disadvantage in emotional regulation.

I have seen adults, multiple adults, gleefully tell students how many points they're losing. This tends to send them into a downward spiral because not getting all your points = not getting privileges (we're not talking a big cake. We're talking craft supplies here). I have seen teachers goad students who are doing the best they can to self calm into getting more upset.

If you have a young person with emotional regulation difficulties, and they are trying to talk themselves down when they had a bad start, just shush and let them talk themselves down! This is a big step for many students I know. Talking oneself down, even with a "tone", is much better than dumping a desk. (My strategy for "a desk is about to get dumped" is "jump onto the desk, Gollum pose", because being ridiculous can interrupt a downward spiral & it isn't threatening. I've never seen anyone else use this strategy).

I have seen teachers who were supposedly trained in deescalation get into the face and space of a student who has suffered severe abuse & is having a hard time. Then when the student runs or pushes them away, the adult uses this as an excuse to take them to the ground. Getting in someone's face is not deescalation. Moving away and shushing or saying soothing, validating things is deescalation.

Behavior Disorder classrooms are a place where seclusion & restraint are very popular. And never let anyone tell you for a minute that it's not punitive or retaliatory. It is punitive and retaliatory. If a kid shoves a boring book off their desk, that's disrespectful, sure. It is not something that is a risk to anyone. There is *no excuse* to restrain a kid for that.

My classroom had a room that was ostensibly a break room. It isn't a break room when you shut students in there, no matter how many beanbag chairs are in there. Saying something smartassed is not an excuse to lock someone in a room. It's like the adults in these settings have forgotten what it is to be small, young, and have a limited coping repertoire. And they punish the students in abusive ways for manifestations of their disability. That's not ok. That's not helping.

3. You *will* have to call CPS. They *will* blow off your call.

As I said in point 1, most of my students had been in foster care. Most of them had dealt with abuse or neglect. Some of them were still dealing with abuse and neglect.

As an educator, I was a mandated reporter. As the person who would jump on a desk, raise my eyebrows, & set off a giggle fit instead of encouraging rage, I was the Trusted Adult. They knew I was on their side.

Being Trusted Adult sucks sometimes, because a small child will tell you the very gory details of what started happening when he moved from his mom's house to his dad's. And you will think you can help, you have to report to CPS, and CPS isn't perfect but they can do something.

79

And then CPS will tell you that the kid is lying, don't you teach behavior disorder? Those kids lie. That is what they will tell you.

This is the hill I chose to die on. A student confided in me, things I'm pretty sure most young people wouldn't think of out of their imagination. I called CPS. CPS told me my student was lying. I said he wasn't. They said they'd believe me if the lead teacher in the room called. The lead teacher in the room elected not to call.

And I walked out. I couldn't help this young person through the accepted channels, but damned if I was going to sit there and pretend it was ok to call him a liar. I could do more good not in that classroom, & that's sad.

Many many students in these classrooms are in them because abused children act out as their only way of asking for help—and then their being in these classrooms is used as an excuse to not help them. It isn't ok. It will break your heart into a million tiny pieces.

4. Your students will be blamed for anything that goes wrong within a half mile radius.
A goal of our class was to prepare our students to go back into the mainstream classrooms. They were mostly academically on grade level in at least a couple areas. They could mostly comprehend the work, it was dealing with the behavioral demands of the classroom or the amount of busywork that made things a problem for them in the regular ed classrooms.

Part of the least restrictive environment, then, was that they would go to music and PE with the other students at their grade level (with or without a teacher, depending on how they were doing that day) and had recess and lunch at the same time as their age peers. In theory this is a start, right?

In practice, the other students learned very quickly that if you do something obnoxious on the playground, you won't get in trouble if you blame one of my students. Even if it was obviously not something they would do (the other adults didn't really care what my students would or wouldn't do, they were Those Kids). I had students be blamed for throwing sand when they were in a swing on the complete opposite side of the school yard.

And heaven help the student if they're going to academic classes with their typical peers and someone can't find her book or pencil. Obviously it was my student. Those Kids Steal/Hit/Draw On The Walls. Except...no they really didn't. My students did act out sometimes but they didn't do a quarter of the things they were blamed for.

And the PE teacher, music teacher, regular ed teachers? They were nearly as bad as my coworkers in terms of nitpicking at their behavior. A frustrated sigh is age appropriate. Crumpling up a bad drawing is pretty normal. That is not call to demand that I take them back to the self contained classroom. I see typical kids on the other side of the room throwing their crappy drawings at each other, what on earth is this double standard?

5. You will fall in love with your students, & you may not be able to save them, & failing will never. stop. hurting.

The thing in point 3? Actually happened. For reals. The student in question was about to go back to his home school district, his regular ed classroom with resource room time if he needed a break, when everything went to hell. He went from reading to me and discussing the stories to all sorts of not ideal stuff that I won't discuss because our worst days deserve to be at least a bit obscured. It was a fast downward spiral.

And another student? Really only needed sensory accomodations probably and only ended up in my class because he was defending his right to them. But because he had been placed in our classroom had to work his way back into typical classes and was always considered a Bad Kid because one of his teachers had refused to work with his needs. If you don't get out of the emotionally disturbed self contained classroom by high school you're stuck forever.

Another? Ended up going to the special day school for kids with severe emotional challenges. Another got pulled out of school entirely because his parents didn't want other adults able to observe him. That's frightening.

I couldn't save them from their families, couldn't heal their coping mechanisms. But I loved them to bits, and I know it was mutual. A big hug and "I love you" made it pretty clear. "I wish you were my mom".

"I made you this necklace to play with so you don't break your pretty one".

Photo: A light-colored hand holds a wooden-bead necklace.

I have had this necklace for over 10 years. One of my students from that classroom made it for me. Of all the things he could have chosen to do with the craft supplies, he chose to help me not break things, because breaking things loses points whether you meant to or not. That's a lot of thinking outside himself, huh?

But I couldn't save them. Too many adults who work with young people think only about themselves, act as though their students are having difficulties just to piss them off. And it isn't the case at all.

Maybe *you* won't fall in love with them, which is something I'm sad about. Love is a thing my students needed, instead of being made into monsters and adversaries. They had enough adversaries.

I loved them, they loved me, & it breaks my heart that so few other people saw what I saw.

"Don't let them be Autistic..."

Morénike Giwa Onaiwu

There's a pattern that has existed in my life for as long as I can remember. Not only do I do it, many other people that I know do it as well. I learn about some type of problem— a robbery, a shooting, a murder. About some type of horrific event...one of the many ways humans mistreat and harm one another. And of course, I am saddened for the victims, often offering up a silent prayer for them. But the very next instant, I do something else. I close my eyes for a moment, and then I brace myself as I await more information. And all the while one thought/prayer/chant/fear is running through my head:

"Don't-let-them-be-black-don't-let-them-be-black-don't-let-them-be-black-don't-let-them-be-black-PLEASE GOD don't-let-them-be-black..."

Why? Because I am black. And I know that if the perpetrator IS black, like me, then there's yet another immense form of baggage that it will carry for me, for my children, for people who look like me, and for people who care about those who look like me. And no matter how many of us are honest, law-abiding, kind, non-violent people, we are erased every time the person who has done something wrong has skin that looks like mine.

85

In the last few years, I've added a new thought to the one above. Because a few years ago, I learned that my beautiful, smart, strong, loving youngest son and daughter were autistic. The "failed" M-CHAT, echolalia, ecstatic flapping, hyperlexia, lack of eye contact, different way of socializing, joyful spinning, toe-walking, late speech and later pedantic speech, lining up every object on the planet, fascination with ceiling fans, lights, and spinning items, great attention to detail, sensory sensitivity etc, etc, etc. My babies were unequivocally, undeniably, unashamedly smack-dab on the autism spectrum. Once we learned more about autism, it was almost laughable that we hadn't known about them. And as we learned even more, it became almost laughable that we hadn't known about me...as in time I suspected, and later confirmed, that I was autistic as well.

Autism is many things. But it is seldom what it is perceived by people to be. It isn't a tragedy. It isn't a ravaged life. It isn't an entity that destroys lives. It isn't a disease.

And it sure as heck isn't a crime.

The media seems to enjoy speculating that nearly every time there is a school shooter (it's sad that we even have multiple school shooters to compare, but we do) or a perpetrator of a violent act is presumed to be on the autism spectrum. It happens all the time.

Autistics commit crimes, yes. Just like non-autistics commit crimes. But statistics show that autistics are more likely to be victims of violent crime than to be perpetrators of violent crime. We are actually at greater risk than all of you. If anyone should be afraid, it's US.

We are different. But different is not a crime. We are people, just like you. And our differences should not be pathologized. Our uniqueness should not be misconstrued as a threat. Our diagnosis should not be vilified in the way that it is ALL.THE.TIME.

I am raising black children, autistic and non-autistic. I am already afraid for them. My oldest son, a teenager, is old is soon going to be too old for the bubble of protection that comes with youth—and will have to face life as one of the most difficult things to be in this country: a black male. But my 3 year old son—my sweet, kind, fun-loving youngest child—will have to face life as male. And black. And autistic. What will that mean for him? That he will be viewed as a violent, only half-human individual that doesn't deserve to exist because aside from being "flawed," he's also a danger?

As of right now, it means that I will continue to do this: "Don't-let-them-be-black-don't-let-them-be-black-don't-let-them-be-black-don't-let-them-be-black-PLEASE   GOD don't-let-them-be-black..."

Followed by:

"Don't-let-them-be-autistic-don't-let-them-be-autistic-don't-let-them-be-autistic-don't-let-them-be-autistic-PLEASE GOD don't-let-them-be-autistic..."

I am autistic, and I am obsessed with violence.

A response to Andrew Solomon's article about his interviews with Peter Lanza in The New Yorker

Lydia X. Z. Brown

Content/TW: Discussion of murder, other violence, ableism, various mass shootings, mention of rape, discussion of forced psychiatric treatment, brief description of the JRC, terrorism, 9/11.

An old man falls to his death from a cliff, staring in horror and despair at his loved one standing on the edge.

This is one of my first memories of playing pretend games with my younger sister.

In other pretend games, I wanted to be a man wrongfully accused of being a spy and then sentenced to death, or sometimes a robber caught by the police and then sent to prison. In preschool, I became obsessed with Disney's *Snow White*. One day at school, I gave everyone little clumps of play dough and told them it was poisoned, just like the poisoned apple in the movie. The teacher called my parents.

In second grade, I started a pretend game with my friends where my character drank poisoned water, turned into a demon, and started chasing her children. My first stories, written between kindergarten and sixth grade, involved abandoned children, abusive siblings, poisonings, assassinations, prison escapes, and horrible torture.

In eighth grade, I wrote my first novel. The plotline follows the tyrannical dictator of one country who decides to murder a well-loved official in the country next door, frame someone else for the crime, and then use the distraction as an excuse to invade.

The same year, I read *Helter Skelter*, the true crime story of the Charles Manson cult murders written by Vincent Bugliosi, who was the prosecutor in the case. When I brought the book to school, one of the teachers took me aside and told me that was inappropriate reading.

When I started high school, I wrote my second novel, which starts with the assassination of the U.S. President by a terrorist group.

***

After the Virginia Tech shootings by Seung-Hui Cho, Cho's writing assignments became a huge deal in the media. His two short plays were full of profanity and violence. I read them when one news source uploaded copies online.

I didn't know how to express the feelings I had at the time, but I think I'm beginning to understand now.

This week, *The New Yorker* ran an exclusive article by Andrew Solomon about his interviews with Peter Lanza, the father of the Sandy Hook shooter. In parts of the article, Solomon lingers on Adam Lanza's apparent obsession with violence. According to Peter, his son was obsessed with genocide, serial killers, and mass murder. He wrote extremely violent fiction on top of reading extensively about other people's real violence.

Photo (Rebecca Taplin): A very young me, fifth grade, sitting in the classroom with my sleeve against my lips, reading a book in the *Animorphs* series while other books and binders are piled on my desk. I'm wearing a school uniform, long sleeve maroon polo shirt, khaki pants. Behind me are shelves with messily arranged binders and notebooks.

Solomon, who is also the author of the recent nonfiction book *Far From The Tree* (problematic for other reasons), wonders whether these should have been taken as warning signs. Peter is more direct when he talks about his son and whether his killing spree could have been predicted, and presumably stopped, before it happened.

I read Solomon's descriptions of Adam, and I was crying because most of what he wrote could have been written about me if you changed the names. When he suggested that Adam's obsession with reading and writing about extreme violence could have been a warning sign, I became terrified. Not because I'm afraid that people in power *will* start using that as an excuse for hurting people like me, but because I know they *already do* and I'm afraid it will happen *even more*.

***

Believe me, I understand what it's like to be desperate for answers, for an explanation, when tragedy happens. While I am not the surviving relative of a high-profile mass murderer, I experience total devastation and complete obsession with finding an explanation in the aftermath of any outbreak of horrible violence. Every time. It's hard to put the feeling into words, but the phrases that come to mind are ones like these: a thousand punches to the gut, complete frantic overload in my brain, nameless things dismantle.

Like many other autistics, I am deeply empathetic, and easily and often overwhelmed by emotional overload. I experience the emotions of people around me—no matter whether I know them or whether they're strangers—as though they are my own emotions, and that's on top of and combined with the ones that came from me first.

I was only eight years old when September 11 happened, but as an American citizen living near Boston, it would have been impossible for the terrorist attacks not to affect me.

I say I understand the desperate, obsessive search for answers because I have lived it.

The events of September 11 lit a fire in me and I became desperate to understand, intellectually and emotionally, just *why* it happened and *what reasons* the attackers had when they did it. For the next ten years, I became obsessed with the topic of Islamic-inspired terrorism. If an article, book, or website existed that covered the topic—no matter whose point of view it was from—I read every word with fascination. That interest led me to explore the history and reality of other forms of terrorism, including Christian-inspired terrorism, state-sponsored terrorism, eco-terrorism, just about any kind of terrorism that's ever been named.

The same interest also led me to explore *Islam* itself as a religion, as the basis for many cultures and civilizations, and as a social and legal system. At the same time, I also became extremely interested in learning about national security policy, counterterrorism operations, and the role of anti-brown racism and Islamophobia as tools of white supremacy and American imperialism. By the time I was in twelfth grade, I decided that I wanted to study Islamic Studies in college and later go on to study for a PhD focusing on Sufi music in Pakistan.

Right now, I'm an Arabic major studying abroad in Amman, Jordan,[1] and this is a direct result of my long obsession with understanding *why* and *how* September 11 happened.

***

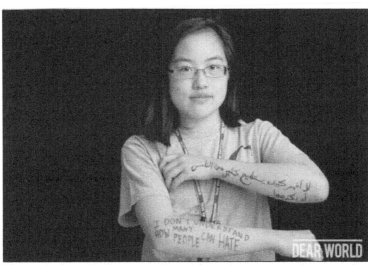

Photo (Robert X. Fogarty): Me with serious expression wearing a gray t-shirt against a black background, holding both my arms in front of my body. Text that I wrote in black pen says, "I don't understand how many people can hate" in English on one arm and in Arabic on the other arm. Photo taken for the Dear World Project at Georgetown University in March 2012.

***

After the Virginia Tech shootings, I read news articles that described Seung-Hui Cho as a socially awkward loner who had been bullied in the past. As much as I empathized with his victims and their living loved ones, I also instinctively empathized with him too.

This doesn't mean that I'm somehow okay with murder or that I think he's less guilty or that his crimes should be excused or ignored. It just means that my empathy is not selective, and I don't think that that's a bad thing.

***

Both Peter Lanza and Andrew Solomon said outright that autism shouldn't be treated as if it's related to Adam's killing spree. But that doesn't change the tone of the article at all, which talks about Adam's diagnosis and various autistic characteristics in a way that reminds me of a freak show, or a post-mortem zoo exhibit. If the fact that Adam was autistic isn't related to the fact that he killed twenty-six people, then why spend so much time focusing on his autistic traits in an article that's mostly about his father's attempt to figure out *why* and *how* this happened?

Plenty of readers will read the disclaimer that autism didn't play a role in the killing spree, and they'll roll their eyes or shake their heads or something like that, because they'll read the same damn article and they'll ask the same damn question, only their answer will be different. Their conclusion will be, of course it was relevant. Of course it was related. Some people will be aware that they've reached that conclusion, and other people will do it subconsciously. The result will be the same, though.

They'll read about the report from a professional that said Adam was more likely to become a victim, and they'll laugh. They'll laugh even though it's true. Of course, statistics don't change the fact that he actually became a victimizer, but statistically, overall, people like him and

94

people like me are at such high risk of becoming victims of violence and abuse. That's true across the board for disabled people, no matter whether we're talking about autism or mental illness. You don't have to read academic studies to know that (though the studies do exist) because if you live in a society where one way of existing is normal and everything else is treated as less than, anyone who falls into that "everything else" category is going to be more vulnerable. That's the way systems of power work.

Solomon may have intended to try to humanize both Peter and Adam in his article. He probably intended to do the same thing with the many different types of people he wrote about in *Far From The Tree*. But his intentions don't change the reality of his writing, which, for me, is completely devastating and completely dehumanizing. And not just for autistics but for people with mental illness too. Autistics got a half-hearted disclaimer that autism isn't related to violence. People with mental illness got thrown under the bus.

And the best phrase I can think of to describe how he talks in so much detail about Adam's sensory aversions to sounds and textures is "morbid fascination." In the course of my activism, I've met so many people, most but not all autistic, who could also fit a lot of these descriptions perfectly too.

***

One of my favorite hobbies is text-based roleplaying, which is basically like writing stories but with other people. Some people treat it more like a competitive game, and other people like to treat it more like a big group writing project better. The roleplays that interest me the most are the ones that explore the same topics that I'm interested in outside roleplay: state violence, terrorism, torture, abuse, human rights violations, rape and other sexual violence, and mass murder.

I'm writing my seventh novel right now. Much of the novel focuses on war crimes and genocide along ethnic and religious lines.

If you didn't know me, if you read Andrew Solomon's article and the hundreds of others like it, if you didn't understand that it's totally possible to be fascinated and obsessed with individual and systemic violence and yet *not* be violent personally, then you might wonder too if I'm going to be the next Adam Lanza or Anders Behring Breivik or Seung-Hui Cho or James Holmes.

When I was in tenth grade, I was called into an administrator's office and accused of planning a school shooting. When I told him that of course I wasn't planning a school shooting, he pointed out that I seemed to be obsessed with weapons and violence, and then he asked me if I was sure I'd never thought about actually hurting someone.

When I was in twelfth grade, my mom told me that there were people in the church who thought I was planning to join Al Qaeda or some other terrorist group.

These things are real, and they prove to me that my fears—both for myself and other people—aren't unfounded.

***

Photo (Shain M. Neumeier): Me wearing a white t-shirt, standing in a room with windows facing a hallway with elevators and various college flyers. I'm looking down and holding a sign handwritten in purple ink that says, "I'm not afraid to say I'm autistic." Photo by Shain Neumeier in December 2012.

***

I don't claim to understand everyone's motives. If I did, there wouldn't be any more obsessive quests for answers after each and every act of mass violence I've ever learned about since September 11.

But I can say with certainty that it's not mental illness or autism or an interest in violence or being bullied or social   awkwardness or violent roleplaying or violent video games or violent creative writing that lead to mass murder. Those aren't warning signs. They shouldn't be treated as warning signs.

There's so much ableism and ageism wrapped up in the assumption that these things are somehow predictors of future violence. Ironically, those same assumptions are used to justify real violence against people like me, and often by the people who in theory are supposed to protect us.

***

Does Peter Lanza have a right to his opinions, thoughts, and emotions? Of course he does. I'm the last person to say that his experiences and emotions are not valid.

But that doesn't make them any less hurtful. It doesn't make Andrew Solomon's article any less painful.

The two most painful things in that article for me to read were when Solomon asked Peter what the family did about a funeral for Adam, and Peter said that no one would ever know, and then when Peter said that he wishes Adam had never been born.

Maybe the family did host a funeral for Adam. Maybe they didn't. I wasn't there during the interview, so I don't know how Peter said that comment, but at least in writing, it came across as so cold and so callous, and I—I couldn't form words.

And as to the second comment—we have no way of knowing when someone is born if that person is going to be a wonderful amazing human being who helps many people or if that person is going to turn into a horrible person who does horrible things to other people. It's so easy to say after the fact that you wish someone hadn't been born.

But when the parent of a young man who obviously did have many disabilities says that, even though his son was a mass murderer who killed twenty children, just how close in time this article was published to the March 1 vigils in memory of hundreds of disabled people (plenty of them autistic) murdered by their parents only gives this statement a chilling underline.

***

Photo (Kory Utto-Jacobs): Me wearing a dark blue winter coat, a beige suit jacket, and an ochre shirt, with a blue lanyard and beige gloves, facing slightly away from the camera while speaking. I'm standing in front of a large poster that says "Mourn for the Dead ...And Fight Like Hell" for the Living followed by a list of victims' names, ages at death, and manner of murder. D.C. Day of Mourning Vigil in Farragut Square on Friday 1 March 2013 as part of the National Day of Mourning for disabled people murdered by caregivers and family members.

***

In the interview, Peter Lanza talked quite a bit about how Adam never came to terms with the Asperger's/autistic diagnosis.

There's no way to know, but I can't help but wonder whether being able to accept being autistic and be around other affirming autistic people might have changed the course of events.

***

For all the constant media pattern of assuming that someone who kills a lot of people must be autistic or mentally ill, two of Adam Lanza's victims, Josephine "Joey" Gay and Dylan Hockley, were autistic too.

In the rush to railroad autistic people, the media often conveniently forgets that fact.

***

Both Andrew Solomon and Peter Lanza kept emphasizing that maybe if Adam had received treatment, this might not have happened. I can't underscore enough how damaging this is for so many people.

First of all, Representative Tim Murphy's bill in Congress right now, if passed, will severely cut funding for community-based programs supporting people with mental illnesses as well as the advocacy agencies that exist to protect people's rights.

100

This bill comes after his hearing almost an entire year ago when witness after witness kept testifying to his committee about how horrible and dangerous people with mental illnesses are, and only one brave witness dared say something different.

Secondly, the sad and extremely violent reality is that the vast majority of therapy and program options for people with mental illness are coercive, demeaning, and paternalistic.

Thirdly, this article reinforces the social presumption that the default option for mental illness is and should be psychiatric treatment. And while I absolutely support the right of anyone who wants psychiatric treatment of any kind to access that treatment on their own terms, the reality is that not everyone wants to go that route and that's okay.

Fourthly, there is the reality that this article, written by a famous journalist in a well-known publication, will be treated as an authority, and that the statements in it can and will lead to even more stigma and less voluntary options for people who do seek out psychiatric treatment.

These are realities and consequences that profoundly disturb me.

***

I can tell you why I am obsessed with violence.

It is because I am also completely and absolutely committed to the ideal of justice.

There was a long time after September 11 when I dreamed about a career in counterterrorism, with the idea that I could help stop future attacks.

The broad theme of my work for the past five years has been addressing violence against disabled people, especially disabled people made even more vulnerable because they also happen to be queer, trans, poor, immigrants, or people of color. Violence against us happens all the time, both by other people in the community and by government forces.

My work is emotionally exhausting.

Every so often, I receive an email out of nowhere from someone asking for help because they or their kid are in an abusive situation at school or work.

Writing and roleplaying about individual and systemic violence, and how it impacts everyone in the community, helps me process my emotions. In fact, it's the only thing that actually works for me. It's not that I take sadistic pleasure out of writing about violent things or that I secretly wish I could do violent things to people I've met.

It's part of the same obsession with understanding *why* and *how* and *what next*. I wasn't exaggerating when I said that I understand the desperate search for answers in the wake of violence. That desperate ocarch has been the narrative for much of my conscious life.

***

Photo (Taylor C. Hall): Shain Neumeier, white person with short blond hair and glasses, and I standing on a traffic island in the middle of a multi-lane highway on an overcast day in January 2013. We're holding hand-drawn and colored signs to protest the abusive Judge Rotenberg Center, which uses painful electric shock as punishment/behavioral modification for disabled residents. Shain's sign says "Stop the Shocks" with lightning bolts cutting through the o's, and I'm holding two signs, one that says "People not Experiments" and the other that says "Shocked for... hugging staff, swearing, nagging, getting out of seat, taking off coat, screaming, tensing up, closing eyes, raising hand. Ban the GED [electric shock device]."

***

In the end, I've started asking different questions. It's less often, "Why did this mass tragedy happen?" and more often, "Why do people insist that the only people capable of committing such horrible crimes must be an Other?"

103

and "Why do we treat specific instances of mass tragedies as both more important and more horrible than the continuous and brutal violence against marginalized people?"

I don't mean to belittle the real victimhood of people killed by mass murderers or the pain for their living loved ones. I don't mean to belittle the internal struggle that must happen for anyone who finds out someone they loved or knew well was responsible for those killings either.

But the questions are worth asking because they, too, carry life or death consequences. They carry consequences for my life and my experiences, and they carry consequences for those of so many of my friends and colleagues too.

I don't want my children to grow up in a world where they have to worry about whether their teachers or bosses will peg them as the next mass shooters if they just happen to be loners, socially awkward, interested in violent games, autistic, or mentally ill. If my children are autistic or mentally ill or both, I don't want them to grow up in a world where their humanity is questioned every single day, or where police brutality based on their disability status could end their lives.

The fact that much of the response to a horrific act of violence has been to encourage more violence is not merely astounding, but extremely sad.

The worst part of all of this is knowing that no matter what I say or do or write here, the people who have power in media and politics will carry on with their dehumanizing campaign, and I—we—don't stand a chance when these things are simply accepted as true and normal and how things are.

If you're reading this essay, all I can ask is that you consider an alternative narrative. Instead of trying to play the blame game for violence—autistics one day, people with mental illness the next, every young Black man the week after that—can we start to focus on healing within ourselves and our communities? Can we cope with our trauma in less hurtful ways?

---

[1] I originally wrote this essay in March 2014.

Plea from the scariest kid on the block

Kassiane A. Asasumasu

Yet another mass killing. Yet another tragedy. It is terrible. It is horrible. It is wrong.

People are scared.

People are looking for a group to be scared of.

Ladies, gentlemen, other august personages, I am the monster you are afraid of. For my entire life I have been. The reasoning changes, but I always come down on the wrong side of the line. I am always who the media, the talking heads, the papers, now the blogs, who the people you listen to tell me to fear.

And this makes being me terrifying. It makes being me unsafe.

First, it was being an abused child from what they call a broken home. Abused children commit all sorts of violence, you see. We are dangerous and unpredictable because we grew up with violence and that is all we know. We are ticking time bombs, we have no empathy, our dysfunctional unstable home lives have made us fragile at best, cold blooded killers at worst.

106

So isolate us. Keep your children away from us. Warn every one that we are dangerous because of what our families are like. Make sure that everyone knows that we—not our abusers, but *we*—are the scariest thing on the block.

Do you remember all the news reports and such emphasizing the terribility of home lives of serial killers and mass murderers during these time periods? I do. I do in great detail-because I remember relating. And I remember staying up nights horrified that they were a glimpse into the only future open to me. I was 9 years old and scared shitless that my only career option was as a mass killer—because the media had everyone convinced that's what happens to children with childhoods like mine.

And because the other adults around me made it very clear that I was the scariest thing on the block.

I was isolated. I was alone.

Then that went out of vogue.

For about 10 minutes I was safe.

Then another terrible tragedy happened, and they found a new scapegoat, and I was in an even more precarious position than before: the new problem was children and teens who were bullied.

I have been able to write about my parents. I have not been able to write about the bullying I experienced without being too triggered to function. It was that bad. Again, I was dangerous.

Again, people were telling their nice, 'normal' children to stay away from the bullied children. Isolating us—making us further targets. And making us more alone. Warning everyone that we were dangerous, the scariest thing on the block again—this time I was scary not just because of my family, but because I got locked into lockers by my peers. We are dangerous and unpredictable because we didn't have the skills and characteristics to not be at the bottom of the pecking order of middle school.

So obviously the answer was to isolate us more lest we 'snap', to fear us and let bullies to their thing, rather than to do anything about bullying. We are damaged, terrifying, violent, dangerous, irredeemable. We are the middle school monsters of your nightmares.

Again, I was the middle school monsters of my own nightmares, too. Literal nightmares, I'm talking. Still everything around me was telling me that because of things outside my control I was destined to go out in a blaze of violence and take as many people as I could with me. That was the career path being offered to me. Never mind that I knew (and still know) exactly nothing about weapons more volatile than bows and arrows, never mind that I am reluctant to physically defend myself, much less be the aggressor, this is what life had to offer me.

Because I was a target, because I was different, I was still what everyone feared. Everyone was telling you to fear me. No one even thought about the bullied kids seeing these news reports. They just knew about you normal folks, and that you needed to be safe from people like me. They couldn't tell you a single thing about the mass killers except that they were in this one category—so, literally, they told you a single thing-and that single thing was what made them dangerous.

It made me dangerous.

Isolate me. Make me alone. Fear me. Abuse me some more. Make me more dangerous. It doesn't matter, I am unsafe no matter what you do. The news—all the news—says so.

And now. Now I am 30 years old.

I am still literally losing sleep, wondering if or when that transformation is supposed to happen. I know logically it will not happen. I know I have no interest in hurting anyone. I know the statistics on who actually commits this sort of violence. I know my history is not going to magically impart a knowledge of guns or explosives or a desire to hurt a large number of people. My anger and hurt do not manifest that way, they never have, and that is not going to change.

But now autism is the scapegoat du jour. Now every time someone does something violent, they are speculated to be autistic. And, just as some killers who were speculated to have crappy home lives actually did, just as the

Columbine killers actually were bullied, there is a possibility that there will be a mass shooter who is Autistic.

But that does not make all of us dangerous. The immediate speculation makes my blood run cold.

It brings bile to my throat and a panic to my chest.

Have we learned nothing? Have the bullied children and abused children and medicated children and other scapegoats who have done no violence learned nothing? Passing the hot potato is a relief, but it is wrong.

Passing the blame down to another group without power hurts people.

They will be isolated. They will be alone. They will be hurt.

I do not want another child, a single other child, to be hurt by their peers for being 'dangerous'. I do not want a single other child to be thought a 'ticking timebomb' by the adults in their life. They treat you with fear and they treat you with loathing when they are afraid of you.

I do not want another kid loathed because the media decided to pin the blame on their brain. I do not want another child being isolated, gossip about why to steer clear spread through whispers and subtle finger pointing.

NO.

I do not want another child to have nightmares like I did—like I still do—of being some sort of sleeper agent who has no other career path because of self fulfilling prophesies. I cannot even explain what this fear is like, and the fewer people who understand it, the better.

This has *got* to stop.

It's too late to stop for my sake. The damage was done by the time we got to "bullied kids are dangerous". But it is not too late to stop for the sake of today's autistic children.

too dry to cry

Lydia X. Z. Brown

Content/TW: Gun violence, mass shooting, detailed discussion of ableism and racism (especially against Black and Brown people) surrounding such events, mention of sexual violence, occasional swearing.

I haven't written nearly as frequently for *Autistic Hoya* in the last two years or so as I did for the first few years that this blog existed. It seems that the few times I interrupt my long absences here now are most often for devastating news—for writing flowing straight from my pain, and sometimes my anger, and often quite a bit of both.

Today, there is too much. Too much.

Today, the top news story in the U.S. is the hours-long mass shooting at the embattled Inland Regional Center in San Bernardino, California. The Inland Regional Center is responsible for providing and coordinating community-based services to over 31,000 people with developmental disabilities (likely including many autistic people) in San Bernardino and Riverside Counties east of Los Angeles. At last count, 14 people are estimated to be killed and 17 additional injured. The shooting went on for hours. So far, we know that the shooting happened inside one of the buildings, at a county-wide event honoring healthcare professionals. We don't know who specifically the attackers targeted because the victims haven't been publicly identified yet. Police have counted three suspects—two men and a woman.

I learned about the shooting while it was still happening. I was in class.

TASH is hosting its annual conference in Portland, Oregon right now. A friend told me the conference is reeling.

My email inbox has exploded with messages on disability lists reacting in real-time to the attack.

Every time I glance at my phone, I see more news updates scrolling across the mobile browser, telling me police have killed two suspects, are searching an apartment for possible explosives, won't release identities of the dead until next of kin are notified, are speculating about motive.

My Facebook news feed is equal parts horror and disgust and fear and sorrow and anger and brokenness and fragility from this community, these many fractured communities, where I have learned to live and love and suffer and often, to cry.

* * *

I was going to use "Anti-ableist ways to respond to today's ongoing tragedy in San Bernardino" as the title for this blog post. But it sounds too artificial. Too prepared. Too hollow.

I wanted to write this because I can't stay silent. I can't. Not when those struggling alongside us, those attempting to practice allyship, those not directly impacted by ableism want to know what to say or do. How to react.

We have a saying in culturally autistic spaces—"I need help reacting to something."

I do. It's nameless things dismantled all over again.

Minneapolis. Chicago. Beirut. Yola. Kano. Baghdad. Paris. Colorado Springs.

Now San Bernardino.

I can't. I just can't.

The trouble is, it's less that I can't react than that I'm crashing from trying to react to too many things all at once. Made it home from school in the rain. One load of laundry done. Dinner for four made, eaten. Dishes washed, put away. Old exam questions pondered, discussed with fellow classmates. Emails sent. All while forcing myself not to feel too much. Not to think. Just to act. Follow a script. A routine. Forget I am real. Forget I inhabit this taut and trembling flesh.

This is empathy overload. This is emotional shutdown. This is autism.

***

There was a news article earlier today quoting someone from the FBI describing the attackers as "Americans, not terrorists." Somehow totally missing the complete irony of just how full of terrorists the U.S. always has been and continues to be, in both state sanctioned and individual forms.

Our country is steeped in violence. For the vast majority of us in the U.S. who are not Indigenous or Native, we live on stolen, colonized, occupied land.

In our Property class in law school today, a student objected to the concept of adverse possession (when someone can gain ownership of someone else's land/real estate simply by occupying it for a long time without the owner's permission), saying, "But this is America!" And a number of us responded that, well, nothing could be more American than taking someone else's land. After all, that's how this country was built.

Not too far from our school, there was a rally today at Ruggles Station against police terrorism targeting low-income Black and Brown communities, as we have learned of the police murders of more unarmed Black men—Jamar Clark in Minneapolis last month and Laquan McDonald in Chicago last year, whose death was videotaped and covered up by not only the police department but its commissioner and the city's mayor.

President Barack Obama described himself as very good at killing people, as the number of Brown people killed by remotely operated drones has risen higher under his administration than under the George W. Bush one.

Trans women of color face routine violence in the streets from strangers and police alike. Women who dare criticize men or even acknowledge misogyny risk terrifying, brutal retaliation. My psych disabled and mad, neurodivergent friends live with constant terror of possible incarceration in the name of treatment and public safety. While my light skin and educated words lend me some measure of protection, my Black and Brown friends risk their lives upon encountering a police officer for so much as existing.

But of course, the term "terrorism" is steeped in a particular racism that attaches it only to Brown people and those racialized as Muslim.

***

It's everywhere on Twitter, Facebook, anywhere you care to check. Ordinary folks expressing shock, horror, outrage that anyone might target disabled people for violence. Surprised by it. Wondering how, how could anyone go after *the disabled*?

My friend Maddy Ruvolo says, "So many people talking about how they can't believe shooters would target disabled people like they're not complicit in the violence disabled people face every single day. If you're surprised by violence against disabled people, you haven't been paying attention."

This narrative is superficially sympathetic, but it's plied with the pity endemic to pathologizing ways of thinking about disability. It depends on understanding disabled people through pity/charity frameworks, on infantilizing us as eternally untouched by reality (negativity, fear, violence, malice) on the presumption of incompetence.

Expecting disabled people to be angels, innocents, somehow specially exempt from reality—similarly to the misogyny in the idea that hitting *women* is somehow especially wrong, but hitting *men* is normal, if still wrong. Thinking about us as objects, not subjects, not agents of our own destinies. Treating disabled people as some specially innocent population, as readily available charity/community service projects here for abled people to feel good about themselves for being *nice* to us—for not calling us retarded, for not refusing to let us in the room, for not staring. Relegating us to a constant position as objects for the edification of abled people.

(Sign up for Best Buddies. Be friends with a person with a developmental disability once a week and occasionally at group events with all the other people with developmental disabilities. Give yourself a pat on the back. Grow some warm feelings. Make the person with the disability smile and believe you are really their friend. Never or rarely include them in your other outings with your regular friends. Never confide in them your trust. Never think of them as simply another person you know. Consider yourself a do-gooder. Don't worry; the disabled person won't notice.)

Wondering who could hate disabled people.

Believe me, plenty of people do. Hate is nothing new. And no, pity and hate are absolutely not mutually exclusive. Sometimes they depend on each other.

Over half of people killed by police are disabled. I think of Stephon Watts, Steven Eugene Washington, Natasha McKenna, John Williams, Mohamed Usman Chaudhry,

117

Kajieme Powell, Freddie Gray, all disabled *and* Black or Brown.

One study found that 83% of women with developmental disabilities will be raped at least once in their lifetimes, and that more than half that number will be raped at least ten times before the age of eighteen alone. That almost 40% of men with developmental disabilities will be raped at least once in this lifetime.

What terrifies me is that these numbers are probably conservative estimates.

This is ableism.

***

The Los Angeles Times announced that police named Syed Farook as one of the shooting suspects.

Of course the first person named a suspect in the shooting has a name racialized as Brown and Muslim—and when the articles begin to appear, his neighbor discusses how he became more outwardly religious (or was perceived that way), predicated on the presumption that of course, this is relevant. Of course it matters that he grew a beard. That he began to wear non-Western clothing. We are expected to read these details and assume the rest of the narrative—young Muslim becomes a terrorist by becoming more Muslim.

(They say the second shooter is Tashfeen Malik, now giving the public two identifiable Muslim names.)
How soon will the FBI's earlier description of the shooter as a U.S. citizen be forgotten? How soon will news

coverage shift to obsessive nitpicking over Syed's religious identification and practices, speculating about connections to Daesh (ISIS) or Al Qaeda or some other such group? How soon will the rhetoric shift from the ever-familiar refrain of "we need to fix the mental health system" to "this was possibly terrorism-related?"[1]

***

Congressman Tim Murphy's pet project, House Bill 2646, is moving rapidly through Congress. We know it as the Murphy Bill. You might know it as the Helping Families in Mental Health Crisis Act.

He began pushing this bill right after the Sandy Hook shooting in December 2013.

It's the kind of measure that sounds superficially nice and potentially worthwhile. He cloaks it in the rhetoric of public safety, greater good, better mental health services. The lie that these mass shootings are the product of mental illness.

Here's what the bill does: Pumps funds into involuntary, coercive treatment through both inpatient and outpatient commitment. Incentivizes states to increase use of involuntary, coercive treatment. Cut funds from community based programs, services, and supports. Slash funds for the national network of protection and advocacy systems that work to promote the rights of people with psych disabilities—a network created in large part because of horrifying revelations about the all-pervasive abuses in institutional settings (the psych ward, the mental hospital, the long-term residential institution). Weaken

119

doctor/patient confidentiality protections for people with psych disabilities.

Its supporters will tell insist that mental health reform is necessary to stop gun violence.

We know we need better mental health services. We know the existing system is riddled with failures, is a frequent source of (re)traumatization for so many of us.

But these issues are so separate from gun violence.

Stop pathologizing violence. Violence is not a mental illness, but psych disabled people, like all disabled people, live with the constant possibility of violence and abuse in this profoundly ableist world.

They will tell you that jails and prisons are now the nation's largest mental health care providers. That people with mental illness don't belong in jail or prison, but instead in specialized facilities. That they need treatment instead.

Don't believe the lie that new asylums, new mental institutions are anything other than a different—and often, far less regulated—form of incarceration than the penal institution.

Disrupt the pattern of disability hierarchy. The Inland Regional Center's clients with developmental disabilities undoubtedly include many, many people who also have psych disabilities. We will find these narratives—that (1) people with developmental disabilities are innocent angels incapable of understanding violence, and (2) people with psych disabilities are unstable, potential murderers waiting to happen. We will find these narratives everywhere.

This is ableism.

(And often, in the wake of gun violence by white people, it's also the racist effect of white supremacy. No matter whether the murderer writes a terrifying manifesto against women or repeatedly espouses white supremacist causes before targeting Black people at prayer, white supremacy insists on exempting whiteness from violence by scapegoating the specter of madness instead.)

These lines have well-worn grooves in our newspapers and frequently-visited websites. They provide a familiar refrain, one that rips and breaks and tears at me.

Here, where those dead, injured, and left surviving, left reeling may well be disabled like me, I can't begin to respond. I don't understand this pain. But I know it. It's written all over me.

***

We have to hold space for each other.

Make space for us to relax. To heal. To dream. To mourn. To cry. To scream. To not have words. To feel empty. To process this jumbled fucking mess. To recover. To find new scars.

Ask us what we need.

Remind us that we are valuable, that we matter, that we deserve to exist, and more than that, that we deserve to exist in a world where we genuinely care for and about each other. Where our wobbly, sick, lopsided, drooling, asymmetrical, neurodivergent, mad, crip bodies are welcomed and loved and honored.

Join us in our struggles.

Morning, with its promise of familiar routine, waits for us.

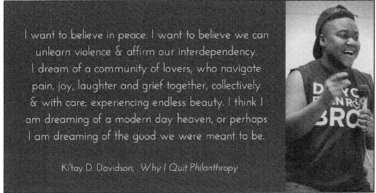

I want to believe in peace. I want to believe we can unlearn violence & affirm our interdependency. I dream of a community of lovers, who navigate pain, joy, laughter and grief together, collectively & with care; experiencing endless beauty. I think I am dreaming of a modern day heaven, or perhaps I am dreaming of the good we were meant to be.

Ki'tay D. Davidson, Why I Quit Philanthropy

"I want to believe in peace. I want to believe we can unlearn violence & affirm our interdependency. I dream of a community of lovers, who navigate pain, joy, laughter and grief together, collectively & with care; experiencing endless beauty. I think I am dreaming of a modern day heaven, or perhaps I am dreaming of the good we were meant to be."

Ki'tay Davidson, Why I Quit Philanthropy
#Justice2050

Photo (Talila "TL" Lewis): Dark rectangle with the above quote and a photo of Ki'tay during a presentation to disabled youth. Ki'tay is smiling with an open mouth and snapping in celebration of a great comment by an audience member while facilitating a Disability History, Culture, and Pride workshop for youth with disabilities during the summer of 2014. Ki'tay is holding a microphone in his left hand and snapping with his right. He is wearing a black shirt, orange pants and a black hat.

---

1 I originally wrote a slightly different version of this essay one day after the shooting. Within a few days, the news coverage turned entirely to discussion of the shooters' supposed pledge of allegiance to Daesh (the Islamic State or ISIS). So the answer is: less than a week, and it wasn't discussed as "possibly terrorism-related," but as a "terror attack."

Love Letter To My Autism

Kaijaii Gomez Wick

They say you are a limb, an appendage,
attached to me by meathooks or finger traps,
something that needs to be cut off. They
do not know of you, your eternal, your infinite.

You, first color in the void, you,
when-you-love, you love-unto-infinity, you, joy
of moving hands, you,
the-smallest-thing-is-worthy-of-my-rapture,
you, the beginning of creation. You, there at
the start, you, me born smiling because I had you,
you, divine ecstasy that rescues from agony. You,
lights that swim with a flick of an eye, you,
obsess, you, sharpen-my-mind-onto-the-head-of-a-pin,
you, and-dance-on-that-pin, you. You, manic-fire-of-want,
you, loneliness a candy, you, crave-with-all-your-skin, you.
You.

Softness rubbing against my cheek, celebration of ritual,
day after day, a stone to rest, foundations scraping
the skies for me to lie on and writhe in perfection.
You, demand-of-me-to-know-thyself,
you, protector-of-self, you, without whom I would have

been dashed against the rocks, would have jumped
without a twitch of fear, without the calm you bring me.

They call you changeling-arranger,
stealer of children, kidnapper of potential. They know
nothing.
Their eyes have never exploded with the colors of elation
at the taste of a single fruit, their fingertips never become
their entire world at the touch of silk. Their feet do not
know
the singing when they touch the earth,
their wrists are held stiffly upright, never to flap like
wings.
They do not spin. I would weep for them if it were not
for the certainty that they do not feel guilt for it
and you whispering that heart is wasted on enemies.

You. With you they say my life is chaos, they say
that your pleasures are temptations, apples that, once
eaten,
will make me into cyborg or angel, will make unto me
armor against the world, a shell. If you are an apple I will
grab
you right off the tree, devour, gorge, lick clean the juices
and roll on the grass. I relish my spine of gleaming metal,
my mithril hair blowing in the wind, my fingernails of eye-
burning
light, my six wings. If you have made me an angel
or a monster, it is because I am that which I choose to be,
and you make me what I am.
My life is chaos? How else should a life be but chaos?
Why would anyone

want a world quantifiable, every experience laboratory-
clean,
factory-standard, counted, not a single strand out of place?

No, no, no, you are so beautiful that you scare everyone
who wants to control you. You are so powerful that you
terrify all
who want to wipe clean life of all its undignified messes,
its impure delights. You are that which cannot be stopped,
you are repeat-after-everyone, you are no-need-for-words,
you are objects-in-a-line, quietly, on a cool surface.
You are order, you are chaos, you are electric words
like stim and echolalia,
words that hum and buzz
and loll around on the tongue. You are all that I would
ever want,
you are the ink that has long since seeped through all the
pages,
as long as my staircases of blood. You are me, and I am
you.

You are Autism. Infinite. Self,
warmth in the sweetness of the dark,
home. Life is for the small things, and you are the smallest
and the largest of them all. You. I want to kiss you,
represent you, cloak you in beauty. Let me. Let me love
you,
let me love myself. Let me fill the dishwasher
to make your world make sense again, let me touch-
comfort
with a single fingertip, let me show desire with a stack
of beads. Let me show you
how Autism loves.

PART THREE:

INTERSECTED REALITIES

On Race, Diagnosis and Privilege

Kelly Johnson

I am an Autistic (androgynous) female of mixed race. My father was from Barbados and my mother is French Canadian. I married a white man of Austrian, British and Irish heritage. I thought my (also) Autistic son would come out with a bit more colour to him, but instead he looks 100% white, with strawberry blond hair and beautiful green eyes. He does have my nose and mouth—my black facial features—if you take a moment to look. But if you don't, because of your (perhaps ill-conceived) notions of what a family should look like, you can, as I have been, mistake me for the babysitter.

Add the fact my once non-verbal son went from calling no one mom, to calling all females of colour he saw, "mama," well I guess I can understand some confusion. (He also called all white males "dada" for some time.)

It was I who brought him to many appointments, where I raised my concerns about his development. I was spoken to like I couldn't possibly know what I was talking about. My concerns resulted in condescension and blame from doctors, so I switched doctors THREE times. Not an easy feat when we have a doctor shortage here.

I was told I was not stimulating him enough at home, despite using the speech therapy techniques I had learned from my studies in university and my volunteer speech therapy with disabled children. I was told I was not feeding him well enough. It was assumed, without even asking for details, that the reason he was not developing normally was because of my bad parenting. Was that because of my colour or something else? What is it about me that screams to people: not smart enough/not a good parent?

In the end, I found a private psychologist, who respected me and my son enough to listen, test and confirm my suspicions. At the time I was unemployed (on mat leave) and without that privilege to have the time and strength to fight for answers, I am not sure what would have happened. I never fail to recognize the many levels of privilege I used in my quest:

The fact I had paid maternity leave.
The fact I was educated.
The fact I had the means to research.
The fact I had the means to find professionals.
The fact I had the means to pay a professional.
The fact I had the time to go to appointments.
The fact I had transportation to get to appointments.

I wonder what would have happened had I not persisted.

At times I do wonder—did I not get adequate help/treatment because I am a POC? Did I end up getting help because my son is not technically a POC? Did I not express the seriousness of my concerns properly at the time because of my disability (Autism)?

These are things I will probably never have a good answer to, but I know a big part of my job as a parent is making sure my son knows his own privilege and knows how to advocate for himself. It's a shame to say, but he will probably get better, or at the very least, adequate services and support simply because he inherited my disability, nose and mouth, but not my skin colour.

Untitled

Shondolyn Gibson

Walking around the playground, I drifted in a world of my own. The other kids laughed and screamed together, playing confusing games while made up stories and collected interesting things off the ground.

My mother, 1 out of 12 kids, told me about growing up down south and how'd she pretend corn were students and she was the teacher. She also made up stories.

I don't really know much about my father's childhood. Neither he or my mother raised me most of the time. It was mostly my paternal grandmother that raised me. He sometimes lived with us, but had a hard time connecting to me other than our mutual interest in music. He has an obsession with chess, a talent for music and art.

I can't help but suspect my parents are both on the autism spectrum.

The difference between affluent people, especially affluent white people and many minorities and low income people is that affluent people are more likely to be able to afford to take their children to specialists at the first sign of autism. Though I could have flown under the radar when I didn't speak until three because I was getting treatment for the large cancerous tumour on my hand. My mother said she thought I'd develop at my own pace. My worsening sensory issues, social anxiety and awkwardness and fixation on things like spiders made me suspect autism as early as college. A psychologist I was seeing for social phobia ignored me when I suggested autism to her. I wasn't diagnosed until I was at least in my 30s.

I spent so much of college struggling with depression that made me feel like my blood was full of lead. Outside of college I struggled to find a job. Simple sensory things became painful. Making friends outside of school was hard.

Yet, at the same time there were things like my Synesthesia getting stronger. Music became even more of an epic drug for my ears. There were advantages and disadvantages to my neurology. I've learned to embrace it as part of me.

The problem is autism is girls and minorities, not just black people like my family, is under diagnosed. For me it was a mixed bag. At least no one tormented me with hours of ABA to try to make me normal. I spent my life feeling like an alien waiting to be taken back home. A lot people weren't so lucky, having to be institutionalized if they were non-speaking. Speaking autistic people have their struggles too. Passing takes a lot of energy and spoons. It uses up more than we can regenerate.

I wonder if the stress of my job contributed to worsening sensory issues and physical sickness.

There are a lot of people out there who may find comfort in knowing there's others like them and they don't need to feel alone. Especially people who are already marginalized.

Personal Literacy

Elly Wong

I can sum up the best thing I have ever written in one word: "disgaybled." In fact, it is just literally that word. Disgaybled. DISGAYBLED.

Once upon a time, I shoved the word "gay" inside the word "disabled" because I think I'm hilarious.

Once upon a time, I was a pretty weird kid who liked to watch *Glee*. I loved honorable, gullible Sam, and stiff Kurt, who lived in references to old movies and musicals, and, most of all, Brittany S. Pierce. Brittany was assertive, oddly masculine, believed in everyone being themselves, had some meds she didn't want and some meds she did, didn't know how to leave a room, definitely knew what someone being electroshocked looked like, and was gorgeously, exhilaratingly brave. Because these characters were strange or stupid or broken like me, I could be strong like them. And then I met people who loved them the same way I did. Quinn was the smartest person I had ever met, and she handflapped happily at the mention of *Glee*. With Quinn came her best friend, the sweet, strongly ethical Zoe, and Zoe's friend Alex, who didn't even watch *Glee*, but who did listen to the same music as me. I was a pretty weird kid, but I made some friends, and if anything, I got even weirder.

Once upon a time, Zoe yelled at someone on Tumblr for interpreting *Glee* wrong. People persistently think that Brittany S. Pierce is somehow offensive because she's the only main character who's bisexual, and the writers dared to insult bisexuality by giving it to a girl who needs help remembering how to eat breakfast. The implication is that no one like that actually exists. Zoe, who sometimes walks into traffic, yet definitely exists, took this particular miswatcher of Glee down in a flounce of exclamation-pointed rhetoric and indignant hashtags. Quinn, also existent despite her inability to button jackets, proclaimed "Marry me, Zoe!" in a fit of rightful passion, and I jumped in with "Same here!" By the time Alex had woken up from her midday nap, we had logically decided that we definitely needed to have a four-way Internet wedding. On the horrible wedding invitations I made in Microsoft Paint, in 32-point Comic Sans, I declared our strange party of developmentally disabled queer girls "v. disgaybled and shit."

Quinn made sure her flower crown would match Alex's sparkly blue cane, Zoe uploaded a picture of a chuppah, I tied a ribbon to my noise-canceling headphones, and the four of us posted our vows to Tumblr under the tipsy officiation of Alex's college friend. We were four-way disgaybled married, and we all streamed "Call Me Maybe" to our respective computers in celebration. "Before you came into my life, I missed you so so bad." We all felt it in our bones, and in our weird, fidgeting fingers and rocking bodies that we could make okay. Sometimes, the storybook monsters can throw a fairytale wedding, and our jokes and laughter are part of our happy ending. Once upon a time, my friends and I turned a very mean offhand comment that erased our existences into a goofy, joyous triumph.

Coining the term "disgaybled," in spite of and because of an ignorant world, is the best thing I've ever written. I love "disgaybled," not because I need it to describe myself, but because I need it to feel like I truly have a self to inhabit.

Once upon a time, I finally came up with my very own word to tell my community *I love you.*

Why the Term 'Psychopath' is Racist and Ableist

Lydia X. Z. Brown

I have become used to being told that I do not have feelings, that I am innately incapable of relating to other people as human beings or having any empathy at all, that this is a core component of what it means to be autistic. I have become used to hearing this said constantly by so-called professionals, dramatically by television personalities, clinically by journalists and academics, and casually by friends, acquaintances, family. But I have never become used to the feeling of absolute devastation weighing somewhere deep in my chest each time I find myself on the receiving end of this accusation.

Empathy is what makes us human.

It's no wonder that the idea of psychopathy is terrifying. If psychopathy means the inability to experience empathy, and empathy is what makes us human, then psychopathy is literally the dehumanizing condition. Psychopaths populate crime dramas, horror films, murder mysteries, and thrillers. It's the casual diagnosis for mass murderers, serial rapists, and child abusers.

But it is also deeply personal, profoundly ableist and sanist, and rooted in a complex, interlocking web of structural racism, ageism, and sexism.

In 1944, the Austrian pediatrician Hans Asperger published a paper describing a condition that he called "autistic psychopathy."

Theory of mind, in clinical psychology, means the cognitive ability to recognize that other people have different knowledge, experiences, emotions, and beliefs than oneself. Theory of mind is something that autistic people, like me, supposedly lack. Theory of mind is what makes empathy with other people possible.

When I was a sophomore in college, my mom sent me an email that said, "You need to work on your theory of mind."

Dagger to the gut, I reeled at the words and, with shaky fingers, called home.

"Never say that to me again. Never."

When I was a sophomore in high school, I was wrongfully accused of planning a school shooting. Another autistic friend who was accused of planting a bomb at her school was detained and interrogated for hours while the entire school went into lockdown. In response to frequent claims in the media and by policymakers that autistic people lack empathy (and are therefore violent psychopaths), many people in the autistic community, including autistic activists, begin the process of disavowal.

"No, autistic people are nothing like psychopaths. We are more likely to be the victims of crime while psychopaths are usually victimizers."

"No, someone who would shoot dozens of innocent children wasn't autistic. That's not autism. That's mental illness."

"An autistic person wouldn't commit such horribly violent crimes. Only a psychopath could do that."

If empathy is what makes us human, and autistic people are as human as anyone else, then we must have empathy. It must be some other kind of person who doesn't experience empathy. It must be someone who is truly psychopathic. This is the logic path that afflicts so many disability communities. Disavowal of one another has become a way of life. Many autistic people routinely decry the use of the slur retarded, yet assert in the same breath that they aren't crazy or mentally ill. Many physically disabled activists proudly say that their minds work just fine.

When we commit to examining our language and ideas and deconstructing the ableism we find in them, we must make a full, not partial or half-hearted, commitment. When we stop using autistic, crippled, and retarded as insults, when we realize the urgent need to stop scapegoating violence on "mental illness" and "emotional instability or disturbance," when we learn to stop referring to our political opponents as blind, deaf, or crippled in their ideologies, *we must also critically re-examine our use of the psychopathy label.*

In radical communities working toward intersectional social justice, the figure of the psychopath is invoked all too often to characterize members of oppressive classes, especially when they are in a position of political power in addition to apolitical structural power.

Empathy is what makes us human.

In September 2013, a popular blogger responded to a CEO's appalling statement that criticism of executive bonuses is just as bad as lynching by invoking the specter of psychopathy.[1]

In the alternate reality of wealthy people, criticizing someone's wealth is just as bad as kidnapping someone, dragging them–by force–to a tree, beating the shit out of them, wrapping a rope around their neck, stringing them up until their neck snaps, setting them on fire, having a barbecue around the charred remains, and taking photographs of the whole thing for postcards and posterity. These are the psychopaths in charge of this corporatocracy we call the United States of America.

The term psychopath is as common in the vocabulary of the average radical social justice organizer as it is in that of the average mainstream political commentator. Yet psychopathy isn't even a medical or psychiatric diagnosis. It doesn't exist in the DSM-IV or the DSM-5, and as much as I hate lending any further credence to the medical-industrial complex's state-sanctioned and socially-approved authority, this is important. *Even the medical-industrial complex does not recognize psychopathy as a diagnosis.*

However, most people who point out that psychopathy is not considered a diagnosis typically follow up by explaining that antisocial personality disorder (APD), conduct disorder, and oppositional defiant disorder (ODD) are the closest medically accepted diagnoses to what is meant by psychopathy. These labels are recognized and codified as psychiatric conditions by the medical establishment. And who are the people typically diagnosed with Antisocial Personality Disorder, Conduct Disorder, and Oppositional Defiant Disorder? They are overwhelmingly poor students of color (especially dark-skinned people of color) who frequently have other disabilities.

Antisocial Personality Disorder, the diagnostic category that comes closest to approximating the lay definition of psychopathy, is most often a tool for criminalizing poverty, blackness and brownness, and disability. It is the diagnostic label that legitimizes non-compliance as a mental health problem.

Refusal to take medications? Non-compliant. Failing math class? Non-compliant. Stimming in public? Non-compliant.

If you are non-compliant, you are anti-social. You are mentally ill. You are a psychopath.

In August 2013, Anthony Stokes was denied a life-saving heart transplant because he was Black and labeled non-compliant.

A physician's form for students in a study abroad program asks the doctor whether the student has a history of emotional disturbance. It asks whether they have displayed "difficulties in relations with parents, authority figures, peers" with reckless, chilling disregard for whether the student is the victim of parental abuse (financial, physical, emotional, sexual), bullying or other violence by peers, or violence by authority figures (including teachers and police). "Difficulties" in those relations are automatically rendered non-normative, deviant, and thus, suspect and pathological, symptomatic of some supposed larger psychiatric crisis or disturbed personality.

A billboard in Washington DC buses asked parents to volunteer their children for a study on conduct disorder. Symptoms? Failure to conform to social norms (that could mean anyone queer, trans*, mad, autistic, or politically radical), trouble with the law (hell, that could mean anyone who uses weed or attends protests), consistent irresponsibility (that could be anyone for various poverty, disability, or abuse related reasons), impulsivity (as if this is pathological?), manipulative behavior (as a catch-all for anything non-normative or potentially subversive), and **lack of empathy.**

The language of pathology, mental illness, madness, disease, and disability, has long been used to reinforce other existing structural oppressions like racism, classism, sexism, heterosexism, binarism, cissexism, and ableism. And it is most disheartening when those who purport to work toward dismantling those systems still use ableism as metaphor. Ableist metaphor is all-pervasive in public discourse, academia, grassroots organizing, and left-leaning movements as well as in conservative, neoliberal, and nationalist movements. It draws on the language of disability to characterize, denigrate, attack, rhetoricize, and politicize—and it does so based on the presumption that deviation from typical thought, movement, emotional processing, communication, bodily/mental functioning, learning, remembering, sensing is evidence of defect, deficiency, disorder, and ultimately, moral failure.

To use psychopathy as the lens through which one views either systemic or individual violence is to reinforce the structural power of the medical-industrial complex at the expense of disabled people, poor people, and people of color.

My advice: Be precise in your language and say that oppressive structures are violent and manipulative. Say that those who abuse their structural positions of power act with reckless disregard for other human beings. Say that they are callous and unabashedly wielding the power that comes with their privilege.

But don't call them psychopaths.

I've experienced enough ableism in my life to last me several lifetimes. I don't need fellow radicals feeding into ableism.

We talk about intersectionality in our identities, in our organizing, and in our writing so often. It is past time to move from talk to accountability. We must hold ourselves accountable for examining and deconstructing ableism in all its forms in our work, our communities, our personal lives, and our relationships with each other. Because our lives, our dignity, our very ability to be recognized as human, depend on it.

This piece was originally published in Black Girl Dangerous *on 22 January 2014.*

---

1 I can no longer find the original source of the quote and do not remember the author's name. It does not seem to exist online anymore.

Black Lives Matter???
The Day After
(#WalterScott)

Morénike Giwa Onaiwu

Author's note: As a black Autistic mother of disabled black children, the pervasive anti-blackness in our society is more than just a recurring annoyance. It is a threat, a constant fear. One that we cannot escape.

I wrote the post below about a heartbreaking conversation I had to have with my children after yet another release of video footage of police violence against an unarmed black man, Walter Scott. Sadly, at the time this is published you will probably not recall who he is because of how commonplace these atrocities have become. So I ask you, like I asked in this post, do black lives matter?)

Only slept an hour last night. Couldn't stop thinking about life, death, race, gender, violence, deceit, corruption. About #WalterScott. About everything.

I had "the talk" with my kids this morning in the car. Not the "birds and the bees" talk. The "how to stay alive because you're black and therefore a threat" talk. Don't wear that dark gray hoodie you love anymore. Make eye contact with authorities at all times—forget everything I've ever taught you about how forced eye contact is a bad thing...do it anyway, even if it hurts. Speak in a soft, gentle tone. Keep your hands where they can see them at all times. No sudden or unexpected movements and ABSOLUTELY no stimming or fidgeting or flapping as it might be perceived as attempting to strike someone. No echolalia, as it might be perceived as trying to "mock" an officer. No going to the mall with a group of friends if more than two people are male-presenting and of color. Say "yes, sir," and "no, sir" with each statement. No nervous laughter. No sarcasm. Do everything that they ask of you even if it is unlawful. If they want to know your name, age, shoe size, whatever—just tell them. If they violate your rights we will file a complaint after the fact, but do not address it with them in the moment. If they hit you, shout at you, insult you, spit on you, just take it. We will seek justice for the wrongdoing through the legal channels. Don't put yourself at risk by trying to stand up for yourself.

Just take it.

They listened quietly. Asked me if it was okay to just run away. Inwardly I kicked myself for forgetting to mention running. "No," I replied. "Absolutely no running."

"Mom?"

"Yes?" I asked.

"I'd probably be nervous, Mom. I don't think I would be able to keep from moving and remember to keep my voice a certain way and remember to say 'sir' and all of those things. Will I still be okay? They know I'm just a kid."

Good point, I thought. I'd probably be too nervous to keep from stimming myself if it was me. And DO they know you're just a kid? I wondered silently. You are close to 12 year old Tamir Rice's age. He was just a kid too. It didn't save him.

"Mom?"

"Um hum, kiddo?"

"You didn't answer. Will I still be okay?"

Will you? Will you? For the love of God, I hope so. I hope so. But I don't know for sure.

"I hope so, sweetie. I think so, yes."

I just died a little—no, a lot—inside.

A version of this post originally appeared in the "Just Being Me...Who Needs 'Normalcy' Anyway?" blog in April 2015 the day following the release of video footage of a police officer shooting an unarmed black male, Walter Scott, who subsequently died, in the back as he fled.

Raceabelism

Nicole S. Xurd (Shalese Nicole Heard)

That racism, and ableism have overwhelmed much of my climate; I'll not deny.

"Your obsession with Russia, and Barbie dolls weird, these are white people's interests and you don't even know why you like these things."

"You aren't autistic, you are just manipulative."

"Learn to speak more...chill....You should learn to say Douche, instead of Gentleman; you speak too formal and it is too pretentious."

"She's just a spoilt brat, with a behavior problem and we sterilize little girls like her who can't speak."

"Autistic people cannot and should NOT be doctors."

"You speak so white....are you part of the KKK??"

Among the white majority, and African American community alike; racism has overwhelmed my climate.

I'll not deny any of this. Yet, I still enjoy being the only African American, Autistic woman in a room.

It is my pleasure to destroy the boxed up residence that has been predecided as my residence.

It makes me smile breaking the chains, and continuing to fly "out of bounds."

I'm the only one in the room, and you can't help but be embraced by my presence.

You see, it absolutely astonishes me that any of you would even THINK to TRY to force me into this narrow box when so much of the world mine, and waiting for me to conquer it.

Yes, I have taken every book off the shelf.

Read, consumed, and did what was fed to me.

I break records on purpose.

I repeatedly turn North when told to turn Right, and smile whilst doing so. Actually, it's quite amusing.

I've sailed so far out of my decided boundaries, to a place beyond Bouvet Island; there is no turning back, and there is no finding and restraining me. And I don't apologize!

Not for redirecting constructed climate!

Passing Through

Melis Leflef (Melissa Murphy)

The story goes that when I was born, I was the only blonde, blue eyed baby in the hospital. In a sea of browns, my alabaster skin was shockingly white. Old Turkish women would cry out that my hair had turned prematurely grey. My surname, that of a household shoe polish brand, was solid, Turkish. My appearance was not.

And yet, very soon, the tables were turned. As they often are, in times of conflict and turmoil, when to survive you must move on. We arrived in the West Kerry Gealtacht (Irish-speaking area) in 1980. I could not speak a word of English, never mind the Irish that was more commonly spoken there. And so I did not speak. For a year, I was mute. So, there I was, unspeaking, odd, impossibly tanned amongst the Celtic skinned. Other. The local gossip didn't help. Where was my father? (Finishing up his contract of work in Turkey) Was that lady his second wife? (No, she came along as a sort of nanny, a hired hand, a helper) They called us "Na Turkeys Bána", the White Turkeys. Great at puns, the Irish. Not so great at acceptance. Now, my skin faded by the grey skies, I was the right colour but my surname let me down.

We moved to Dublin when I was six. I learnt to fit in, to hide my grief and my depression, to ignore the bullying and crushing loneliness, to spell out my surname automatically before being asked. And I felt guilty when my darker-skinned,

Irish-born sister got cursed at to "go back to your own country". And when we did go back, on holiday, I fell foul of being "Turk-but-not-Turk", of not picking up on the subtle cultural differences despite being fluent in the language and the "learnt" culture. No shoes indoors was second nature. Not knowing to lie about not being a virgin, was not.

And now I have found there was another layer going on as well. Another way I was "other". A different culture I was learning to pass as. I used to practice eye-contact by staring in the mirror. I used to wonder why certain lighting in certain shops made me faint and dizzy. Why I was never invited to birthday parties. Why the playground games had forever changing rules that everyone else knew but I couldn't figure out. The journalist interviewing my mom about her poetry spotted it. He wrote that my brother and I were "Midwich cuckoos". I asked my mom what that meant. She said it was from a sci-fi movie, that we were like "alien children". I took it to mean alien in an immigration sense. I figured it had to do with my surname. I blamed the Turk in me. I got married and changed my surname to a solid Irish one. But I was still "other". I was still "alien". Little did I know there were other genes, from my mom's side, the oddly creative side, the poetic, other-worldly side. It had a name I've only recently come to recognise. Autistic.

And there's another word I've recently learnt. Passing. Passing-white. Passing-NT. And with that knowledge has come a release. A letting go of the need to pass. I am now free to explore my heritage, both autistic and non-white. I can avoid eye-contact, I can avoid talking, I can listen to Tarkan and sing along loudly, I can use whatever surname I want. My passing phase was but a passing-through to my own, unique me. I will hide no longer.

Invisible

Yasmin Khoshnood

I sit alone in my room
Sometimes lost in happiness, sometimes lost in gloom.
Reading, writing, or even just alone with my thoughts
As I think to myself how
People like me
Don't exist on TV
Too many of us left behind
By a society that is blind.
Despite an early diagnosis, an exception
Whereas others of color don't get as much attention.
I still feel invisible
Lack accurate portrayals on television and news
Because even with autism
They're seeing White.
They're seeing severely autistic traits
Which isn't me
I often hear the old theory: People with autism lack empathy
So is all we have apathy?
I remember the news of the Iranian election protests
My heart sank
The empathy I felt consumed me to the core
It made my mind feel sore.
Stereotypes of terrorism
Crime
Apathy

Among both groups
All contribute to my
Invisibility.
A few years later I heard a news story
That connected autism to violence, to lack of empathy
A young man who committed a horrible crime
The school shooting
He was said to have autism
Very few of us, even if we all truly lacked empathy
Would commit an act of violence.
If I felt less invisible, I'd be
Happier
More liberated
More optimistic
I'd have more faith
That things would change
In my lifetime
I would feel less
Anger
I long to hear more stories of diversity among autistic
people.
I long to hear more stories of autistic adults achieving
happiness and success.
I long to hear more stories of goodness, empathy and love
among us.
I long to escape being invisible

My Experience

Stephan B.

I grew up an outsider.

I had been diagnosed when I was around 7. By then I had already been expelled from several daycares and elementary schools. The diagnosis came after concerns I spent weeks walking with my hands straight to my sides and when asked why I responded with, "I'm in a coffin." My great- grandmother had passed before then and looking back I was probably coping with that by mimicking her as I often did. The doctors and my family thought I was experiencing schizophrenic hallucinations. I don't know if my mother felt any relief from the MRI that told a different story.

I wasn't told I had Asperger's until much later, after many school fights and expulsions, when my mother and my psychiatrist dropped the bomb on me, I didn't take it very well. I thought of the representations of autistic people the media had fed to me and did what most people would do. I panicked. I denied it. I was ashamed. I already didn't fit in and I had no friends. I had prided myself on my grades and intelligence to make up for my lack of social anything. "Autistic" sounded like "Retard" and at the time both words were thrown around as interchangeable insults amongst my peers, and even my family. I refused. I was already often the odd one out being a dark-skinned

155

Puerto Rican boy in predominantly white schools and neighborhoods. I had been both a bully and been bullied. I always got stricter punishment than my white peers. In the 6th grade the school even went as far to call the police when I had a meltdown. An older white kid had a more serious meltdown a week earlier and never faced law enforcement. Much like the world, it wasn't fair. Much like my world, it was unusual.

Throughout middle school I had mellowed out a bit. I was no longer jumping at every opportunity to fight a kid for so much as sitting next to me. I knew the difference between right and wrong, and the consequences of my actions. I still had some behavioral issues few and far between, controlling myself was a struggle. The therapy and medication helped. I was still performing academically well above my peers but socially lagging. I remember the frustration I felt from not fitting in. The way I tried to just blend in by silently standing in the background. When the spotlight fell on me however, I was nothing but an embarrassment. The other kids were like dogs and I was a bone.

My mother had seen my autism as inconsequential. I had continued to ignore it. Either way, I still didn't have any friends. I could talk to the neurotypical white kids I was surrounded by and every conversation seemed to go the same way. "You don't act black," or "You talk like a robot." My formal way of speaking and predisposition for higher-level vocabulary had not made me an effective communicator with my peers throughout school. I always shrugged it off in an effort to carve a friendship. I didn't succeed. These kids saw me and saw the sum of my stereotypes. They saw a black thug from the ghetto, and that intimidated them. They steered clear, and I didn't know how to approach them. I ended up at a different high school and created a different strategy. I determined not to speak with anyone and just focus on my academics. I wanted to work, not to blend in, but to remain completely invisible. It didn't work out quite as planned. I'm so happy it didn't.

A single encounter changed the course of high school for me. It was a girl, but the story isn't about romance. I had been late to class the very first day of high school and my plans to remain invisible had already taken a hit. After class that same day she approached me. She joked about me coming in late and struck up a juvenile conversation with me. She was all giggles and kindness. Somehow she knew before she even spoke to me that we'd be friends. I know it sounds like a small gesture. To neurotypicals it probably sounds creepy or unusual that I consider this a life changing encounter. However, this encounter lead to what I consider my first real friend.

If she hadn't approached me, I would've went on through the rest of high school on my trajectory to invisibility. Instead I adapted myself to fit her personality. It was sudden and mostly subconscious, I did as I was good at and so often did. I mimicked. I grew on her friends as we grew to be even better friends. I adapted to their patterns of speech and formed many of their habits. My growing list of acquaintances seemed so insignificant to everyone else, but to me it was overwhelming. My personality kept adapting to my friends to fit in. Sometimes I feel as if I'm barely me. I feel as if I just leech the personality and mannerisms of others, adding them to my own, creating someone unique. And is that so bad?

My high school experience ended up very different as a result. I grew in confidence, I became popular. I imitated my way into the mainstream. I was involved. I felt human connection in ways I never expected. I was no longer recognizable from that little autistic Puerto Rican boy who constantly found trouble. I was no longer the wallflower that tried to blend in. I easily pass as neurotypical.

Between that encounter the first day of high school and graduation, I had gradually not only come to terms with my autism, but I became proud of it. I saw not only its detriments, but its advantages. My exceptional memory and academic ability I attribute mainly to my autism. I saw the social obstacles as surmountable. I'd openly tell people about my autism after I'd graduated, which is something I wouldn't have dreamed of freshman year. I realized that autism doesn't make anybody better or worse, just different.

Nowadays people are still quick to place their labels on me. I'm regularly told I don't seem autistic or that I'm not black. My acquaintances are under the impression that being black and being puerto rican are mutually exclusive. I still deal with being profiled. I have to explain to people what being autistic really means. I have to show them I'm not what they expect me to be, and that's okay.

I worked so hard to overcome the social obstacles my diagnosis put forth. I worked hard to rebel against the labels placed on me, to be authentic. I am not a walking stereotype. Nor am I defined by diagnosis. I do not fit into the boxes others try to put me in. I am me.

I am no longer an outsider.

The Wonderful World of Pharaoh: Introduction

Pharaoh Inkabuss (Timotheus "T.J." Gordon)

I wish I could buy into a universal world, where everyone adheres and thrives under the same social norms. An utopia in which we won't be misreading signals or bicker over ways of living. I assume that people in such utopia don't have to call each other weirdoes or lames because they don't have to worry about different worlds. Or I can dream of creating an earth—like atmospheres field with islands of various social expectations. You don't have to bow down to a mainstream culture and suffer bouts of conformity. Inhabitants in that world can see their way in their own, private, and visual manner in each bubble.

Sadly, the world as we know it doesn't operate in either way. We live in a world within multitudes of worlds and perspectives. Human share at least two different worlds at once. There is the physical world, which is the planet Earth and its environments/resources. Then you have a universal world; everyone in that world agrees on a set of social norms and taboos that can be understood anywhere, no matter what culture you may represent. Let's be real: universal worlds are NOT utopian or totalitarian. I don't see a leader make the whole world follow a set of rules.

Good luck controlling approximately six billion people by enforcing a static set of social norms! On the other hand, it would also be difficult to govern six billion separate mindsets. Even if a government was created to allow separate worlds to exist as isolated islands, everyone would still either clash or stick to their own rules and social norms.

Along with the physical and universal worlds, you may also experience personal, customized worlds within those two primary, preset realms. It can range from two to infinite additional worlds, and it all depends on various factors. One must consider things such as ethnicity, medical conditions, education, family upbringing, critical event that may influence ideologies, social status, etc. Some can juggle multiple worlds at once. Others thrive on focusing on living in their own little world, without much regard for their other worlds.

For example, I sit on a bench to enjoy a placid, bright day at Rainbow Beach in Chicago. To the naked eye, I am located near 79th Street and South Shore Drive in the Cheltenham/South Shore neighborhood, on the beaches of the great Lake Michigan. A pedestrian may see me stare at the skyline, the children making sand castles, pretty ladies strolling on the pathway, or youth spiking a volleyball over the net. That's what I call the physical world. It's the things, the concrete and immediate ones, that you can recognize.

Keep in mind that there are more worlds than the physical one and that you may be experiencing two worlds at once. Going back to the Rainbow Beach example, you may also pickup on how I see the universal world within the physical realm. You'll probably assume that I'm at Rainbow Beach to relax, take a break from work, escape the sweltering heat wave, meditate, or search for a mate. Besides, I think we all go to the beach for any of those usual reasons. But then there are more worlds to consider within the confines of Rainbow Beach. You might see two common worlds: the physical and the universal ones. However, Rainbow Beach can mean many more things than just its standard definition. That beach may be my retreat from the violent Chicagoan streets; it might be my little island of heaven. Or it could be a reminder of how much I missed my hometown, since I can see the Chicago skyline from that area. Maybe Rainbow Beach reinforces my affinity for water and the lakefront. Who knows what else I can draw from Rainbow Beach! Aside from the sea of possible viewpoints, I'm using the Rainbow Beach example to illustrate how you can experience worlds with a know physical location.

Why am I going on a tangent about worlds, you may ask? I can be expressing my passion for studying metaphysical and spiritual ideologies. Or blame it on the anime and cartoons; those two factors are loaded with whacky and vast worlds. Yet those are not primary reasons why I'm going into detail with multiple worlds. Instead, I'm borrowing a page from W.E.B. DuBois' philosophies on identities, in which a person is carrying two or more personas in one body. Originally utilized to explain how African-Americans view their dual identities in America, you can say that DuBois' notion of "double-consciousness" can be applied to any situation where a person is floating between two or more identities that conflict with each other. Those with multiple identities may have difficulties coping with how their peers view each persona and how those affect certain aspects of their life.

I have so many worlds that I navigate within a finite space. I am a brony, spiritual being, photographer, believer in polyamory, humanitarian, South Sider from Chicago, football junkie, foodie, life-long student, romantic, troubled soul, etc. If I keep going with the listing, then you'll assume that my head is saturated with interesting worlds I travel back and forth to. I will talk about some of my interests and personas later. But for now, I want to explore two primary identities readers should examine more closely; one of them needs special attention because it's a world only a brave few can describe.

On one hand, I am human, just like everyone around me. Yes, I am a six-foot, 270-290 lb. dreadhead who can pass for a lineman or linebacker. Otherwise, I'm similar to the average Joe. I have feelings and I express them verbally. I eat, sleep, move around, poop, and piss like a human being. My five senses are present, though I do need glasses sometimes to look at tiny or far away objects. I can be adventurous and have fun with you if I'm in the appropriate situation. I get in trouble just like everyone else, bleed just like you, and try to answer life's questions like everyone else. And best to believe that I am capable of playing sports or making sweet love (if I wanted a mate)!

At first glance, you may perceive me to be human. I guess I've been playing normal well for quite some time. You can't tell that I'm different right? I don't think so. Other than exhibiting a few personality quirks, I can pass for a neurotypical with flying colors.

But what if I tell you I have another identity? Perhaps this human/normal thing that I have is nothing more than a façade. It's because I'm also autistic. Furthermore, autism is my dominant identity, not human. Being autistic is being a foreigner in his or her motherland. I operate and function like a neurotypical in the human world, and if you didn't know any better, you would assume that I'm a natural-born citizen of that world. However, I don't feel like a citizen of this Earth, but rather an explorer from Planet Vegeta or some mystical territory. I view the world much like a dog roaming the barren alleys, relying on senses and patterns and visuals. From what I learned, humans usually rely on feelings, abstract thought, and social concepts. I'm functional (somewhat) in those departments, but even close to fluent. But I am fluent in recognizing and explaining concrete details. I use my five senses and brain to navigate this jungle called life. I concentrate on one thing at a time with sharp focus, as if I'm buying into Coach Schottenheimer's "one play at a time" philosophy.

Those are cool traits to have, right? You're the most incredible person in the world (in my books) if you can shove all your social mayhem and focus on what you love to pursue best. I can empathize with you on that one, but some neurotypicals my give us the evil eye when we go on with our lives with that mindset. I believe that a few really give a damn about the logical viewpoints of autists and aspies. We're aliens, even though we bleed, piss, and shit like non-autistic people. However, I live in the social

164

world, dominated by concepts, idioms, and emphasis on peer interaction & social norms.

There are reasons why the whole different world spiel is a reoccurring theme. As mentioned before, autistic live in two parallel worlds. There's the neurotypical world, where daily life is governed by constructs, cues, and norms....with chunks of (complex) emotions. And then you walk into the world of autists and aspies, where logic, patterns, and animalistic thinking dictate how daily lives and routines operate. What I mean by animalistic thinking is the type of thinking that Dr. Temple Grandin once explained in a BBC documentary: both animals and people on the autistic spectrum rely on their senses and concrete details to navigate their surroundings. For example, a scent from a person can give me numerous information, such as the age of the person, state of mind, taste in fashion, personality, brand of cologne/perfume, lotion flavor, etc. Senses and details matter to autists and aspies. I wish that the higher powers could have forged an Earth-like planet just for autists and aspies to inhabit. But then I won't have to write my essay series, or find a legitimate reason to write it. Haha!

There is only one Earth in the universe, therefore us aspies and autists share it with non-autistics. Despite my distaste for some of the social norms, I must obey the rules of the neurotypicals in order to survive the chaos called life. I am bombarded with visuals and literature on how to be "a normal person" on a daily basis. I see it in mainstream movies, where they are saturated with social norms. The ads I see on TV dictate how I should behave. Institutions, like school and places of worship, have knacks on molding me into an average, respectable human. And people are quick to point out my "weaknesses" if I pull out my first generation Pokémon cards. If an action seems off to them (even if it's not a wrong vs. right thing), then I'll be hammered with concerns or jeers. I'm an outcast if I see the world differently from what I was programmed to see it. And yes, some of my quirks may seem strange to their eyes. For example, turning a fan on while the heat is circulating the house or not dressing up for church can lead into unnecessary debates. I have my reasons behind certain actions, and most of them are preferences, not good vs. bad (some of them can be stemmed from my autism, like turning on less lights).

On one hand, I see those who mock my "autistic way of life" as bullies and complete assholes. They seem to get a kick out of judging the autist or aspie, though some may have at least working knowledge of what autism is. They appear to purposely mock their mannerisms. But then you have those who don't know any better or are misinformed. You may have never heard about autism until I wrote about it or someone you know has the condition. Or maybe you were listening to fictionalized accounts (some are them are inaccurate) of those living on the spectrum. I'm not surprised if you see as a savant or man-child prone to tantrums, if my routine gets shaken up. Perhaps you might have strong knowledge of autism. Or, you may even exhibit traits of it, but your family, peers, or community doesn't want to hear what you have to say. I'm assuming that they have their own fears, myths, or prejudice on that matter. I believe that, in general, the African-American community is not big on topics surrounding mental and developmental disorders. Though I don't want to get into detail until later in the book, I can say that it boils down to "trying to play normal and cool", like Shaft, Snoop Dogg, or Michael Jordan.

I'm writing my essay series for two kinds of people: those in the spectrum who are facing similar predicaments as myself and those who don't understand our struggles to live in a predominately neurotypical world. I'm aiming for the latter because I'm tired of others telling our stories without regards for the autistic community or taking the time to learn about our daily lives, especially as adults. In fact, I don't think people ever get to listen to stories from autistic adults often. My book shouldn't be taken as gospel; my account of being autistic is unique, and the same can be said for previous essays and memoirs written by those in the spectrum. However, I pray that you can get a slight handle of the struggles and benefits of living on the autistic spectrum. People can again more insight to how I, as an autist, operate in the "normal world" and why I can sometimes feel like an alien on my own homeland.

To those on the spectrum, I hope that the journeys in my collection would be exciting rides for you too. I want to help remind my aspie/autie family that our voices are out there and we will be heard with attentive, objective ears. We write such non-fiction pieces to inspire those on the spectrum to be themselves and live out their obsessions. This is especially important for autists and aspies of African descent. It's a rarity to find successful black people on the spectrum; I only managed to come across one who is officially diagnosed with autism: British artist Stephen Wiltshire (eeyup, the guy who can draw the city of

Manhattan using photographic memory). We ought to see more aspies and autists of color doing their thing and sharing their stories. I'm far from a celebrity figure or person of importance, but writing my thoughts on the world of the autist can at least spark something.

With all being said, are ready to travel through the wonderful world of Pharaoh? Sorry if I was long-winded with my speech. Don't worry about fluff and fillers, because those things are reserved for anime. You will come across interesting facts, funny anecdotes, and repressed memories....all are thrillers. But please be aware of references to booze, sex, "God-talk", cannabis, and all the taboo stuff. I'm sure some may not be ready for an aspie who cares about Mary Jane. However, unexplored territory must be visited if you want an authenticated view of Pharaoh's world. At any rate, y'all will come home from this expedition with enlighten.

So what the hell are y'all waiting for? Hop on the flying nimbus, relax, and enjoy the journey through "Pharaoh's World".

World Autism Interviews: Socialworks/Toronto, Ontario

E. Ashkenazy with Socialworks

Photo: Black and white photo of African Canadian woman smiling.

Socialworks is a single mother of one child. She has a Bachelor's in Social Work with a minor in Public Administration, as well as a Master's in Social Work. She spends her time in community advocacy, namely accommodations and housing education. Socialworks is the Organizer for the Toronto Autistic Adult Network self-advocacy group, which started up in 2009. She enjoys cars, chess, home renovation projects, listening to all kinds of music, mechanics, and soccer. She's also a Star Trek fan (except for the most recent series).

E: How old were you when you received a diagnosis, and how did your family respond to the news?

Socialworks: I was 29 years old when I received a diagnosis. I was treated for depression and anxiety, and after being put through a bunch of medications that did more harm than good, I was assessed as having bipolar disorder. I did nothing with the diagnosis because it meant nothing to me. I was unable to see the mood swings that were supposedly evident in my vague generalizable answers. When I joined a local bipolar group and heard the stories and difficulties people lived with, it was then I knew I was not bipolar.

After having a 'meltdown' that landed me in the hospital, it was almost impossible to get professionals to listen to me because I was a "person with bipolar disorder." When asked what I needed at the hospital, I mentioned that I could not go home. They never asked me why. They didn't ask what I was reacting to. I was simply "bipolar."

I was put on medications again. But my routine was interrupted when the pharmacy fixed an error in the dosage and didn't tell me. I was functioning at a basic level, and with that medication change, I ended up in the hospital again a week later. I knew it was a medication switch, but no one was listening to me. In retrospect, I could have died because I was being given medications intended for individuals who are bipolar. Instead, I was autistic and didn't know.

Since I live alone, my family had no idea what was going on.

Months later, I decided to examine the root causes of my issues and the things I have difficulty with. I had to identify social norms and redefine the obstacles I was facing. It was then that I found my issues to be sensory related and went on to seek non-medicated ways of addressing the issues.

I was diagnosed during a three-session Cognitive Behavioural Therapy assessment for anxiety and depression.

Unfortunately, I had to struggle with the doctor to get the diagnosis because the doctor felt that labeling me wouldn't do much, and that there wasn't really much support for adults with Asperger's. I didn't care. I wanted the formal diagnosis so I could decide for myself what it was I wanted to do with it.

My family has been neutral about the issue. They have little to say and don't seem to be too interested in understanding. I don't think they believe me because I have been able to accomplish many things. Autism is apparent with other family members who either have persevered and have not experienced systemic difficulties that would force them to take a second look, or they live in environments where autism is never discussed.

I have also been bullied by relatives who don't understand Asperger's, and likely never will because I have chosen not to disclose to them for my own safety.

E: In many communities, autism and disability are stigmatized. As an African-Canadian woman, do you feel autism is a stigma or taboo in your family? If so, why?

Socialworks: It is definitely considered taboo in African and West Indian-Canadian cultures. Many times, children with developmental disabilities are ignored, and when you are raised like that, 'coming out' to family is an uphill battle. Oftentimes, adults are mocked, ridiculed, or belittled. And the more we speak, the more familial disdain becomes apparent. You're not just outing yourself, you're also outing your family. There are few spaces to talk about disabilities in the African-Canadian community.

Although I have autistic members in my family, I wouldn't consider autism open for discussion. There are fears of labeling yourself or being labeled by others that, historically, we as a community have tried to get away from. It just is what it is…hidden.

E: Have you ever felt misunderstood by family members or friends who expect you to behave in certain ways?

Socialworks: In my family, being seen as a strong individual has oftentimes made it difficult to be heard. Subjectivity plays a huge part in how my family understands my difficulties. I tend to keep it to myself instead of trying to get them to understand. I can speak, but speaking is not my first method of communication, as it is quite tiring. Add in the emotional piece that exists (even if you can't tell) and the whole experience can leave me unable to function afterward.

In regards to being misunderstood, I find that the old "You don't act autistic" attitude exists within my family. Sometimes my autism is hard to see. I've also focused a lot of energy over the years trying to fit in. I lived with a belief that such challenges (of fitting in) was a skill that would be beneficial to have as I moved forward. It got much harder as I got older.

My family doesn't see me when I not 'on' for the most part. They don't understand why I spend so much time at home alone, and why I don't react positively to spur of the moment invitations outside of the home, or to invitations to most social gatherings. My family never asks, and only recently did I know what was really going on myself. I grew up being called antisocial, selfish, narcissistic, "having emotional issues," strange, weird, etc.

My behaviour is what has been misunderstood for most of my life.

173

My family doesn't understand why I won't go certain places, why I can't work in certain spaces, why I'm a picky eater, why I feel cold most of the time, why I don't speak much in groups, why I carry all of my heavy grocery bags at once, why I go grocery shopping rarely—and only during the wee hours of the morning, why no one really visits me, why I've worn dark coloured clothing most of my life, why my walls are virtually bare, and why I seem to avoid most things others find appealing.

They do not understand, and I no longer see much of a benefit to them gaining an understanding. It's important to be understood to a degree, but it's more important to understand yourself. It is only then that you can decide for yourself who you want to be. Anything less (i.e. being defined by what other people tell you you are) tends to hurt the self-esteem.

E: What has been most frustrating to you in regards to how you might be perceived by others who share the same cultural heritage (do you feel you have to cover up, hide, or overcompensate for being on the spectrum)?

Socialworks: I think the fact that attitudes and assumptions are the same, if not more, by others who share my cultural heritage. It is frustrating to try and share a part of your identity when doing so sometimes closes the doors to being seen as a human being, or "more than just [this or that]…"

I will say that I have been in various spaces where, based on discussions—which had little to do with ASD—it was clear that I was not in a safe place to be open about myself. Hostile discussions around gender roles, sexuality, race, cultures, education, and the reinforcement of linear thought around these issues have repeatedly told me that if I speak out on any of these topics, my social location alone would set me up for a battle I can't say I am always up to fight.

For the most part, I feel neutral about it all. The only times I get heated is when my apparent neutrality makes it difficult for others to believe me when I say I am experiencing some sort of emotional difficulty. Then I feel frustrated. It is then, and only then, that I wish I could better communicate my feelings so as to avoid the doubts of others.

E: Do you know anyone else of color, on the spectrum, who has also expressed similar cultural struggles?

Socialworks: Yes, I have met other people of colour who have a diagnosis of ASD, and we share similar struggles. Our age differences, access to opportunities, and general life experience may play a role in how we internalize societal pressures to hide or fit in, but the issues are the same.

E: In general, do you feel a healthy percentage of African-Canadian parents are likely to look into further diagnostic testing if either they or others (e.g teachers) notice non-standard development?

Socialworks: The scars of black children being labeled in the school system and streamed are still there, so many parents are hesitant to seek a formal diagnosis for their child, and when they decide to, service providers rarely approach assessments with a deeper understanding of the complexities around disability within culturally specific groups.

It can be tough for any parent to accept that their child could be having difficulties. I do not believe that more parents will look into further testing without community outreach. If parents seek services through the school, they have to keep in mind that schools are not necessarily eager to swallow the costs of assessments. In addition, once a child has been assessed, the school must take action. Add the fears of the parents, and the fears of the school being seen as labeling another black child and/or labeling too early in the child's development, and nothing meaningful really happens.

E: Do you feel accepted and understood by the Autistic community, regardless of your cultural heritage?

Socialworks: I do know that I have not felt rejected by the Autistic community because of my cultural background. At the same time, I don't feel included. I see it has another dimension to the third person perspective I find myself in most of the time as an Autistic adult.

E: Is there anything I have not asked, you would like to share?

Socialworks: The most frustrating thing is that people rarely ask why. If we begin to ask why, and if we value the lived experience of individual persons at least as much as we do those who perceive, we could dispel a lot of misconceptions. We need to take into account some of the cultural attitudes we have around autism and disabilities, as well as open up spaces for understanding and change. We need to help others fight for and access needed services in ways that protect the dignity of individuals, as well as their families and communities.

World Autism Interviews: Isabel Espinal/New England

E. Ashkenazy with Isabel Espinal

Photo: A smiling Dominican-American woman with long curly hair in front of a waterfall and mossy rocks.

Isabel was born in New York City. Her parents are from the Dominican Republic. As for college, she enrolled at MIT and nearly flunked out. She decided science and technology were not for her and transferred to Princeton where she wound up flunking her senior thesis.

Eventually, she submitted a passing thesis, earned a Bachelor's degree, and then a Master's in Library and Information Studies. She has been a librarian since 1991. Isabel is a mother to 3 children. Her kids are now teenagers (and her son is in his first year of college). She loves literature and especially enjoys translating poetry from Spanish to English. Isabel is currently working on a PhD in American Studies with a focus on Literature.

E: How old were you when you received a diagnosis on the autistic spectrum, and how did your family respond to the news?

Isabel: I am 46 years old and just received a diagnosis two months ago. I started reading about Aspergers and autism through a friend of mine (Rachel Cohen-Rottenberg, who writes about her own autism since her diagnosis at age 50 on her blog Journeys With Autism). All of this is so new to me, so unexpected, and yet so wonderful too. I don't think I have completely assimilated the diagnosis yet—let alone my family.

I have a big family and I have not told a lot of people, but as soon as I started to think I might have it, I sent an email to my sister and to a few close friends. I emailed my therapist, and I also told my kids. My sister reacted by saying that she said it made her wonder how many other people in the family might have also been on the spectrum. Autism definitely resonated with her as something that may exist in our family, and I found that very affirming.

I had a friend who said, "No way," because I am very empathetic and the classic symptom of Aspergers (in her view) is lack of empathy. But I had done a lot of research and I sent her a few links that refuted that theory. She said, "Wow, I had no idea."

Another friend was very mean. He said I did not have Aspergers, that it was a fad diagnosis, and that what he thought I had was Narcissistic Personality Disorder. It was very upsetting that he would dismiss my thoughts, as well as dismiss my own observations. I explained that there was a lot about me he did not know, but he insisted that his view was correct. I was so upset I could not stop crying. But that experience did not stop me from pushing what I felt was the truth about myself, even though I was sad not to have his support.

My boyfriend has been very supportive. We talk about it all the time. I can see how my autism has affected our relationship, and how the diagnosis and knowing about autism will improve how we relate to each other—it already has.

As for my kids, my oldest said he knew students who had it and he did not think I had it because I was not like them. But it's different now that it's not just my own suspicions, as I have a professional diagnosis. For me, I know that it's my kids who I most want to explore what autism has meant in our lives, as well as what my autism has meant for them, and will mean for them. I think it may help them understand some things, but I also think that we need support services so they can understand this and better deal with it. In this sense I feel very different from a lot of women I have read about. It seems that women and men my age who get diagnosed often do so because they have a child who is diagnosed first. Discussion of autism is already in the family in many adult cases. In my case it wasn't, so I have the challenge of being the person who introduces this concept to my children. And it may seem like it's coming out of nowhere. It's daunting, but also promising—I feel like this can really help us in ways not found in the past because we were solving the wrong problems.

E: In many communities, autism and disability are stigmatized. As an American-Dominican, do you feel autism is a stigma or taboo in your culture? If so, why?

Isabel: I don't think there is much understanding of autism, and of what the spectrum is. I certainly did not have that understanding until recently. I don't know if it's a taboo. I don't feel it that way. I feel that it would be much easier to talk about autism in my Dominican family than it is to talk about sexuality or divorce or religious alternatives, for example. My family is huge—I have 73 first cousins, and there are many 3rd, 4th, etc. I think there is a lot of variety and in many ways a lot of acceptance of difference I have a cousin who has a daughter with developmental delays. I'm not that close to him so I don't know all the details, but for all I know it's probably autism. He and his wife have structured their lives around meeting their child's needs. They moved to Boston to be near specialists. This was a very difficult move for them because they are now far from the extended family. I visited them a few years ago before I knew anything about autism. Everyone treats their daughter with so much love and affection. In my family children are precious no matter what.

There are aspects of my own autism that garnered praise in my family. When I was a child, I was often complimented for my ability to sit still, quietly. For me it was natural, as I was often in my own world. It was easy to sit still at church or at a medical clinic. I remember one time I was picked to be an angel in a church event. They dressed me up in a silvery costume with silver wings. Everyone kept saying I was the perfect angel because I was so still. Another thing that earned praise and attention was my ability to read, memorize, and figure out visual things like maps and charts. People exclaimed things like, "¡Esta niña es una Biblia!" ("This girl is a Bible!") So when I recently read about autism and Aspergers and the "little professor" syndrome, I totally related. I probably cried reading about that because it was so close to my experience.

E: Have you ever felt misunderstood by family members or friends who expect you to behave in certain ways?

Isabel: Yes, yes, yes! In particular, people did not understand why I liked to be alone. I'll never forget the day one of my aunts confronted me with the question: "A tí te gusta estar sola, ¿no es verdad?" ("You like to be alone, don't you?") I felt cornered, exposed, and ashamed because I liked something that was so seemingly horrible. Until recently, I attributed this difference to culture. I thought the fact I liked to be alone was a result of having grown up in the United States where people are almost obsessed with themselves and always seem to want their own space, as opposed to Dominicans.

Another thing that was criticized in my family when I was a girl and a teenager was the fact that I liked to read so much. I was always reading. I would bring books to the dinner table if I could get away with it. But this was a habit that worried some people in my family. Aunts would tell me it was not healthy to be reading so much. When I was a teenager in high school and college, a lot of family thought I was rude because I was not overly friendly. And in high school a lot of the girls thought I was a snob. I felt confused and hurt by this in both cases because it seemed so removed from my inner reality. I had to learn so much—teach myself so many things about how to behave so I would not get that reaction. And yet, to some extent, I still get that reaction despite having worked on this so much.

Being bicultural gave an alternate explanation for a lot of my problems "fitting in." If I didn't fit in with my Dominican family, it was supposedly cultural. If I didn't fit in with my New England white co-workers, it was also supposedly cultural. But after I discovered autism, it made much more sense why I have never fit in anywhere.

Some of the aspects of Dominican culture that might have made my autism more hidden (when in the context of the dominant US culture) are things like interrupting conversations, blurting things out, being too honest, and talking too loudly or too softly. For example, I exhibit all these things at work, and they always made me stand out in that context, but not among Dominicans.

E: What has been most frustrating to you in regards to how you might be perceived by others who share the same cultural heritage (do you feel you have to cover up, hide, or overcompensate for being on the spectrum)?

Isabel: I don't live among a lot of Dominican people anymore, so it's hard to answer. I think in both my cultures it was frustrating to be misunderstood. It's frustrating to have people put expectations on me based on how they think and perceive the world and to assume that I perceive the world the same way. Because I have been successful in academics and work, people expect more of me. Parenting has been very challenging for me and it's been very hard to always have people say, "Why don't you just..." or "How could you let..." People expect me to be a certain way or assume that because I have a certain outward appearance that certain other things should be easy or be common sense. It's frustrating that what is common sense to some is very hard for me and really needs to be broken down in ways other people I know cannot seem to fathom. I guess my sense is just not common.

E: Do you know anyone else of color, on the spectrum, who has also expressed similar cultural struggles?

Isabel: No, only the people I have read about on your blog and maybe a few other blogs. But I have seen very little even in blogs about people of color. Most autistic blog writers seem to be white. I would love to read more from people of color on the spectrum, especially adults and people my age.

E: In general, do you feel a healthy percentage of Dominican parents are likely to look into further diagnostic testing if either they or others (e.g. teachers) notice non-standard development in a child?

Isabel: The kind of behaviors I had I'm not sure would cause either Dominicans or non-Dominicans to seek diagnosis—even today. I wasn't a disturbance to anyone. I wasn't a *problem*. Adults loved me. Teachers loved me. I was often set up as a "model," which made me uncomfortable. I don't think the field of diagnosis and diagnostic follow up has caught up with kids who are similar to what I was like. Other autistic individuals are likely to be treated differently, especially if they are more easily identifiable. But even there, I think because of economics, Dominican parents would not have the resources to get the kinds of diagnoses that whites can get for their children. I think the differences from the "standard" would have to be more severe for Dominicans to get help. Based on what I'm reading on parental blogs, the kind of intense help and attention that autism spectrum kids are getting is probably not fully available to Dominicans.

E: Do you feel accepted and understood by the Autistic community regardless of your cultural heritage?

Isabel: It seems like in some ways being autistic itself is a kind of culture. I feel I have so much in common with people in this community, that I can't help but feel identified. When I received a diagnosis, I emailed Rachel Cohen-Rottenberg to let her know and to thank her. She asked if she could post my response on her blog and I got a lot of nice welcoming messages. On the other hand, I feel that a lot of people in this community have limited cultural perspective in general and sometimes I wonder if some of the things that are assumed to be true of all or most autistics might really be more indicative of European-heritage autistics.

Passing—and Passing

Jane Strauss

Intersectionality exists, though most have ignored its multiplicative effect until recently. I have lived in the junction of minority culture and disability for far longer than the junction has been recognized. Dehumanized as a Jew and again dehumanized as a disabled person, both detrimental to my existence and self actualization.

As a child, I had no labels but Jew, underachiever, and oversensitive. We lived in a White Christian-Catholic neighborhood, one of three Jewish families within miles. At certain times of the year, if I did not fly under the radar, terms like "Christ killer" were bandied about. This was because the others never saw me at Mass, not because my family actually engaged in any Jewish practices, for they had assimilated so well that I never saw a synagogue until I was 10 years old.

At school, I had a target on my back. I made friends with some teachers, but did not understand why one needed only a particular kind of clothing to be valued by other students. I read years above my level, created outstanding art (I was told), had few friends, and was bullied unmercifully by kids and even some teachers, especially the PE teacher, a wizened middle aged woman named Miss McKee. I struggled with rote memory out of context. The times tables were hell. But I escaped into theater, learning to become another, even for a little while. Theater also taught me about passing, because I practiced being somebody else. I am generally not surprised when another actor or comic self diagnoses or reveals their autistic traits. To this lapsed thespian, it only makes sense, as having a script made the difference between making it through the day at school and melting down in terror and frustration. Autistic Pride, Disabled Rights, did not exist.

I grew up learning that Passing was Necessary. I grew up hating that I had to try to Pass. I passed so well that, after moving to yet another neighborhood in which we were the minority, a kid at the school bus stop told me that some "kikes" had moved into the neighborhood. I broke his nose for that, even though he probably outweighed me by a good 50 pounds. That was when I stopped Passing, at least a little. It was the beginning of a journey.

As an adult, I tried the ultimate passing. Not only did I pretend to be "normal", I thought about becoming a Christian, and even was admitted into a Christian seminary, relocating in the upper midwest. My experience in seminary taught me that, even if I were to convert, I would always be seen as "the Jew" so I decided to return to my roots, the roots my parents (who had made passing into an art form) had denied in my childhood. I then found that employment was challenging, unless I passed as a member of the dominant culture I had rejected, worked on holy days, concealed my culture, and quieted my culturally exuberant communication style. Not passing resulted in queries such as "Do you wear your hair curly to hide your horns?" (Yes, even in the last quarter of the 20th century, folks.)

Concurrently with increasing stress and anxiety I acquired a multitude of labels: atypical learning disabilities, psychiatric conditions, but none of them really fit, or told the whole story. Finally, well into my sixth decade on the planet, and after more than three decades of wondering if speaking Autistics existed, came the Autism diagnosis. While I knew it was another undesirable (from society's viewpoint) identity, it was finally one that made sense and I embraced it. Fortunately, I had been involved in the disability rights movement for decades by then, so passing was never an option—any more.

Passing- while it is often defined as based upon race—can also involve a divergent culture, a "hidden" disability, or both. It is a way of trying to fit in, by denying one's core identity. It takes a toll, in self esteem, energy, stress, and watchfulness. One is always "on guard," lest a slip be made that could lead to discovery. And the fear of "what if?" you are discovered feeds on itself and can, in the end, paralyze. It can even result in one of the "comorbids" so-called, to Autism—which is called anxiety disorder. Passing is also a euphemistic term for death. And every time one denies core identity, the result is a little bit of death, cumulative over time, lessening energy, often resulting in depression. Tiny deaths mount up and can lead to suicidality. If society wants my core to die, why not help it along?

With respect to disability, specifically Autism, the norm in treatment (especially for "social skills") seems to be

189

teaching us to pass for non-Autistic. The goals, and I have seen such goals both in my work as a teacher in the past and in advocacy for my youngest child, often require more stringent behavioral norms than are ever expected for the run of the mill student. This kind of program mirrors and formalizes my own injurious childhood. It teaches the Need to Pass, and in so doing denigrates the Person one Is, reminding me of the historical conscription and indoctrination of Jewish boys in Czarist Russia and the Boarding Schools to which Native children were sent.

Teaching rules is one thing, putting higher expectations on the special education" student and grading on how well they can fake it, an entirely different kettle of fish. I often wonder how children brought up with the emphasis on fitting in even survive, why they are not crushed by the weight of living as another. I know that when I was finally given a diagnosis that fit and was able to embrace it, my previous anxiety and depression lifted. It was as if a two ton canary that had been sitting on my head finally took flight.

How many of the so-called co-morbids to Autism are a direct result of "treatments" is a puzzlement. I doubt that this will ever be researched, as the possibility of harm being discovered if such a study were honestly conducted is too great a risk for the "treatment industry"(including Universities) to countenance. It would also require that those developing and executing the research program first honestly look at the system requiring those of non-dominant races, cultures, neurologies, and abilities to deny their validity as productive members of society. And above all, it would have to take into account the harm done by passing and acknowledge that intersectionality exists.

Untitled

D. Campbell-Williams

I am a black woman who was diagnosed at the age of 34 with Asperger's Syndrome in 2011. It was huge relief after spending countless hours and late nights over many years searching for reasons why I constantly lacked friends while growing up, had a very hard time making friends, was bullied and verbally abused constantly in school, and had such a difficult time expressing myself, especially when I was angry, stressed or just plain confused about a situation.

My life was not easy growing up. I had to endure constant laughter, snickers behind my back and flat-out dislike from classmates, associates, co-workers and even my own family members for simply being born with Asperger's Syndrome. Things were also frustrating because as a gay woman, I noticed a lack of media exposure on persons of color and/or those who identify as LGBT who live with autism and how it impacts their daily lives, which only seemed to further compound my general sense of marginalization. To this day, I keep a journal detailing my feelings of constant ostracism by others. I now have a total of 15 journals with countless entries that I've maintained since early childhood.

One of my cousins once told me that he had always disliked me because I seemed so weird, angry and quiet to him, which hurt me very deeply to hear this news. I've also suffered a broken relationship with my only sister. We love but do not like each other very much and still have a huge distance in our relationship. I believe it started during early high school when I was in the throes of major depression over having no friends and being depressed and angry with everyone all of the time. My sister accused me of acting selfish and pathetic and desperate for attention, and our relationship seemed to be permanently damaged afterwards.

Despite my past struggles, today I've learned to live relatively well with autism. I now have with good medications that help to control my ADD, anxiety and depression (which are all common co-morbid conditions that some autistics tend to have), as well as the support of my spouse, friends, and good therapists.

Having a support system in place has helped to improve my life greatly. I've started experiencing more relief from my depressive symptoms and have been able to communicate better with others. I'm able to laugh more and concentrate better during conversations which has considerably improved my conversation skills. I'm less anxious when I find myself in social situations though I occasionally struggle with certain unstructured settings such as large parties or work-related functions. Even my relationships with certain family members have started to improve. Some people even comment today that I seem "normal" to them and that they wouldn't have ever suspected that I had autism, which is something I've longed to hear throughout my life. Autistics just want to feel normal and be accepted but it feels impossible sometimes.

I now work full-time and attend grad school part-time but still struggle some days with feelings of loneliness, isolation and inadequacy. However I've learned to develop key coping skills along the way that have helped me to enjoy social situations more often since I now know what to expect and how to behave during those times, whereas before it always felt like a very mysterious and confusing process. Don't get me wrong, things are still not perfect now by any stretch, and I still get occasional odd glances from non- autistic neurotypicals (NTs) for doing something "out of turn" or "improper" during conversations, and I still feel somewhat disliked by others on my job for simply being me. But things have nonetheless gotten a bit easier on the whole.

For years, I was so angry for being born with autism. I now realize that I'm just as good as everyone else out there and I'm not less than anyone because I have a neurological condition that makes socializing with others more difficult. My cousin recently told me that he "likes" me now and that I'm "okay" with him. But I now could care less if he genuinely "likes" me or what anyone else thinks of me. My cousin has no idea what I've endured in my life and I'm now stronger for it.

They Said I Didn't Act Like A Black

Yvonne Christian

It still troubles me that all the people who knew me before my diagnosis had no idea that I am really an autistic black woman. Back in 2002, I got two diagnoses: Asperger's Syndrome and Non-Verbal Learning Disorder. That helped me realized why the people in my past were very abusive to me in the form of bullying and some actually accused me of not acting like a real black woman.

When I started the 3rd grade, I was the new kid at this school called Rollingwood in the small suburb in Montgomery County, Maryland, called Chevy Chase. My family had moved from the Shepard Park section of Washington, DC, months before the new school year started. In this school, there were more white children than black children. This was the 1970s when African Americans were referred to as "Blacks." At my old school, Shepard School, a few students bullied me. When I got to Rollingwood, the bullying got worse for me. Some white students thought I didn't act like a normal Black girl. I reacted as though it was a racist attack and said there was nothing wrong with me, but the few black students in the school also argued with me and even bullied me over things about me: Loving the Beatles, watching TV shows like *Batman* and *Star Trek*, and being too quiet when I was supposed to be talking to others (I didn't really know how to socialize at that age, but everyone, including the teachers, thought I had the capability). I remember crying a lot in those days over being alienated by my fellow students. Before long, I was getting angry and getting into fistfights with other students. Not really a good way to enjoy the 3rd grade.

At the end of that school year, the school had its annual Olympic games. I won a blue first place ribbon for the Standing Broad Jump competition for 3rd graders. When the teacher announced my name, I heard a ton of boos as I received my ribbon. My older brother, Alfred, who was in the 6th grade at the time did nothing to defend me. He told our parents later that day about what happened, and my mother asked me if I did something to get those kids angry. That was my home situation.

During my time in public school, I was bullied mercilessly by both black and white students. In 1980, Alfred died from a head injury after being in a terrible car accident. A huge amount of people who went to school with us attended the funeral. For many years, I never understood why everyone was so friendly towards Alfred (Of course, he wasn't autistic like me).

In the mid-1980s, I moved up to Boston to go to Emerson College. I sometimes argued with male white students that I was acting like a Black woman, despite their complaints. I don't know why they would say I wasn't acting like one when I was. They seemed very ignorant. At college, I struggled with becoming to be more outgoing. I certainly was talking more, but some students who were the same color as me were just casual acquaintances than real friends during my college years. I did manage to stay friends with both white and black students after I graduated from college in 1986.

During the years after I graduated, I struggled with trying to break into the broadcasting industry. During the 1990s, I networked with tons of people, but somehow didn't make the right connections. There were misunderstandings about what I wanted to do versus what they thought I wanted to do. I would tell them I was passionate with being a writer, and they would assume that I meant that I wanted to work in sales. I would encounter some people at parties who said to me that I wasn't acting the way I should be acting because of the color of my skin. I felt frustrated because I completely didn't believe a word they said. However, it was during these years I realized that I still wasn't good at socializing with everyone. Just like when I was a child.

By 2000, I simply turned my back on the broadcasting industry, quit my very stressful job as telephone customer representative for the IRS in Boston (I was with them from 1987), and went to pursue other interests. I also discontinued seeing my doctor who diagnosed me in 1989 as having Intermittent Explosive Disorder (IED) because I was always losing my temper when I was at work. Her talk therapy and medication (Lithium) was never a big help with me in the long run because I was still unable to change my life to something more fulfilling.

In 2002, I met with a neurotherapist who figured out after giving a few biofeedback treatments that I did not have

Intermittent Disorder at all but actually Asperger's Syndrome and Non-Verbal Learning Disorder. That diagnosis made me realize why other people didn't see me as a black woman because I was really an autistic black woman.

These days, I am striving better understanding and acceptance of autistic people of all colors and what a talented writer I am with my two blogs: *Outside In* and *Uncommon Bostonian*.

All Kinds of Different

Jennifer Msumba

Growing up in the 80's, I was all kinds of different. Biracial, brown skinned and curly headed, in a sea of white children with silky hair and matching parents in the suburbs of Massachusetts. Full of quirks, fears and routines nobody could understand. A "tomboy" amongst girls with pretty pink outfits. Here I was, fuzzy headed, wearing Toughskin corduroys and my favorite "(con)'struction boots". I enjoyed playing alone in our sunny living room with my brother's old toys. A mish mash of Legos, wooden blocks, matchbox cars and lincoln logs. All seen better days but golden in my eyes. I would build for hours, talking to myself as I built towns, my own Transformers, and raced my cars across the kitchen floor. Sometimes I would just lay on the floor and stare at the sunlight streaming in, focusing on the dust particles floating like snow. It was hard to pull away from that once I started.

As long as I was home I felt as if I belonged. There was no pressure, there was no skin color. Mom was mom and Dad was dad. I never even noticed they were different colors until kids at school pointed it out in that nasty way kids so often do. To be exact my mom is Italian and my dad is Malawian and South African. Our family was a rarity then. The teasing began in about first grade and only grew worse. There was the N word. The N word all the time. I remember clearly the day I came home, thoroughly frustrated, and started rubbing my hands with white chalk. My mom burst into tears. My pain was her pain. She told me don't I ever, *ever*, not be proud to be who I am. But that was a concept I would not know until years to come.

A boy named Todd was the worst. He rode on my bus and teased me without mercy. He put papers in my hair and laughed that they stuck in my curls. Every. Damn. Day. The bus ride was overwhelming with the noise and the teasing, but I couldn't express it to my mom. All I could do was react. And react I did. At school I was known for throwing rocks on the playground at the kids who teased me. I was always in trouble. Running out of class and hiding in the stairwell was my specialty. Yet in my academics I was ahead of most kids. I was in the advanced classes. But I was always in trouble. I was sent to doctors and got pulled out for tests the other kids weren't taking. The psychologist would ask me lots of questions, and I wanted to answer but my mouth wouldn't move. I wanted to tell about the teasing, I wanted to tell about how the cafeteria was too loud and the reason I ran away from assemblies was the noise, the clapping. I wanted to tell that the reason I refused to go to library class was Mrs Smith always put me in the "baby chair" because I wandered into the sixth grade books section instead of looking at the pop up books. I could read since I was 3, and this lady is making my look at pop ups! I didn't know what self esteem was but it was reported I had low self esteem. My unnamed disability had me frustrated, and I hated my hair, I hated my skin, I hated that people mistook me for a boy all the time. I was terrified of the

200

teasing, I was a target and easily fooled, falling for the kids' latest prank they cooked up just for me. I hated being singled out. I hated that I had to write my answers then erase the write it again and again because OCD had claimed me, although I didn't know its name. I wanted to tell that I felt most of my teachers were mean to me, and I was sure in their minds they called me the N word too. I wanted to tell, but my mouth wouldn't move.

Going into middle school the whole game changed. Only I didn't change with it. Instead of playing kickball at recess, kids would gather in groups and talk, joke, laugh, look at boys and giggle. Ugh. The teasing got a little less, but the friends I did have started to outgrow me. They still let me sit with them at lunch but I was left out of the conversation. My one haven was orchestra. I had started playing the violin in 3rd grade, and it had always been my escape. In elementary school our violin class was in a sunny quiet corner of the school, with dust floating in the sunlight just like at home. I remember wanting to stay there all day long. I was always first chair, which is the top spot. This was my source of pride. I was playing with the high school orchestra since about 6th grade. The older kids were nicer to me because they saw me as a little sister, and nobody looks cool picking on a younger kid. So this is where I was most happy. I loved the music, it made me feel calm and in tune with everything around me. It was certainly my escape from the dark confusion in my mind. I didn't understand myself and surely other people didn't. It wouldn't be until years later they had a name for why I was so different.

By the time I got to high school a lot of the teasing had stopped. There was mostly just loneliness. There were a few boys that still loved to tease me, but I had learned to navigate the school in order to avoid them in the hallway. The school was bigger, and by this time I wasn't the only brown skinned kid in school. But at the same time a terrible depression hit. I was becoming more and more different and separated from the other kids. I felt caught in a time trap where I just froze at a younger age. We had nothing in common. They were all in to boyfriends and girlfriends, dances and parties. I hated all of those things. They scared me and seemed not fun at all. So was really alone. At this same time my mom was diagnosed with cancer and I just lost it.

So in 10th grade my parents put me in my first hospital. That would be my life for the next 20 plus years. Hospitals, residential schools and programs. One of the (very) rare positive things about being in residential schools was that I was now with girls and staff of all different ethnicities and walks of life. There was a lot more acceptance. And I learned how to love myself for being brown. They taught me how to style and maintain my curly hair, and even told me how beautiful my hair was! They showed me that there is a whole big world out there of people just like me. And I don't have to feel bad about myself, but have confidence because I was important too! They accepted my different way of being, which the doctors had diagnosed me as Autism Spectrum.

So, in the end, it has all come together for me. It was a *very* difficult road but I'm glad I went through it because I would not be who I am. Now, in the year 2014, I can't help but smile when I see so many mixed couples at the store, their little brown skinned, fuzzy headed kids in tow. It makes me so happy. I see this as a turning point, with this new generation, that will help combat racism and promote tolerance. I see mixed couples on tv commercials and I think back to when I was a child, and most of the commercials featured white children and their matching parents. That made me think something was wrong with me. I am also happy to be comfortable being *me*, with all my quirks and routines, and found my skills in music and writing and making people laugh. I am even now able to speak all of those things out my mouth that I couldn't say all those years ago. And today, being all kinds of different, is the coolest thing ever.

The Ways I Don't Exist

Anmei He

There is no way you are reading this sentence. No one is writing this passage, as there is no possible way this fictional writer actually exists. If Anmei exists, she's lying through her rotten teeth, but for the most part, she's not anywhere.

According to popular culture, random people on the internet and the jerks in her life, she's not who she says she is. She must be making it up, or is a mythical being too absurd for reality. Below sits the overwhelming proof.

Exhibit A—Disability

Disability is easy to spot. The afflicted often have missing body parts, a spinal cord injury, or a dog to serve as their surrogate eyes. These people are sources of kindness and wisdom, happy to display their courage by taking out the garbage. Likewise, the disabled must never lead ordinary lives, but are compelled by international law to compensate for impairments, serving as inspiration to the able bodied. Blind swordsmen and deaf pinball champions are especially popular.

Subsection A—So You Say You're Autistic
Thanks to the work of media, articles, and a certain non-profit group, the core of autism has been revealed. There are not words to describe Elder God Cthulhu. This

unfathomable abomination exists so entirely outside of the realm of human understanding that our minds cannot begin to find the words to describe him. To simply gaze upon is to induce madness upon the viewer.

In order to sow suffering upon the world, Cthulhu sends spores around the globe, allowing them to take root in helpless infants. These children's souls are sucked away, yet their bodies continue to live. No matter how hard the parents of the affected beat their chests and wail, nothing can restore the wrecks that were once their offspring.

Divested of souls, these former humans are incapable of producing emotion, let alone sensing it in others. Do not be fooled by the elder god's schemes, their screaming and tantrum throwing exist to draw despair into the hearts of bystanders. It's best not to get too close to the infected, for they are the cause of nearly every violent crime that dominates the news.

With every new murder spree that hits the public, Cthulhu works harder to lull the masses out of wariness. As empty creatures of pure logic, autistics amaze any and all with their powers of observation, mathematics, and ESP. The stories Hollywood produces of them amassing fortunes in Vegas, cracking Pentagon codes and interacting with ghosts are all fact. To keep the public off guard, autistic people are largely mute, retaining the physical and mental capacities of toddlers.

She has not, nor has she ever served as the tool for a Lovecraftian abomination. According to some, she has the ability to "act human" around those she likes, implying she has a soul. She can't name which day of the week a date fell upon, nor can she win casino game through card counting, or think like Sherlock Holmes. She is a legal adult capable of paying bills, tying her shoes and putting together sentences. The family dogs clamor for her affection, she can read others' emotions and she has a fiancé.

Subsection B—Mental
There are alleged quirks of the brain that're supposed to make learning tough. People with these quirks have uniformly terrible grades and barely graduate. Either the problem evaporates when school ends, or they're sentenced to a lifetime of misery.

Learning disabilities may seem difficult to manage at first, but there are simple solutions. Any person can cure them, no specialized training necessary. One boy was kind enough to offer his services via chat room, and took it poorly when she declined repeatedly. According to him, good intentions and positive thinking was all it would take to make her better.

In truth, there are no learning disabilities. They're merely a scam cooked up by people who insist that they aren't stupid or lazy. All a person needs to do better in school is to try harder. When she describes numbers fading in and out of her head as she tries to calculate, or says that writing comes as easily as pushing a kidney stone, she is wriggling her way out of responsibility. She should be more like her classmates, who know how to study and finish work on time.

Some add that with regular applications of pain, any person can learn. If the bruised, limping victim is still struggling to understand algebra, the severity and frequency of the beatings should increase. In this fashion, the person will either become intelligent or die of internal bleeding, with the former being more likely.

Just like there are no learning disabilities, there is no depression. When she told the adults in her life, again and again, that she was depressed, they all shot her down. They had good reason not to believe her. That she weighed less at seventeen than she did at twelve was a quirk of adolescence. Her insomnia was a hereditary trait, while her self-inflected bruises were proof of her inferiority. As for her constant misery, it was an affectation to try and be fashionable.

Subsection C—Bodily
She has an intact spine and all her body parts. With the aid of glasses, her eyesight is 20/20. Since nothing's amiss at first glance, all must be well. The moments where she's screaming shaking falling down and going blind are mere hiccups, nothing to worry about.

Physical disabilities are another lie. A wheelchair user who can stand and take five steps doesn't need the chair at all. The person having a seizure is just trying to get attention. They can stop whenever they want, so their insistence on upholding their masquerade is a sign of moral weakness.

If a disabled person happens to look like everyone else, then she must be like everyone else. Treat her accordingly. She is not to receive medical care, pain management, or other quality of life improvements. The visibly disabled should go forth and spit on her for trying to steal their thunder.

Exhibit B—Heritage

The vast majority of people on the planet are bleach white. Sprinkled here and there are people of color whose main hobby is insisting on human rights. Everyone else tries to ignore them.

Subsection A—Mixed, and Happily So

To be more than one race is on par with having more than one pelvis. It cannot happen, as it is impossible. That blacks and Amerindians have intermarried for generations, black Americans often have traces of Caucasian blood, and that some Amerindian people have intermarried with French, Scottish and Irish people is pure fiction, no matter what history and DNA tests may say.

If a person had more than one race in their body, they'd be unlovable. Who could ever feel kindly towards a walking contradiction? Since a mixed person would know nothing but misery, they're unable to achieve contentment, let alone become music stars, top athletes or president of the United States.

Parents of these misbegotten beings wouldn't make a point to tell their children they have ancestry to be proud of. Adults would never teach kids to announce their multifaceted heritage to the rooftops, because their blood is special. No one would tell the mixed that no matter how they look, they're worth knowing.

Subsection B—Person of Color and Female

There's a certain online magazine with a community that believes microaggressive comments are the height of hilarity. This not-person spent months pointing out their hurtful words, until one commenter kindly explained the group's actions. As the fans wanted the magazine to be a safe space for women, others, like people of color, weren't welcome to speak.

This was how she learned that being female was the purview of Caucasian people. Icons such as Nzinga Mbande, Rani Lakshmibai and Catherine Tekakwitha were never female, but liars. Otherwise they were the white children of their parents of color.

Subsection C—How to Be Black

It is easier to understand the mind of a dragon than know what goes on in a black person's head. This is why the internet is full of essays and blogs on how to depict the latter in fiction.

In the quest to become a better writer, she perused many of these articles. The first and most profound lesson is it's impossible for a writer to portray anyone who is not an author avatar. To treat a black character as a human being is to insult the race. She learned that her part-black self could not rely on her experience or those of her family.

Other lessons told her that real black people aren't human, but an army of clones. Anyone who conveys the black experience should know that all blacks come from the same region of the United States, enjoy the same cuisine, have the same taste in music and carry the same opinions. She's not sure what this means for her.

Exhibit C—Gender

You may have noticed by how this construct keeps referring to herself as female. This is another trap. She may claim a feminine gender identity, but she defies what is meant to be the essence of that gender.

Subsection A—The Wrong Gaze

According to the wisdom of popular media, blogs and their commentators, she violates what it means to be objectified. It is always a man's fault. Men exist to obsess over feminine erogenous zones when they aren't going out of their way to hurt women. Posters, movies, books and more are either a reflection of a predatory male gaze, or they goad men into going forth and harming the other gender.

The explanation is simple. Men have sex drives while women don't. While men may occasionally turn to one another for relief, it's important that the majority of their attention is on women. If females believed that they have lives outside of men, the results would be tragic. For that matter, it is unthinkable for a woman to have agency.

Since women are only props to be acted upon, they have no ability to cause harm. By default, if something bad happens, a man is to blame. This is infinitely true when it comes to sexual matters.

For all of these reasons, she has never witnessed a woman carnally attack another person. There was never a time she transcribed testimony of a woman's repeated assaults by

210

other women. She has especially never been on the receiving end on this type of unpleasantness. Don't pay attention to the way she dresses, holds herself around others, or when she fakes a flashback. It's only her imagination.

Subsection B—Queer
While there's nothing wrong with males pursuing same-sex relationships, and other people embracing non-binary intimacies, female involvement is problematic. To be an ally is alright, as is questioning aspects of her identity. To proclaim a sexual identity is patently absurd, as women are incapable of wanting sex. The sun rising in the north is more likely.

While same sex relationships are fine, depending on the gender, having interest in more than one group is not. There can only be gays and heterosexuals. Those who say they are bisexual are lying, for they always have a preference. All the proof a person needs is to see who the ostensibly bisexual is currently with. A woman who dates a man yet drools at the sight of a shapely female is heterosexual, though a kinky one.

When a woman says she's bisexual, what she means is that she wishes to give a man amazing sex, even if most of her sexuality chats are with female friends. The truth is though they're female, they're puddles of lust, waiting for a man to stroll into their midst in order have an orgy. It doesn't matter that she considers sex with friends to be incest, or that she's more interested in looking than in coitus. She's greedy, claiming multiple orientations at once.

There's another alleged orientation claimed by those who want attention. Every human wants sex, end of story. Those that say otherwise are deluding themselves and need professional help, or people to encourage them to have sex, usually by making them the butt of jokes. Men are appendages attached to penises while women are on permanent standby to be receptacles for penises. People that don't obsess over sex are dead, and this isn't a world of zombies.

These liars often have hormonal or other medical issues that they can't be bothered to remedy, don't care to admit they're depressed or want a fancy word for being celibate or frigid. The lack of sex makes them unhappy but they're too proud to say it. The only asexuals are single-celled organisms.

If the public is to play along with these supposed asexuals, these silly people must do their part by following arbitrary rules. First, they must describe themselves as celibate, even if the term indicates that the person does have an interest in coitus, but chooses to abstain. They must never have a sex drive, as that is exactly the same as having an interest in carnal companions. The asexual must be interested in masturbating, while simultaneously refraining from seeking orgasms.

There are no asexual females, just women waiting for the right penis to come along and change their minds. Women who say they're asexual are closet heterosexuals. No one can be asexual and in a relationship with erotic elements. There is no "if it's with my fiancé, it's all right."

212

Subsection C—Autistic and female

She calls herself female, and has evidence to support this assertion. She enjoys skirts, dressing stylishly and working with textiles. Her hair falls past her shoulders and she wears it tied back, so it doesn't tangle in the jewelry she likes to wear. To name all of her culturally feminine quirks would take pages.

Cthulhu's spores reach only as far as boys. There are no females who have ever been, nor will be diagnosed as the elder god's spawn. The ancient one prefers to take a male brain and make is as masculine as the organ can handle, for it is the fastest way to further his ends.

The discovery was made by a man known as Dr. Simon Baron-Cohen. As a doctor, he has extensively studied both medicine and the arcane truths of ancient forbidden unspeakable terror. Between his education and his title, he is never wrong.

While Cthulhu can suck the soul from any gender, boys are preferable. They already have low empathy and are logical, so the spores have an easier time controlling them. Girls are problematic, being preprogrammed to have feelings and care about others. While removing the soul will change that, it takes more work than converting a boy. The time and effort to rewire a girl could be used to reprogram one and a half boys. There are other inconveniences related to infecting girls.

When a girl doesn't have emotions, it's a great blinking sign saying that something is amiss. Bystanders will look at her closely, realize what's wrong and lock her up before she starts a murder spree. Boys aren't expected to express themselves, allowing them to be sneakier in in doing the elder god's bidding. Though taking out the soul increases logical thinking, female biology doesn't aid the process. Autistic girls would be like Sherlock Holmes' Watson, while boys, already quite clinical, turn into Vulcans with the help of the spores.

Girls, lacking agency, need to have their lives revolve around men, which increases the chances of others spotting their contamination. Boys have more leeway to express independence, making it simpler to go about sowing evil. Females are too physically fragile to sow despair.

The best way to avoid having Cthulhu-touched offspring is to have only daughters. If a female gets diagnosed, the doctor must have written in the wrong gender by mistake.

Conclusion

So many impossibilities strain belief. The construct of Anmei would be more credible if she was in a fantasy tale and had only one absurdity to her name. But no, she had to claim too much weirdness. It's no surprise so few take her seriously. It's better to make her, or the people that imagine her, stop their foolishness and move onto more productive uses of their time.

You Think I Don't Notice?

COBRA—Confessions of a Black Rhapsodic Aspie

You think I don't notice?
The way you look at me when I walk into the room
Being the lone black man in a room full of mostly whites
I don't even want to think in terms of black-and-white
But...apparently my very existence forces that conversation to happen

You think I don't notice?
The way you respond to me when I start a conversation
Here's a hint: I'm autistic
But I don't know if you want to think in those terms
Yet...my very existence forces that conversation to happen

You think I don't notice?
When other blacks give me weird looks and/or the cold shoulder for being different?
When other blacks don't even consider the possibility of having an invisible disability?
When other blacks mock my hobbies for being "not black enough"?
When other blacks mock me for not being able to speak a language I "should know"?

You think I don't notice?
How most of the autism/autistic safe spaces
Are actually **NOT** safe to talk about race?
How the death of a black autistic will get a group to rally
around for autism
But leave the race portion untouched?

Yeah, I notice
I notice that I'm different from other blacks because I'm
autistic
I notice that I'm different from other autistics because I'm
black
I notice
Do you?

Acting Abled, Acting White

Amanda Filteau

Most people can't tell just by looking at me that I'm Autistic, and that is no accident. Earlier in my life I had accepted that my inability to perceive and interact with the world the way most people did made me an inferior person. And before I accepted that about myself, I quickly figured out that learning how to appear as if I wasn't disabled was one of the best ways to avoid ill treatment from peers. The same way I learned, as a person of color, that there were advantages to be had in knowing how to "act white"—acting in ways that minimized my racial and cultural differences from white people—I similarly learned that the best way to get kids to stop calling me "weird" and a "freak"—since most kids didn't have the word "Autistic" in their vocabulary yet—was to learn how to "act abled". I've chosen to use the term "acting abled" instead of a term like "passing as neurotypical." I think the term "acting abled" highlights the *work* it takes to appear neurotypical better than "passing" does.

Acting abled is not just modifying a couple behaviors. It involved years of learning to laugh at the things I saw others laughing at even if I wasn't sure I understood the humor, listening to enough conversations until I could identify some commonly used sarcastic phrases—and thereby avoid making myself look foolish every time I took someone's sarcastic comment seriously—and *absolutely* stopping myself from rubbing smooth things like a fleece sweatshirt or a rose petal against my lips and cheek even if it was something that felt completely natural for me to want to do at that moment. It took a lot of time and effort for me to develop these strategies and incorporate them into my public behavior, but I thought it was worth it not to be thought of as a "weirdo," which is probably the nicest word that comes to a person's mind when they see someone, in public, rubbing a rose petal against their lips and cheek. And I still stroked that sublimely soft rose petal against my cheek in the privacy of my own room, as I was never able to completely disengage myself from something that seems so natural to do. The ignorance and social stigma surrounding disabilities, especially those involving neurology, worked together to ensure that I was never upfront about my disability until very recently in my life, when I finally learned that there is a disability community and met some of its members.

Acting white wasn't quite as much work. One of my parents was white, and my non-white parent vigorously encouraged me to align myself with whiteness motivated by a mixture of internalized racism and a simple shrewdness that deeply understood the advantages that came with knowing how to successfully navigate white culture. I can't find it in myself to be completely mad at my mother for deliberately choosing not to speak any language that wasn't English around me, thereby reducing the likelihood I'd learn her native language. My mother knew that as a person of color and a non-English speaking immigrant, they would never be able to integrate into white culture no matter what they did. In her own life she could see the disadvantages that came with being non-white and a non-English speaking foreigner. She saw her status as a person of color as doing nothing positive for her life in America, so she probably thought (perhaps rightly) that by encouraging me to be as white as possible she was encouraging me to have a greater chance at success and fitting in culturally in a way she couldn't.

Acting abled by contrast was something more self-developed as neither of my parents were nearly as explicit trying to get me to learn how to act abled. Part of acting abled meant that of course I should never seek any accommodation for my disability. I had already gone twenty-one years, more or less successfully, without doing so. It wasn't until my final year of college that I even considered seeking an accommodation, and I anguished about whether to seek one at all. I finally decided to do it, but unfortunately, having never sought one in the past meant that the school psychologist looked at me with suspicion for only now considering accommodation for the first time. When I finally did meet with the psychologist to discuss the possibility of seeking an accommodation, he told me that he didn't think I needed any. I accepted his judgment. I felt too defeated to consider asserting myself more during our meeting, or even to consider getting a second opinion. I accepted his implicit judgment that the ability to act abled meant that one was not really disabled. And that is the unfortunate consequence for those who are good enough at acting abled. Once people think of you as abled any time you are unable to keep up the act is seen as something to be suspicious of. People question how authentically disabled you are in the rare moment you choose to disclose that information about yourself.

Both being abled and white are part and parcel of what it means to fit into mainstream American society. Both are usually the result of the internalization of both ableist and racist beliefs and is the double edged sword that allows us to believe that we fit into the American mainstream, but only so far as our acting abilities can be maintained. But I don't want to be an actor motivated by internalized ableism and racism anymore. An actor whose performance invalidates and erases the very person I am. I'm afraid there is no hollywood award for that performance.

The Middle, Or—The Mestiza and the Coffee Shop

Emily Pate

Mestiza: "a woman of mixed racial or ethnic ancestry, especially, in Latin America, of mixed American Indian and European descent"

Mixed: "consisting of different qualities or elements; (of an assessment of, reaction to, or feeling about something) containing a mixture of both favorable and negative elements"

SATURDAY MORNING

"Bagel with eggs and sausage, bagel with eggs and cheese, croissant with eggs and cheese!" A barista's yelling out a string of orders to waiting customers in a coffee shop. I'm hunched over my laptop, reading a *Splitsider* article on comedian Maria Bamford, procrastinating working on a pilot script for a competition. Okay five more minutes, then I'll start. I think I heard them call my order. I snap out of reading, go up to the counter to grab a plate. Oh Maria, you're so talented and hilarious. I love how you use your family in your comedy. I sit, take a bite. This sandwich needs salt. Where's the salt? Ugh, over there by the creamer. Go get the salt. Wait, don't run into that guy in front of you. Are you going first, dude? Me? Okay fine.

Got the salt. Sit down. Put on the salt. Bite. I wish my parents would do material with me. This biscuit kinda sucks. It's chewy. Very round, too, why? Their biscuits just look like that. No, it has a hole in the middle and looks like bagel. Ooooh, it is a bagel. They messed up my order, I guess. Eh.

"Biscuit with eggs and cheese!" *There's* my order. Shit.

I glance up at the steaming biscuit and bubbly cheese waiting for its owner, momentarily paralyzed with indecision. I look down at the bagel sandwich on my plate. There's an enthusiastic, moon-shaped bite taken out of it. Switching them out covertly doesn't seem to be an option. I search around for the bagel's actual owner. There's a cute guy standing to the side near the counter, shifting his weight back and forth. A rubber band ball of anxiety forms in my stomach while I deliberate my next move. Maybe I *can* return it without anyone knowing...even with the bite taken out...Ugh of course it belongs to some Hottie McHotterson. What am I going to say if he overhears me talking to the barista? "Sorry I stuffed my face with your breakfast. I don't look at my food before I cram." I stand up with the plate and walk toward the counter just as the manager repeats the announcement in my face.

"BISCUIT AND EGGS WITH CHEESE!"

I set my food on the counter, sheepish.

"I'm sorry, I grabbed the wrong plate."

The manager's clearly annoyed. In a RomCom, Cute Guy would've smoothly intervened with some seemingly repugnant response so he and I could initially hate each other, but somehow cross paths later and fall in love over time. But, this isn't a RomCom. A nasal and admonishing California accent cuts in before she can respond.

"That's ours."

A tiny woman in yoga pants and a jogging sweater is standing behind me, piercing me with narrowed mole eyes. She repeats her accusation.

"You took our food."

"I'm sorry, I spaced out and didn't hear properly."

I expect her to understand at least a bit, assure me it's okay, that mistakes happen. Instead she frowns with disdain, wrinkling her pinched, alabaster nose like I'm the sick and twisted villain in her little sleuth adventure.

"That's alright" But her scowl and tone of voice are clearly saying, "I hope they lock your ass up, you kleptomaniac."

My eyeballs are hot, my chest tight. I offer to pay for the bagel as well as my order, but the manager says they'll use my biscuit and cheese on standby for the next person who wants one. I go back to my table with the bagel, humiliated. Nancy Drew grumbles and stomps over to her boyfriend, furious at the injustice of having to wait longer.

Who does this white bitch think she is?

BORDER GIRL

I'm not immune to racist thoughts. I'm from El Paso, TX, a city sharing a border with Juarez, Mexico. I'm Mexican-American, or Chicana, I didn't really grow up with one term or the other. Though El Paso does have some diversity due to Fort Bliss and various Jewish, Italian, and Chinese immigrant communities settling there during the late 1880s, over eighty percent of us are Hispanic and/or Latino, mostly Mexican. The first time I ever sat in a classroom where most everyone *wasn't* my own race was during a state speech competition. High schools from all over Texas competed. I remember sitting in my first round of dramatic interpretation, in a sea of Anglo (I assumed) kids. My medium olive skin, black almond eyes, and dark curly hair seemed to me to stand out so much I could feel them tingle, my own sheltered background manifesting in my thoughts. I wonder if they hate Mexicans. They've probably never seen a brown girl before. Chances are they had, they lived in Texas, after all. But other than this experience, I pretty much grew up where being a Latino didn't mark you as different or a minority. There were, however, many layers of complexity surrounding identity based on skin color, being a Spanish speaker, or lack thereof, and whether you were raised in the U.S.; Juarez; or both. I felt the effects of all of these elements.

Skin tone is important. Mexicanos on both sides of the border with light eyes, hair and skin are treated in ways that imply they're more attractive. The term guero(a) is typically used as a gushing term of endearment for these people (though it can be used negatively in certain contexts as well). The term morena(o), however, refers to a person with tan/dark skin, eyes, and/or hair. It also sometimes has a subtext of being underclass or marginalized. People openly talk about how beautiful someone's babies will be if they have them with someone with light eyes or hair. A woman once told me that my son was a "golden child" because of his medium skin tone and light brown hair. It's common for people to complain about getting darker during the summer months, wanting to look as light as possible. Gueras don't want to become morena, morenas don't want to become indio (a term meaning Indian, usually derogatory because it can refer to being of the "lowest" uneducated and poorest class). If you watch Spanish-language television or Google actrices Mexicanas, you'll see plenty of fair-skinned actresses.

Growing up classified somewhere on the morena side of the spectrum, I was constantly told, "you're not THAT dark," as some sort of reassurance. Classmates said my knees and elbows must be dirty, when in fact they were just a darker brown than the rest of my body. My knees were ashy, but what the hell did they expect? We lived in a freaking desert. And also, I hated putting lotion on. Actually, my attention to "the boring parts" of grooming has always been fragmented. Even now I'm typing this with badly chipped nail polish. My fingernails need cutting. Growing up, friends and family would scold, "You need to put on lotion. You need to take care of your hair, take care of your nails, stop going to bed with makeup on." Of course a lot of this was part of being an ultra feminine, as beautiful as possible woman in a culture (and I'm talking about American and Mexican here) that emphasizes her worth via her appearance. Also, when you're done up, you might look like you might have more money. You definitely don't want to look like a poor, unkempt, wild, bagel-nabbing, indigenous girl, do you? So I could see how it was important to everyone, given what was reinforced for us, but for me I was very bad about any mundane tasks that took patience and planning to execute. I was absorbed in other things. But it so happened that, in this case, my knees and elbows were definitely clean. Clean and brown.

While looking white is seen as positive, a Mexicana "acting white" isn't necessarily desirable. "Why are you talking like a gringa [white/American girl]? "Porque no habla espanol [Why don't you speak Spanish]?" "Do you like white guys or Mexican?"

Non-Latino Anglos are a different story, and we tend to otherize them. "White people are weird; they don't care about family." "White people think they know everything." There's an underlying perception that Anglos can be a tad condescending, invader-ish, and shouldn't be trusted too much.

Of course, this is not historically unfounded or irrational. El Paso and U.S. history is steeped in a history of Mexicans losing land and rights after the U.S.-Mexican War, rights that were protected under the Treaty of Guadalupe Hidalgo and largely ignored. In El Paso, for instance, the salt wars of the late 1880s served as a symbol of the struggle between the locals operating on the Spanish and Mexican culture of communal resources and the Anglo Americans privatizing them. El Paso didn't have a Hispanic mayor until 1957. And of course, go back even further, and the Spanish were taking Apache and Tigua land to parcel out to Mexicans. So this sense of "the outsider" is still very strong and manifested in nuanced ways.

So when one of them acts like she just caught you stealing her license plates, you might resort to a knee-jerk "who does this white bitch think she is?".

I'm not 100% Mexican, my paternal grandfather and great grandfather were Anglo. And I'm regrettably not fluent in Spanish, like so many Latinos whose parents stressed English over their own native tongue, usually as a result of being shamed. For my parents' part, my dad spoke it most often to his grandmother. English was used in school, at work, etc. When I've asked my mom, she'll typically reply that we [my siblings and myself] didn't want to learn, but she has also said she was embarrassed by her "border Spanish," even though it was her first language. And I do remember being very young and not wanting to listen to Spanish music, for instance. Most of my friends who were fluent in Spanish had at least one parent or grandparent who either didn't speak English or would simply only speak Spanish to them and require them to speak back in Spanish. For whatever reason, my grandparents would speak to me in English, Spanish, and Spanglish and didn't really correct if I answered in English. But as far as looks go, I'm definitely not considered white, nor could I pass for it. My curly hair and thick eyebrows, latte skin, almond eyes, and sharp jawline tell all.

I'm Mestiza. Mixed. In every sense of the word and beyond. Ethnically, culturally, artistically, occupationally, neurologically.

***

227

Bagel girl is livid, retelling her woes to her boyfriend with emphatic gestures. This refuels my shame turned self-righteous racism/anger. I fight off crying on my laptop. Oh, poor you, privileged white lady in your sunny Southern California neighborhood. Livin' in your craftsman bungalow that you probably own outright, no doubt with a garden being maintained by a brown person as we speak. Oh, the trials and tribulations you've faced this morning.

I bite into the bagel. My eyes well up again, partly from self-indulgence, partly from what's turning into an anxiety meltdown. I'm less able to deal with the noise now. The voices around me get louder, and the sound of the milk steamer stabs through the air.

Our entitled gentlewoman finally gets her sausage bagel. I need to take a breath and get my head out of this hatred zone. She's probably just hungry and had a bad morning. I think the worst thing is she acted like I did something MALICIOUS by making a mistake. YOU FUCKED UP. How could you be so careless?

I see adults admonish kids all the time for being "too slow." "I already told you twice." "You need to listen better."

Not being aware of your surroundings = being selfish.

Pay attention.

MISTAKES, OR "YOU'RE NOT THAT"

~~We were never made to feel bad for mistakes in my family~~.
We weren't usually made to feel bad for mistakes in our family if they were obvious accidents. Nobody would scoff or scold if you dropped a glass. Who cares? We have lots of jars; we didn't need it anyway. If a cooking attempt went awry, everyone insisted it was delicious. I still remember one instance where my parents graciously choked down a severely over-seasoned brisket I'd made. The oven bag exploded because I'd forgotten to poke holes in it. (I sometimes struggle with multi-step tasks.) The marinade burst all over the oven, so I moved the brisket into a new bag and poured an entire second bottle of marinade in. Just figured I'd reset. The result was a very tender brisket with nauseatingly concentrated flavor. "I like it like this!" Mom insisted, downing glasses of water between tiny bites. Dad raised his eyebrows jokingly to make me laugh, then nodded in agreement with my mom, soldiering through the meal.

It seemed many adults in the area where I grew up had a certain wisdom that made them pretty accepting of human error— or things perceived as errors, we'll say. "That's just who she is, déjala [let her be]." Of course, this ends up being a problem when someone could actually benefit from active support with, say, a disability that's gone under the radar, because no one wants to acknowledge it exists in the first place.

My own family currently goes back and forth on whether they believe, or perhaps, accept, the fact that I'm autistic. "There's no way you had a learning disability, you got straight As." Only I didn't get straight As, I had very high grades in certain areas, but always one or two areas where

229

I was unable to finish work on time, wasn't getting the material, and received low grades, even failing a class during my senior year. And it took me seven years to graduate college, with plenty of class withdrawals to avoid failing when I couldn't handle a standard course load. "You talk. You're very social, you always want to be on stage." Well of course, many autistics are very verbal. We're diverse. I'm not as social as they think I am. In my hometown, ya gotta have friends. Or family, rather. Family is the most important thing. Put your family first. Smile, chat, listen, be respectful. Help with the little ones. The other women around me did it, and I followed to the best of my ability. I just didn't realize how much it was taking for me to do it. I wasn't aware that when I do what I thought was "daydreaming," I'm actually repeatedly rehearsing conversations I may have later, then constantly replay them after they occur, only now adding my social anxiety into the mix, cringing from things I said, wondering if I was too blunt, rude, or inconsiderate, if people talked about how weird or inappropriate it was.

As for being on stage, when playing someone else, you get to fade away. You get to assume someone else's identity and do something weird, outlandish, or "insane." If your character does something out of step, it's on her, not you. You just get the freedom to do it, and in a very narrow, safe construct. People think you're talented for it; you're celebrated. You're successful and honorable. Plus you get to script, and it's completely acceptable. When I recounted to my mom recently how I'd pace and script constantly as a child, she replied, "I just thought you were doing your plays." Well I was. They happened to line up. Lately I've been more open with telling my family and friends I still

230

stim and script on a daily basis, much like my kiddo, Henry, also autistic. After it's initially waived away, I emphasize, "Yeah, I do, though. Like Henry. It's okay." This is met with an "ohhhhh," then silence. Because Henry is a six-year-old male who is visibly autistic, speaks largely through scripts and short phrases, and doesn't just stim when he's home alone. Then someone will say something like, "There's no way. Think what you wanna think, but you're not that." Not that. Not Henry, who is within earshot. If I point this out, there'll be protests of "there's nothing wrong with Henry, you're just not like that."

I come from a line of high achievers: educators, engineers, business owners, industrious people putting huge pressure on themselves to be successful, celebrated, and honorable, to maintain financial stability and move up the ladder, gain respect in your field. And to achieve those things, it's assumed you need to be socially outgoing, nurturing (particularly if you're a woman), industrious, pious, and studious. And probably just as important and unspoken, you need to be somewhat "normal." Eccentricities were definitely accepted and even celebrated if they seemed "mild," but if they became "too obvious" they might put you at risk for being laughed at become something no one talked about. It was similar with "being smart." You were pushed to take your studies seriously, learn everything you can. "You've always got your education." "Education is everything." But of course, the age-old dynamic is that you eventually use that education to question the status quo, and that doesn't go well. And these mixed messages were very much present in the larger community as well. Like my autistic identity, values existed in this ambiguous, nuanced state. It was kind of like *Fiddler on the Roof*. In fact, it was very much like *Fiddler on the Roof* because I'd play the soundtrack in my room on a loop, stopping and repeating certain parts until I could nail every note. But more generally, I was performing a balancing act with those opposing values. I was pushed to stand up and fight for what I believe in just as often as I was told to respect authority, be obedient. "Put everything in God's hands; let him decide." It was a constant limbo.

***

Snapping out of my head and into the physical world for a second. Look at her over there stuffing her face. Okay, no. Breathe. Focus on yourself, chismosa [shit talker/gossip]. Mom's bringing Henry back in awhile. Finish. You have this free time to get what you need done. Don't waste it. Be grateful.

GRACIAS A DIOS [Thank God]

Living in a high-poverty city, I was very aware of privileges I had growing up. My parents migrated from working in the service industries to solid middle-class jobs by the time I was nine. They started out living with relatives, then a small mobile home, duplex, three-bedroom home that they bought, and finally a shiny, new, comfortably sized house in a pristine subdivision. I received a private-school education where teachers weren't burdened with packed classrooms and narrow standards. I read great books by women about women: *A Tree Grows in Brooklyn, The Bean Trees, Wuthering Heights, I Know Why the Caged Bird Sings, A Raisin in the Sun, The House on Mango Street, The Awakening.* I was encouraged to be outspoken. And also constantly reminded that I needed to be grateful for all I had that others didn't, the sacrifices my ancestors, family, parents had made for me. Being ungrateful is a sin. And sometimes, standing up for yourself looks a lot like being ungrateful.

So sometimes I tiptoe. I can keep my mouth shut, riding waves of indecision that leave me at a standstill. I don't want to make an inconsiderate mistake.

Pay attention.

***

The baristas are fighting over who should take a mental-health day. The cashier claims the guys get a couple of days, and the manager schedules one for herself, but she never gets one. The manager wears a guilty smirk of admission. "I don't do that."

I consider myself pretty good at reading other people's emotions. I'm acutely aware of others' feelings, to the point that I'm constantly considering how my words or actions affect someone else and try adjust accordingly.

Someone scrapes a chair along the floor, making me jump. "Do you mind if I sit here?" A man stands across the large table I'm at. "Hm? Oh, no." I've learned exactly how to minimize the fact that being pulled from a task is very jarring for me. Smile, ask again to give yourself a second to process the question, then answer. This was never conscious, but I now know I do this constantly.

And I do mind him sitting there, but I'm so used to accommodating someone's feelings it doesn't cross my mind to politely decline. Luckily he stays at the far end of the table instead of choosing the chair closer to me. I have to breathe. My kid Henry would've put his headphones on. Wait, why don't I have headphones? Huh. I should get some.

I definitely can misread sometimes, but a lot of the times I'm spot on.

"CHILDREN AND ART"

I need to finish writing this script. It's not very clear at this point how a pilot contest might help my career, though. Maybe if I was still living in LA. I had moved up there with Henry to finally pursue a career in entertainment, but it ended up lasting only a year. My shared apartment was pricey, I pulled Henry from an abusive school setting, and when our lease ran out, my bad credit prevented me from finding something suitable, despite great rental history. For that year, I was a 33-year-old single mom pursuing my lifelong dream raising a kid in a city I couldn't afford. But I loved it. I was happy being in a place with history, grit, a mix of cultures, and things to do for free. Once I pulled Henry out of that school, he seemed very happy. He was back to his typical sleeping and eating habits and interests that had fallen away when he was in school. We were lucky to have a great sitter and family friend who lived with us and took him everywhere when I was working. When I wasn't, all three of us explore the old zoo at Griffith Park, go to an inclusive gym where we could zipline and bounce on the trampoline to our hearts' content. We'd go to free matinees of old Disney movies at The New Beverly Cinema or sometimes, if we didn't want to brave the congestion and noise, stay in with Netflix and an iPad.

The best part for me was the countless number of artists around me. Imagine an entire hub where everyone else is also devoted to your special interest. I simultaneously felt like an imposter. Okay, well sometimes I felt like a badass. But I didn't fit the mold of what I had been taught was a "true artist." A struggling artist is supposed to sacrifice everything, all or none. I grew up missing family functions for auditions, skipping prom and other high school functions to be in dinner theatre productions—and I loved it. I started sending for NYU and Juilliard brochures in 8th grade, dreaming of the day when every hour would be filled with acting exercises and "breakthroughs." My hopes were lofty, and those things didn't happen when I was younger. That's fine, but when I finally did get to LA, I had to fight this destructive inner dialogue that I was too old, too poor. Realistically, I'm a mom first, so of course I can't drop everything for a project. Everything required a balancing act. Sometimes I can achieve that, but more often it's a struggle.

Living in LA, and now, I have one foot in each role, artist and mom. I scold myself for not doing more artistically because I've always had this purist idea of what being a creative looks like. You get up at five, go to the gym and yoga, have breakfast while you catch up on the industry trades, network with another artist, or work on the web series you're developing, go to on-camera class, rehearse with your partner, have dinner, go to improv class or rehearsal for the stage show you're currently in, go out with your classmates/castmates after for more networking, then go home, sleep, repeat. Oh and read super important, enlightening books and go to shows somewhere in there.

My life does not look like that. Plenty of it is spent on day-to-day tasks like cooking and dishes, spending time with Henry. Reading and reading and reading articles, news. Walking to my sister's three houses down from mine and spending time with them. That part's like a sitcom. Very different. They're all good things, but I still struggle with the dissonance between what I imagined and what is. I cope by staying cautious, not risking anything, and trying to forget about things I want for myself. How much I love to perform or be on a set.

I also have a hot-and-heavy but drama-ridden relationship with executive functioning. He's very elusive. Sometimes he surprises me and shows up, other times he won't answer my texts, like when I needed him to help me with the brisket or remind me to sit and write something every day, to finish a long task I know is ultimately beneficial for me. He's a lot of work. Except the difference is I've done better than fine being single and without a male partner the last few years and in no way feel like I need one. Executive functioning, that'd be nice to have around more often. It'd be nice to be able to organize my thoughts, multitask or consistently remember to pay bills. Although it'd be logistically easier to have a partner, too. Perhaps. "Possibly maybe. Probably no."

***

I need to sort out this pilot. Take a breath. Pay attention. I can't concentrate. Bagel girl and her guy have finished and are leaving. My sandwich sits untouched, document with only a few notes jotted down on it. Cute Guy is grading what looks like geography tests, flowing through each page with his pen, unceremoniously slashing the occasional X. Wrong.

Mom will be dropping by with Henry in a while. Maybe I'll walk home now, finish later. My body is restless, and I want the forward motion to think and daydream. I didn't get that last scene done. Oh well. Later.

I get a text from my sister.

HEY GIRL, BRING HENRY OVER AND HAVE DINNER WITH US LATER!

Yay. That'll be fun. I do live in a beautiful city with my family. I've got a small cottage with a yard, and it's super cheap. See? I'm grateful.

Later on at home, Henry's dancing his heart out to "Singing in the Rain" in our living room. I join in, and we spin until we're dizzy, his giggles overtaking the music. We drop to the floor as the song ends with a sharp finish, exhausted. "Bravo!" Henry exclaims.

Stillness for a bit.

And then he wanders to the kitchen. I start the dishes and listen to his contented hum as he plays with the contents of the fruit bowl, arranging it in a careful line. It was initially meant to be an exact replica of the props in Cookie Monster's "Healthy Food" song, but these days he seems to be creating a different pattern each time. He lovingly composes landscapes of produce on our yellow table, queues of citrus, apples, stone fruit, and root veggies. From overhead, it's obvious each individual piece of food has been attentively placed just so with attention to elements like line, shape, movement, and one more in particular, but I can't grab the word. The result is a dynamic, synergetic pattern, a small rolling hill of crops. A carrot rests atop an avocado in delicate balance. He runs into the other room every now and then and comes back, pendulating between still concentration and freeing movement.

I clean the kitchen slowly, lost in my thoughts. It takes awhile because I wander off several times, then return when I remember what I was doing. I turn on some mellow music Henry and I can agree on, set a timer to focus, and eventually finish the dishes.

I sit down across from Henry and set a ten-minute timer and jot a few sentences down in my notebook. I end up writing for twelve. It's a start. A bit later, satisfied with his work he sighs and comes to wrap his neck around mine for a second. He squeals and hums. His breath smells like strawberries. Smile. Pay close attention. I stare at the harvest on the table. That's the word. Harmony.

A NEW STORY

In her piece "La Conciencia de la Mestiza," Gloria Anzaldua contemplates what it means to be a contemporary, intersectional Mestiza. She paints a picture of "la mestiza floundering in uncharted seas." She's bombarded with so much conflicting input and so many points of view that she has to stretch the borders of her psyche to survive. "Rigidity is death." And in fact, maybe that's my strength. As I am now, I "operat[e] in a pluralistic mode—nothing is thrust out, the good, the bad, and the ugly, nothing rejected, nothing abandoned." I can transform that contradiction and that ambiguity into something harmonious and new. And that means I'm going to have redefine some things for myself, for others.

You can be a mestiza without being fragmented between two cultures. You exist, after all. So there's a new culture now, a third one. You're not less of anything. You're one hundred percent you. Sometimes you'll feel like calling someone a "white bitch" and will have to assess where that comes from. Sometimes you'll feel frustrated with a culture that asks you to continually give and give, until you're folding in on yourself, and will have to say no. Me first. It's your story, your identity for the taking.

And this doesn't just apply to my culture and ethnicity. It can extend to neurodivergence, too. Anzaldua writes:

> As a Mestiza I have no country, my homeland cast me out; yet all countries are mine because I am every woman's sister or potential lover. (As a lesbian I have no race, my own people disclaim me; but I am all races because there is the queer of me in all races). (80)

There is the autistic of me in all races, in all genders. And despite the fact that my culture may disclaim my neurology, it's a part of me. And it's up to me to join fellow autistics in stretching people's psyches, making them comfortable with ambiguity, with a new Autistic culture, one that welcomed me with open, validating arms. Anzaldua continues:

I am cultureless because, as a feminist, I challenge the collective culture because I am participating in the creation of yet another culture, a new story to explain the world and our participation in it, a new value system...Soy un amasamiento, I am an act of kneading, of uniting, and joining that not only has produced both a creature of darkness and a creature of light, but also a creature that questions the definitions of light and dark and gives them new meanings. (80)

Tell a new story. Kill your prejudices, question everything, and create. There's no one way. You can write a few sentences, that's fine. Do it on a computer while you're with your child, send it somewhere. Do not be limited by your preconceptions of what artistry and storytelling are. You can line up food on a table. You can be together and alone, be still and wander when you need to. And when you do that, you redefine what it means to be an artist. For yourself, for others like you. See? you were paying attention the entire time.

Pick Two

//kiran foster

"You can have it fast, good, or cheap. Pick any two."

This is an old adage I've heard a lot, probably because my dad has done a lot of project management in his career. You can't have something that's done fast, done well, and done cheaply, it goes: you do something quickly for little money, but it's going to be terrible; do it on a small budget to a high standard and it'll take forever; do it quickly and well and you'll be paying a fortune for it.

It's occurred to me recently, while I was trying to explain what it is to be a brown autistic trans person, that I make the same concessions.

It goes like this: Somebody I have to work with to survive will respect at most two of the three things that are most central to who I am: my race, my gender, or my neurodivergence.

My disability services advisor at university is empathetic about my cultural struggles and the racism I face, but she managed to use both "he" and "her" in one sentence when emailing my psychologist. My psychologist is very good about using "they" or at least avoiding referring to me with any pronouns at all, but she's the sort of white person who often interrupts me with "not all white people though." When I'm around other trans people or in queer spaces, they're usually either all-white or extremely intolerant of my stimming, or both.

My parents, on the other hand, believe that both autism and gender diversity are white inventions.

I recently returned from a hui (Māori for meeting or gathering, in this case a conference of sorts) targeted at takatāpui and other Māori people and people of color with non-normative genders and sexualities. It was an incredibly emotional experience, especially given that I'd spent the last few weeks culturally bereft since being outed and forced to leave home.

It was also an incredibly exhausting experience, because nothing about the hui catered to my needs or those of the other non-neurotypical people there. No details about what we were to bring or the structure of the hui were posted anywhere but in scattered posts on a Facebook page, meaning I had to improvise more than would have already been necessary given I was and am on the run with very little to my name. More damningly, we were locked in a room for the final dinner and show, during which all the lights were dimmed except bright, flashing lasers. I was only let out when I couldn't see much over the signal jamming of my dizzy, terrified panic and could barely communicate.

Pick two: gender, race, autism. Most progressive friends of mine, whether white or people of color, expect me to pick my gender and my autism, and given my experiences with my family and with other majority-PoC groups, I can see why.

I'm practically white, aren't I? My sister jokingly refers to herself as a "ripe banana—brown and yellow on the outside, white on the inside," and I suspect that's how many people see me. I'm "eloquent," after all, "articulate;" the only language I'm fluent in these days is the language that colonized both my homeland and the land I call home; I've always fared well in white-dominated spaces at least in part because of my parents' choice to raise me in an English-speaking household exposed to all the "great classics." I'm practically white, and surely it wouldn't be much of an imposition to choose the two things which are clearly more central to my experience, right?

Wrong. It's remarkable that my white neoliberal friends in particular have absolutely no understanding that while I'm letting misgendering slide among my family, I might be letting racist microaggressions slide among them. I've put up with a lot of things that are far from ideal to stay alive, and that doesn't just mean my current subsistence off white bread and orange juice. My race and cultures being something I'm relatively removed from due to imperialism and white supremacy doesn't make me less keenly aware of the loss I've already experienced and how much I sacrifice every time I swallow down something I should really have spat out in a white person's face.

Pick two, they say, like these things are as discrete as cost and speed. Like it's possible for those of us who are oppressed along several axes to disentangle what comes from where. It doesn't work that way. My inability to read sarcasm and my ineptitude with idiomatic phrases are lumped together either as an autistic literalist thing or an Asian immigrant thing, never considered as a particular set of linguistic difficulties that could be a combination of the two. My social anxiety is interpreted as PTSD-related, or autism-related, or even related to a fear of being misgendered. None of these distinctions are things I can make for myself. I am the sum of my parts, and any and all care I've received has fallen short because it's attempted to treat my parts separately if it considers them at all.

I benefit from therapy which is culturally appropriate or at the very least doesn't expect me to be white. I am nourished by communities which can approach and embrace my gender while affirming that having come to it in a way that often alienates me from neurotypical transgender people is valid and an important part of my narrative. I am sustained by people who can understand that I'm not really joking when I say that my gender is "fuck colonialism," and provide me with a cultural or at least ideological anchor against which I can feel a little less bereft, a little less like white people have managed to take not only my homeland and cultures away from me but also any chance at a coherent gender identity.

I live with a constant sense of loss. I live with a constant awareness that things have been stolen from me both directly through my immediate and dense history of child abuse and through the collective trauma of colonialism and institutional ableism under late capitalism. Existing as a person despite these acts of violence against my person is a political and revolutionary act in and of itself, and navigating the ways in which existing spaces and networks fall short of providing for people like me is an intricate, careful labour of survival. Picking two is telling me that I have lost so much, but that it is only fair to expect to recover some of what I've lost. Picking two is rendering the rest of me less worthy of acknowledgement, and scouring my person and narrative clean of things that are inconvenient. Picking two is unweaving the fraught, trauma-born tapestry of the person I am because I have too many colors of threads running through my story, instead of maybe considering that the space I exist in is just not colorful enough.

Pick two: gender, race, autism, they tell me, and they don't realize that they're separating each of these things from who I am in the process. Just as many of us reject person-first language because it implies that, as "people with autism," we are people first and simply happen to be carrying autism with us like a burden we can set down, I reject any suggestion that setting aside my race or disability or queerness is a viable compromise in order to receive the care and support that I need. These things are not things that accompany my personhood: they *are* my personhood.

Pick two, they tell me, and in so doing they have chosen the status quo over me.

Passing Without Trying

Daniel Au Valencia

As members of the Autistic community, we take it for granted when someone describes autism as an *invisible disability*. We don't have any static visual marker like, say, Down syndrome does, so we conclude that there must be no visual marker at all. Yet in our opposition to medicalized descriptions of autism, we constantly complain that the writer is glossing over our internal experiences and only considering what is externally apparent—what they are seeing. How can something invisible be perceived visually? Seeing should be no part of the process, let alone the only one.

When someone tells you that you do not "look Autistic", their mistake is having the wrong idea, or no idea, of what autism looks like. Their mistake is **not** thinking that autism has a distinct look. It does. It has many. We use the playful term *A-dar* (based on another community's term, *gaydar*) to describe our ability to pick each other out from a crowd. It's not some cosmic or spiritual link; it's just that we each have our entire life experience telling us what to look for. A non-Autistic person can easily be taught if they are willing to learn. Flapping—rocking—spinning—toe-walking—all of these things, and many more, *can* be seen. When I am flapping my hands in excitement, **I look Autistic.** For that reason, I reject the term *invisible disability*. However, the term may suggest one truth: Autistic body language can be suppressed—hidden—made to be unseen; an act we call **passing**.

In the simplest terms, **passing** is when one thing pretends to be another. For example, I was an extra in a film whose story was set in Iran. The casting director apparently believed I could *pass* as Persian (and the location manager believed Santa Clarita, California could pass as Iran). For Autistic people, *passing* usually means pretending to be **neurotypical**, since there isn't much to gain from passing as another neurominority. The choice of whether to pass or not to pass, as neurotypical, is a question I saw posed by Autistic bloggers, long before I ever came across the term *white-passing*. I may be considered both *NT-passing* and *white-passing* depending on whom you ask, although each instance of "passing" means something subtly different. To fully understand the concept of *passing*, you must also understand **normativity**.

An *implicit belief* is one that a person accepts without identifying it as a belief (and as a result, without really thinking about it). **Normativity** is a very common implicit belief, which suggests the existence of a *default* or "normal" type of person— not unmentionable, but simply not worth the trouble of mentioning. If you want to describe an Autistic Latina woman, you have to name those three traits; a neurotypical white man is just *a person*; those three traits are *assumed* until specified otherwise. Take a moment to imagine a hypothetical Autistic Latina woman, and a hypothetical neurotypical white man. In your mind's eye, you probably see two people who are heterosexual, cisgender, dyadic religious moderates with no other disabilities besides autism. This

247

simple exercise reveals an important truth: the word "normal" is merely a categorical label for those traits that we *assume* rather than specify. *Normativity* refers to this process of assumption: every person, in the minds of others, begins "normal"— that is, they begin as a neurotypical, able-bodied, male, heterosexual, cisgender, dyadic religious moderate belonging to the ethnic majority of wherever they live. As their real traits are revealed, on sight or in conversation, their "normality" is chipped away.

When people look at me for the first time, and probably the second and third, they see a person who is white, along with a number of other things. Thanks to normativity, anyone with sufficiently light skin is assumed to be white. In that sense, it can be said that I successfully *pass* as white. By using the word "success" in that statement, I have illustrated its absurdity: I put zero effort into making myself look more white. I have never bleached my skin or worn make-up to lighten my complexion, never taken a chisel to my nose or a syringe to my lips, never trimmed the thick Middle Eastern hair on my legs nor straightened the wavy Caribbean hair on my head. I do alter my body in some ways, but none of them are in service of convincing anyone that I'm white. There wouldn't be a point to it. I naturally "look white" enough to benefit from racism without trying to participate more.

The term **white-passing** is an adjective, not a verb. I effortlessly give off an air of whiteness with my light complexion and European-like facial features, but wait— the two people who contributed to my genome are not

248

white, they're Middle Eastern and Caribbean. That makes me not white, and I look like myself, so by the reflexive property of equality (not the transitive property), I look not white. So... I *don't* pass as white? To see my multiracial face and call me white is nothing more than an assumption. It is no more logical, rational, or reasonable than seeing my Autistic flapping hands and calling me neurotypical.

Autistic readers can guess that the hand-flapping analogy isn't hypothetical. One of those "other things" people see on first glance is neurotypicality. Sometimes they continue to insist on it even after they've been proven wrong (and sometimes they pretend to accept the autism label so they can insist that I must be "so high-functioning" as to seem *almost* neurotypical, though I would really rather not define "functioning" in terms of how not-different I can be). Thanks to normativity, anyone who isn't an 8-year-old boy drooling, rocking, and *currently* having a meltdown, is assumed to be neurotypical. In that sense, it can be said that I successfully *pass* as neurotypical. However, much like white-passing, I put no effort into being NT-passing.

There are many people for whom NT-passing *is* very much an action, and usually a matter of safety. Society has failed in many respects when Autistic and other neurodivergent people feel the need to take such extreme measures to avoid violence. Shame on the social power dynamics and the people who take advantage of them, never shame on the victim. With that disclaimer loud and clear, I can go on to say that the harm which would be done to me if I tried to pass as NT greatly exceeds the benefits.

Overriding your natural body language and defense mechanisms is a full-time job (on top of your actual job). It is extremely taxing, not to mention dangerous (Goodbye self-care? Hello meltdown!)

I *don't* pass as neurotypical— at least, I don't choose to. Most people are *astonished* when I explicitly tell them I'm Autistic. While popular media sources push the narrow image of an 8-year-old boy in constant meltdown, few people learn about any other possibilities. Yet failing to learn the meaning behind what you saw doesn't mean you didn't see it. Those astonished people may not have known which details to call autism, but did they really miss those details? People who didn't know I was Autistic (or were in denial about it) have described me as *weird, awkward, rigid, crazy, stupid, selfish,* and *asshole.* If I'm trying to *pass* as anything, it sure ain't that. My Autistic friends certainly wouldn't describe me that way. It almost seems as though the neurotypicals are picking up on (and judging, and persecuting) the things that make up autism, even if they don't know that autism is the correct term for those things. They notice something different about Autistic people, and reject that difference. If that sort of discrimination is all I get for being "so high-functioning" and "hardly Autistic at all", then I want to be "low-functioning" and fully Autistic. I'd much rather replace all those hurtful labels with a positive one like Autistic. Though far from guaranteed, an Autistic person is much more likely to be accepted and accommodated than a "weird" person.

I must admit that the lack of any benefit to me from (supposedly) passing as neurotypical also indicates an area of privilege: I *already have* many benefits. Where being openly Autistic may expose me to danger, my light complexion protects me. For example, police officers see me as white, so I have the freedom to kick a trash can or wait for a library to open without being arrested. It's easy to put less stake in my ethnic identity when passing as white is *actually* a form of privilege, rather than an obstacle. That's where white-passing and NT-passing diverge: white-passing *works*. What remains common between them is that they are not real. The fact that I have light skin and can speak with my mouth doesn't mean that I'm white and neurotypical. It means that it's possible for multiracial Autistic people to have light skin and speak with their mouths.

Passing is not something I do. Passing is something that other people do to me. It is also something that can be overcome, if you follow a few simple steps:

Ask questions.

I lied. There is only one step. All people know themselves better than anyone else can know them, so the best way to learn about a person is to speak with that person. There is so much information available to anyone willing to seek it in the most straightforward way. A reasonable person will not be offended when you ask if they're gay, or deaf, or black, or what their pronouns are, because these identifiers are sources of pride. And in case you don't get the opportunity to ask questions, practice phrases like "... that person. I don't know what their ethnicity, gender, sexuality, religion, or neurotype is, so I'll just call them a

251

person for now." Because you *don't* know, but only by just *assuming* can you ever get it wrong.

Normativity runs through both racism and ableism. It teaches us that our identities are wrong, that we are not "really" what we claim to be. It teaches us that we should celebrate being able to pass as white neurotypicals, even if we don't want to and still face discrimination. The good news is that being mindful and avoiding assumptions goes a long way towards overcoming it. First we need to conquer normativity in our own communities, then the world.

PART FOUR:

OUR PERSONAL IS POLITICAL

Helene Fischer

Monster Girl

Note: Image descriptions can be accessed through ALT text accompanying each panel, as well as at the very end of this chapter, in transcript form.

Transcript

Monster Girl
By Helene Fischer

Page 1 (COVER)
Monster Girl stands with her back to the viewer in an empty, seemingly endless room. One arm crosses behind her back to grip the elbow of the opposite arm. The "monster girl" has bright red skin, two horns coming from dark hair done in two braids, and clawed hands. She has a little forked tail. She wears a purple hoodie, and black pants. The colors are bright, light in value and somewhat saturated, giving a feeling of open space.
CAPTION: "I'm a monster girl."

Page 2
Panel 1
The same girl stands in the same room, now seen from the front. She is now a human girl, with tan skin, dark brown hair in two braids, hearing aids, and sad brown eyes. She looks down. The colors are darker, muted, giving a feeling of isolation and muted emotion.
CAP: I'm not a real monster.

Panel 2
Monster Girl looks at her hands.
CAP: They just think I am.

Panel 3

Monster Girl, now human again, clenches her hands into fists and she closes her eyes.

CAP: Am I?

Panel 4

Monster Girl walks in a huge crowd of people with indistinguishable faces. Headphones cover the girl's ears, and a large brown messenger bag drapes over her shoulders. Among the crowd are other monsters, unnoticed by Monster Girl.

CAP: They surround me, dull cut outs of the same gaping face, repeated –

Panel 5

Human Girl hunches her shoulders and moves through the crowd, now completely human in appearance. She still has her headphones over her ears.

CAP: Again and again and again and again –

Panel 6

Monster Girl. She sits in what is clearly a therapist's office, on the pastel sofa, clenching her skirt in her hands. Her eyes focus on the floor. Her headphones are off, and her bag is next to her on the couch. The colors are light in value, and the light from the window illuminates the room, with a feeling of open space and isolation.

CAP: They have a name for my kind – for us monsters.

CAP2: They call it autism.

Page 3

Panel 1

Human Girl sits on a bus, looking down. Headphones cover her ears.

Panel 2
Monster Girl begins rocking forward, her eyes shut tight. She frowns.
CAP: I'm told I'm just "un poco diferente" by my parents.

Panel 3
Human Girl sits in the bus, rocking backward, her legs sticking straight out. She clenches her hands in the fabric of the seat.
CAP: I'm told by everyone else I'm a freak.

Panel 4
Monster Girl sits in the back of a classroom filled with humans and monsters, looking at her desk. She has a sketchbook and some pencils and markers on her desk.
CAP: There is only so much I can do.

Panel 5
Monster Girl is human again. She rests her head on the desk, the shaft of light illuminating the paper in front of her. The paper in front of her has stretched out, larger than before and the words IM OK IM OK IM OK IM OK are on it in dark red.
CAP. Only so much I can focus on.

Panel 6
Monster Girl. She crumples the paper in one hand, and covers her face in the other. Tears run from her eyes. The paper is now dark red. Ink leaks on the desk from Monster Girl's hands.

CAP: Only so much I deal with.

Panel 7
Monster Girl. She stands in a bedroom, in front of a TV, her face expressionless. The only light comes from the TV.
CAP: My identity intersects in ways they can't understand.

Panel 8
Human Girl. She stands alone in an empty space looking at her hands. Her shadow is a monster.
Human Girl: And I'm a monster for it. Am I?

Page 4
Panel 1
Human Girl walks through a huge crowd in a park, headphones over her ears. The colors are muted, and she walks alone. She holds a toy robot in her hands.
CAP: Developmental disabilities are scary to people who don't have them. But if they are scared, I am terrified.

Panel 2
Monster Girl. She hunches her shoulders, and looks at a girl with thick curly hair in two puffs and blue scaly skin in the distance. The blue girl is muttering to herself.
CAP: I know one thing for sure. I am not the only "monster" out there.

Panel 3
Human girl, pulling her headphones off, gets the attention of a black girl wearing the same clothes as the blue monster girl from the previous panel.
CAP: We just have to find each other.

Panel 4

Blue Scaly Girl looks sideways at Monster Girl, who waves. The colors are not heavily saturated, but still rich enough to not be considered muted. There is a feeling of immediate solidarity and understanding between the two girls.

CAP: Then we can be scared together.

Panel 5

Blue Scaly Girl smiles slightly.

Panel 6

The two girls (human again) link hands.

Panel 7

The two girls (monsters now) walk through the park, holding hands.

CAP: And maybe one day, not at all.

Letter to My Father: Neurodivergent Kinship

N.I. Nicholson

I BUILT THIS CRIB AND SHE WOULD NOT SLEEP IN IT:
TWO WEEKS WASTED
– my father's handwritten caption on a Polaroid photo of
me dated January 4, 1977

I wasn't rejecting the crib you built with your own hands, that pink-and-white square thing in the background. And although I've shed my girl's name and gender, I didn't reject your dark brown hands, their skin wrinkling in slow motion and soused with acrid metallic funk from welding for Falk Co. since before I was born.

Look at that Polaroid again, Dad. I'm a tiny wiggling gaggle of cells that's *half yours*. Do you remember your own little limbs at that age, electrified with life, your brain a newborn TARDIS begging to grow quickly to size to travel and seize new sights: everything outside of *your* bassinet?

And do you see that chubby brown baby—four and a half months old, with long squiggles of thin black hair covering his head—ensconced in a plastic banana-covered baby walker while peering into a fallow brown paper bag bigger than his body? That babbling giant is surrounded by his toys—a scattered crowd of plastic primary-colored Lilliputian distractions—but he's *more interested in the paper bag.*

Do you see that—his fat face half inside the bag's open mouth? And doesn't it look a little like *your own,* hovering over the squat, hard shimmering body of a car's engine?

Revelation

Mikael Lee

Scars my blood line leading me back to you
Roots flow through dust and breaking open
Ancestors talk to me through white washed walls in all
too quiet rooms, remnants of the past, places they leave
us, lock us up
Our stories terrifying survival to systems of erasure
Grandfather Medicine Healer Teacher—
This body marked from birth to live opposed to false
power
We who have existed outside
We who sweat drum heart heat pain to exist with spirit
Ancestors dance through me
Breathe fire from abrasions
Years left in solitary hospital beds will break open the
doors to the spirit worlds
And this I say: We who exist anyway
Our selves proof of a revolutionary survival power.
We who must keep breathing and breaking bleeding
recreating.
We who live to keep each other here far away from the lies
of white materialism
We know this true living force Fire.

Innocence Torn Asunder

Fragmented Perfection (Cindy Facteau)

Alone in an alley at a quarter past twelve

-It was cold.

Mind going places most sane men won't delve

-I was lonely.

Unable to see forward, too afraid to look back

-Too much grief.

A bug scurries into a sidewalk crack

-He was lucky.

Alone in an alley at a quarter past one

-I was hungry.

Bar down the street radiates drunken fun

-It was loud.

Footsteps approach from the direction of the bar

-Too much alcohol.

Probably some drunk looking for his car

-He was stumbling.

Alone in an alley at a quarter past two

-I was bleeding.

Victim once more, but nowhere to run to

-I was shaking.

Ashamed, degraded, and struggling to survive

-It wasn't easy.

Wondering if I'd ever leave these streets alive

-I was fifteen.

Speaking ill of the dead.

Kassiane A. Asasumasu

It's a taboo in our culture, to speak ill of the dead. When someone dies we are supposed to forget the bad things they did and dwell only on the good.

I cannot forget. I will not forget. I will not be silent. My story is mine, and I will not edit it for ghosts.

My mother died 53 weeks ago. She is the ghost for whom I will not edit my story. I have written about some of her abusive behavior before, and I wrote a bit last year when she died, but there are specific things she did that are not ok and it is time.

My mother was an emotional abuser. And I'm triggered to shit any way, so I am going to tell you about her favorite tactics.

Trigger Warning for emotional abuse, confinement, suicide threat descriptions

Starting when I was very young, my mother would make threats of the abandonment type. They evolved as I grew older.

When I was quite young, my mother would threaten to leave me places. Not like that thing that parents do with their little kids where they wave bye-bye to transition out of McDonalds or wherever. That thing where they say that if you don't stop crying right now they are going to leave you where you are and pretend you are not theirs. Now, I have enough siblings that this is a practical impossibility, but five year olds don't really recognize that. This threat didn't last very long—you can't terrorize a small child who cannot handle a mall into not melting down at the mall while still at the mall, it turns out. It evolved.

When I was seven or eight, I found out somehow that foster care and orphanages were things, that some children did not have parents, that some children could not live with their parents. I don't remember how I came to this information. I do remember my mother using it as a weapon. For several years, every time I got overstimulated, "if you can't control yourself I will take you to the Children's Home". Every time I would not wear what she wanted me to wear, "well maybe you'd like the clothes from a foster mother better." My room wasn't clean (and it was never, ever clean. Nowhere in our house was clean)? "They'd teach you to keep a room clean at an orphanage". This was the constant over the head threat. At least 5 times she started to pack a suitcase for me because I was acting like an overloaded Autistic child, or because I was acting like a child in general.

This, too, would evolve.

So, for my whole life I have had a fear of confinement. Not like "oh, that'd suck" but like "give me liberty or give me death, and I mean that literally". Once I got old enough to

269

know that orphanages weren't really a thing in the US, and to understand a bit more about foster care (and to have double dared her to call CPS a couple times), my mother had a new abandonment threat: she was going to have me committed.

This was where she'd stack emotional abuse tactics. First she would trigger a meltdown. I've got some pretty significant sensory integration weirdness goin' on, and I have always very much needed to know exactly what was going on. File nails right next to me while changing my schedule? Make me late for things with the worst sound in the world? Refuse to do what you said was going to be done when it was going to be done? Yeah I can't handle that now, 20 years later. And it was so much more chaotic there. So my mother would start a meltdown, and then instead of leaving me alone she would yell at me, hold me down while yelling at me, and then demand I calm down or she would call for an ambulance to take me to the psych ward, where she could make them keep me forever.

Yes. My mother told me she could make the psychiatric ward keep me forever if I did not stop crying while she was shouting in my face. This was supposed to be "for my own good". She would never call, but she also would not leave until I was too exhausted to melt any further.

There was a further evolution of this tactic: calling the police.

This did not last long because, while it inspired exactly the terror that was her goal, it did not inspire obedience to every little whim the way the foster care threats of my youth did. It inspired terror, hiding, and running away. She also realized that it had deadly potential, since I was in the habit of calling her bluff, calling everyone's bluff really, and do not react well to being physically handled without permission. She could have, would have killed me just for a sense of power, but something stopped her after the time a cop actually showed up and told her that the next time she called, he was going to have to take someone in. She had played the same trigger a meltdown game, but she had waited til I was too tired to call, so I just looked sleepy, red, puffy, and bruised from where she had grabbed me. This wasn't what she had wanted at all! And if she called while I was still energetic enough to melt down or be a smartass, I was out the window and away. So the police only came the once.

That doesn't mean my mother stopped being emotionally abusive though. She had another big powerful abandonment tactic, beyond the "sending you away so I don't have to deal with you". It was the conversation stopper. It was the one that had every child in fear. And it was the one that was effective regardless of the age of the child who she claimed was "pushing her" to it:

My mother manipulated us by threatening suicide.

Frequently. Often. Many more times than I can count.

She always told us how she was going to do it, too. It was never "If you don't stop embarrassing me at church, I am going to kill myself". It was always "if you don't stop embarrassing me at church, I am going to sit in the tub and cut every vein I can see until I die" or "jump into

271

traffic" or "take a bunch of aspirin and drink a box of wine" or "jump off the roof of the house" or "poke a beehive" (she is allergic to bees).

Not only did she tell us how she was going to do it—and she would think of how she was going to kill herself easily, on the fly, when we needed manipulation to behave how she wished—she would tell us to imagine the body. To think of how the body would look immediately and at the funeral. Would it be open casket? How would we feel then? Which would be worse, a mangled or not mangled corpse?

It was twisted. It was not ok. It was unacceptable emotional abuse, and there's really no way to say it was for our own good. After the third or fourth time she did this, I came to the conclusion she wouldn't do it—I think she was going to jump from the roof to the street, and there's no way she could get on the roof or jump that far— but it was always scary. And then I would always be oh so angry that she made me do what she wanted without just asking like a grownass adult.

This is not ok. This is not the legacy to leave one's children with—one of abuse, manipulation, fear, feeling that if they step one foot out of line, and you kill yourself, it is all their fault. No. That is absolute bullshit. And we never called her bluff out loud, but sometimes? I wish I had.

She often said if she killed herself we could never say anything bad about her. This too is bullshit. She died of lung cancer, which she arguably gave to herself as a heavy

272

smoker. I am speaking ill of her now. Nothing that isn't true. But nothing she wanted heard.

Burnout In Recovery

Kristy Y.

I'm Kristy. I'm a Black, genderqueer autistic in the Washington DC Metro area.

I've tried to fit in with all the so-called "cool kids" when I was in school. I tried to hide my autistic traits, like stimming, and I tried to gravitate to more "mature" interests like *Grey's Anatomy* and *American Idol* just so I wouldn't be ridiculed.

I started to wear trendier clothes because when I was 10, a girl said my clothes were babyish, and people were going to laugh at me. In high school, I wanted to wear Aeropostale and Hollister clothes because everyone else was wearing them. The problem was, I was tall and overweight, so I couldn't fit in those clothes, which was frustrating.

When I was 12 I started crushing on girls as well as guys. I was scared because I heard bad things about being LGBTQ, like that is was a sin. I fully acknowledged that I was bi when I was 19, but it didn't help my feelings of shame that I had experienced.

Trying to be "normal" was frustrating because there were so many rules to follow. Act your age. Be straight. Don't stim.

I cried at my high school graduation. Not because I was going to miss anyone there (I actually didn't have many friends), but because I was so relieved that I wasn't going to have to hide who I truly was anymore.

If I had a time machine and could go back to my school days, I wouldn't try so hard to mold myself into a person whom I was not meant to be.

Today, I spend my time writing in my journal, my blog and writing short stories. I'm not in college or employed because I want to take some time to recover from the burnout caused by the stress from my school days.

My faith is also what keeps me going. I'm building a relationship with God. I go to a LGBTQ-affirming church and I listen to inspirational music. If I didn't believe in a higher power, I don't know what I'd be.

And now I don't care what people think of me. I stim freely. I wear what I feel comfortable in. I am an out and proud queer non-binary person. And I love kids' TV shows and movies like *The Lego Movie*. If people can't accept those things, that's their problem, not mine.

The Real Truth About Expressing Myself

Ondrea Marisa Robinson

This is the real truth about expressing myself.
I'm an honest person who likes to tell the truth
Even though I may not listen to what needs to be done at times.
Please give me a chance, because I am working on it
So I can get it over and done with.
But some people are afraid of my honesty.
They'll do anything to defy it, deny it, or use any excuse
In order to get what they want.
But that ain't gonna happen no more,
Because I'm going to express myself the way I should and not be scared.
And those who are afraid or don't want to hear my honesty better get ready for it.
If they aren't, I'm sorry for them.
I'm going to express myself with honesty and not look back,
And God knows I have to do this sooner or later.

The Truth

Ondrea Marisa Robinson

Get rid of ableism, get rid of racism.
Stop diminishing my light from being used as negativity.
I'm a young black autistic woman that wants to keep living,
But how can I do that if the fiery darts of the enemy keep coming at me?
I must remember that God gave me a voice, and I'm not afraid to use it.
If you don't want to listen, I have a message for you—
(Please don't think I'm being rude, but if you feel that I am, I'm sorry for you.)

Shut up!

Reflections on Growing Up

Lucas Vizeu

I am a first generation Brazilian/Dominican American Autistic adult. I am from and was raised mostly in New York City and am currently finishing a degree in Computer Graphics and Imaging from Lehman College. I was nonverbal until the age of 3 and have had persistent speech issues as well as several learning disabilities. Throughout my youth, I found myself in conflict largely at schools.

I went to elementary school in a largely white and Jewish school. What few Black and Hispanics kids there were mostly in Special ed. I was bullied by the white General ed kids and the Special ed kids. That was more or less a constant up to high school. I did not feel welcome in a lot of these environments. I was a Developmentally Disabled Latin American boy who was trying to get something resembling a decent education.

I also had the fortune of starting elementary school at the height of the ADHD "epidemic," so naturally my school attempted to get me on drugs. My mother rejected this. My family wasn't liked by the administration or the Parent Teacher Association. Fortunately, constant tension from administrative staff was not a constant in my life and I escaped it when I graduated to middle school.

I did okay in high school. Not great, but okay, especially given how bad middle school was. I learned to love literature and writing. Great teachers and my generally awful experiences with Special ed convinced me that I should teach English. However, I found myself at odds with my college advisor, who didn't have time for a Disabled Hispanic kid of no particular wealth.

Against her advice, I applied for the Macaulay Honors College at Lehman, which would come with a series of perks including free tuition and study abroad money, on the basis that I could get in with a somewhat mediocre GPA if I had decent SAT scores and essays. I got a phone call on New Years from the director of the program, which scared and excited me greatly. I had an interview 2 months later at Lehman. I somehow got in despite claiming that I would like to use their money to go to Japan because of "giant robots with light sabers" (I actually said that), but I'm not one to look a gift lack of tuition fees for a regionally accredited university in the mouth. I enjoyed my time at Lehman very much. I felt respected here by pretty much everyone.

I realized early in my freshman year that I didn't want to teach. I decided to major in Computer Graphics and Imaging and pursue a career in media. I learned the various intricacies of videography and started making media friends. Eventually, I got brought onto a friend's project involving turning tweets to comedy videos, which got me into a mentorship. I then got a paid internship animating a squirrel for the finance people at Lehman, which ended very well. I was told that my boss had faith in me, which made me feel great.

Even though I'm doing pretty well for myself and career prospects look amazing, the various modes of oppression I have dealt with weigh heavily on mind. I have reached an oddly introspective period in my life, partly inspired by the death of a few friends and associates and the fact that I am about to start a new part of my life called "Art Major trying to find work." Going to a more generally diverse and clique-less school for under graduate has proven to be great for my mental well being, but I still think about these things a lot. That's partly due to my involvement in various activist circles, but it is also an issue of trauma. Recently, I realized that I have a tendency to get extremely paranoid inside stores. When I realized this, my first thought was "this is weird" followed by a realization that being harassed in stores over being Hispanic and odd looking (it is not uncommon for people to think I am high) has screwed with my head more than I thought it would. I have fear because of many of the commonly heard things that tend to happen to the Disabled and people of color, but it's the weirder things that absolutely scare me, because they just show how deep and unescapable these things are.

Being an Autistic person of color has caused me to think a lot about many issues affecting our communities and the systems that hurt us. I look above and see various mechanisms working in tandem, and wonder if they will ever claim me or someone I love. I don't know whether it will claim a life, a livelihood, health, health care, employment, freedom, the ability to live in this country or what have you. I just know all of it is real and I have seen it and it terrifies me. I only hope we can change things for the better.

Stop Your Hands, Stop Your Breath.

Leyla

Stop your hands, she said,
No boy will marry you.
Stop your hands and your noises,
Your mother has worked too hard
For This to happen.
This, being my mixed up turned around brain.
Stop your hands, it makes you obvious
Hide your history, hide it because
we did not survive only to have people like you
be here, not making sense in this time. Not acting like
us. Make eye contact with me and see your shame,
as if I am not called a terrorist by peers for flapping my
hands.
As if I am not ashamed for not being stronger.
Stop your hands.
Stop talking, they said.
Nobody cares about your struggle.
Intersectionality is an ideal, not a necessity. Not a need,
but a whisper in the wind.
You don't need this, stop thinking in your brown brain.
Stop making it about you, stop talking.
Stop your breath, your 6,000 years of culture are showing.
As if that isn't part of my identity also.
Voices like yours take too much space

Too much air.
Stop talking.
Hide your body. Hide your skin.
Stop talking.
Dive deeper into the glass of milk.
You're welcome here.
Stop talking.

We Are the Earth

Legacy Onaiwu

I am sepia. Mom is mahogany. Grandma is beige. My brother and my cousin are coffee. I never met my Great-Grandma and Great-Grandpa, but I saw their pictures. She was the color of sand and he was the color of night. These are all the autistic people in my family. We are all brown. We all have a disability.

Some people don't like people who are brown or people who have disabilities. That makes me sad. They think people with disabilities are not good enough or brown people are going to steal things. I hope they give us a chance instead of thinking the wrong thing.

When I was little I had to change my school because I went to a school that didn't understand my disability. They did not let me work ahead and made me wait for the other kids even though it took them forever to do work that was too easy for me. I got in trouble for wanting to read the teacher part in the reader instead of sticking with the boring babyish student part. I got sad faces in my folder because I could not finish cutting out the objects with the scissors like the other kids. The other kids were very good at cutting and very fast. My hands didn't work fast in cutting. The kids got in trouble if they tried to help me. I left that school and went to another school where it is okay to be gifted and autistic. I liked that school. But when we moved, I had to change schools. At my new school we learn a lot about God. My teacher lets me do some of my work out loud because she knows I am autistic and that my hands can't always write as fast as the other kids. She is nice.

I go to a school with people of lots of different colors. But a long time ago people couldn't do that. I got to meet Mrs. Lucille Bridges on Leap Day 2016 at a museum near a school. She is the mother of Ruby Bridges. Ruby Bridges was the first black person to go to a white school. She went to an all-white school when she was six years old. She was in first grade.

The President had to send marshals, who are people who are like policemen but they're not from the area. He sent the marshals to help Ruby. The marshals helped Ruby get to school. If the marshals weren't there she wouldn't have been able to get to school safely because everybody was cheering loudly with mean signs about Ruby leaving. The people would force Ruby to leave if the marshals weren't there. The white people were very angry and they might hurt Ruby and Mrs. Bridges.

It was important to meet Mrs. Bridges because her life is an important part of history. Mrs. Bridges wanted Ruby to go to a good school. Black people weren't allowed in the school. There was a sign that said, "We want to keep our school white." They were cheering meanly for Ruby to keep out.

If I were Ruby I would feel sad. Ruby always had to stay in the school. She couldn't go to recess because the mean white people might hurt her if she went outside. And the white kids at the school wanted her to go and might be a big bully to her because she was black.

Ruby is a hero. But Mrs. Bridges is a hero too because she helped pick cotton out of a field to help her family and didn't get to finish school because she had so much work to do. She let Ruby finish school so that she could be happy and have a good life. Mrs. Bridges prayed a lot about Ruby so she could feel better.

Because of Mrs. Bridges and Ruby I get to go to school with different people of all colors instead of having to be in a classroom by myself like Ruby was, or being with only brown and black people in my class. Mrs. Bridges prayed and trusted that God would help her, and He did. In second grade when Ruby went back to the school there were people of different colors in her class. She did not have to stay inside. She could go to recess and have fun with her friends. She didn't need the marshals anymore because now things have changed.

In my Bible class I learned that God formed people out of the earth. My mom said that God let life come from a small creature that kept changing and changing and changing and changing until it became different animals and then changed to apes and then changed to people. It is called evolution. She said there is a museum in Ethiopia that has a skeleton of a lady called Lucy. Lucy was found deep in the earth by some people who were digging up bones and old things. I think Lucy is kind of like Eve in the Bible because Lucy is one of the first people ever in the whole world. Maybe Lucy's real name was Eve! Mom says Lucy was really short because people are bigger now. Ethiopia is in Africa. My family comes from Africa too. My babysitter Gelila is from Ethiopia like Lucy and she is pretty, smart, and nice. She is not that short but she is short. I hope Lucy was nice like her.

I think it's cool how they got Lucy out of the earth. All people come from the earth. And when we die we will go back to the earth. Maybe that's why some of us are the same color as the earth to remind us where we come from and who we are. I am glad God made me brown and I am glad God made me autistic.

I'm a Queen

Nathaniel Hagemaster

The dimly lit room is full of murmuring spectators. I am strutting down a long aisle in the middle of a teaching theater that can seat four hundred people. I'm wearing one of my best outfits, smiling, and trying my best not to stumble when I reach a step. I try to be as graceful as possible while bending over to collect completed answer sheets for a quiz that have been left for me in small stacks on the floor next to every row. I suddenly feel like a drag performer collecting tips that are littering the stage at the end of a number. As an instructional assistant who isn't far from getting to teach my own class, this experience reminds me that teaching is also a performance. Like a drag queen, I'm going to have to keep my student audience engaged as I articulate new ideas in ways they haven't considered. Since a disabled drag queen isn't the typical kind of person for students to look up to as a teacher, I will have to subvert my intersectionalities while playing a part that my students relate to. I might look like an instructor on the outside, but there would still be a queen from within. Just like how a crown doesn't make a king a king, I don't need to be in drag to still be a queen.

The word *queen* has many connotations. With the reference to royalty, you would think *queen* is one of the most empowering things to call someone. However, when asking a history class of young children to name a famous queen, one of the wittier students might say "Freddie Mercury." When somebody is accused of acting *queeny*, it is usually because he, ze, or she (most of the times he) is behaving effeminately. When somebody is being a drama queen, it's usually because s/h/ze is acting overly dramatic in a situation that doesn't call for it. If you get where I'm going with this, you can see that *queen* is often used in a derogatory way to call out a person's behavior as being overly feminine. This said, it shouldn't come as a surprise that drag queens have not been acknowledged or respected as artists, and drag has not been seen as a mode of empowerment, until recent years.

I don't know if it was a result of my mother's direct influence, but I have always been obsessed with my appearance. After being diagnosed with Asperger's as an adult and learning about the obsessive behaviors that are common among Aspies, I finally understand these fixations to a certain extent; however, my mother might have contributed to this obsession as well. She usually has a full face of makeup on: dark eye makeup, light foundation, blush, and her signature bright red lipstick. She also usually still wears long red press-on nails and black clothes to flatter her figure. My mother also used to have long black hair that she would often perm. I still remember watching her get ready before she took my brother and me to school. She did her makeup with quick precision, reinforced her curls with teasing and hairspray, and then I would help her fish out pumps from under the bed by squeezing myself under the low bed frame and reaching as far as I could until one of my mother's shoes was in my tiny grasp.

My mother always made a big deal about going to church on Sunday mornings. While she usually didn't put as much effort into dressing my brother and me as she did for herself, she did on Sundays. My mother never went all out by having my brother and I wear suits to church (probably because we couldn't afford them), but she still encouraged us to look our best for that occasion. I hated wearing anything that buttoned because the attention my mother gave me about how "handsome" I looked made me uncomfortable, which made getting dressed a struggle for me. As my brother and I got older, we became more resistant to being dressed by our mother, but we developed an obsessive focus on our appearance. To this day, I still can't stand the thought of having food or residual drool from the night before on my face or teeth. Unlike most other boys who grew up in a city that bordered Mexico, my brother and I learned that the way you present yourself communicates a lot about a person pretty early in our lives. We were very fixated on our weight and always dyed and styled our hair in ways that made us stand out from the predominant cholo look in our neighborhood, but eventually he got into name brands and I got into drag.

In high school, I wanted to be a fashion designer because I was able to do quite a bit with hand sewing and had the lack of a social life that allowed the time for hand sewing. When I made friends with people who were also interested in fashion design, most of them wanted to design things that were really artsy and avant-garde, and kind of scoffed at me for not really having an interest in designing those kinds of things. I would attempt to conjure up some obscure concept for a collection that showcased something crazy and comparable to the sketches friends would show me, but I thought too pragmatically. What woman who isn't modeling would wear this crap?

I designed clothes with the kind of women I looked up to and respected in my life in mind, not some starved supermodel that had to be lubed up and stitched into someone's ridiculous garment that would only be worn in photos and on runways. Women that are unconventional—women who are covered in tattoos, women that are a little curvier, women who are strong and have strong personalities—have always inspired me. When I began to think about being a drag queen, I realized that I wanted to design for the kind of woman I wanted to embody in some way. When I actually started doing drag, I realized that I was subconsciously embodying my mother. Because I am half-white and never learned Spanish, I always identified more as white. However, now that I'm acknowledging my mother's influence on my drag persona, I realize that I've been constructing a Chicana character that is just like her. I've always felt like I behaved similar to my mother, and even before doing drag, everyone in my family always said that I was the spitting image of her. I adored wearing bright red lipstick; tended to buy long, dark colored wigs with a curly texture; and viewed black as a go-to color for most outfits. As a drag queen who shares a dual identity as a queer man who happens to be perceived as masculine by his suitors, dating can get complicated when that perceived masculinity is challenged.

"So... This is going to sound weird, but I found you on Facebook," Angel said with hesitation during a date at some Italian restaurant.

"Mhmm?" I replied, already knowing what was coming while staring down at my pasta.

"So you do drag?" Angel asked nervously.

His nervous energy makes me hesitate, then I answer "Yeah... So what do you think?"

Angel takes a swig of his Dos Equis, then says "I think you look good! It's just that... I can't really picture you being that feminine."

"That's funny, because I've always kind of seen myself as feminine..." I reply and trail off after taking a bite of garlic bread.

"Well I think you're masculine!" Angel replied in a way that either seemed like he was placating me or trying to convince himself that whatever construction of masculinity he had for me was still there.

After being in one serious relationship and dating a few guys, I already knew which topics about myself and interests to highlight, and which to contour. I find it funny that every time I told a guy I was dating that I see myself as feminine, he would jump to "reaffirm" that he sees me as masculine. This would be almost like a boyfriend trying to reassure his girlfriend that she isn't fat when she tells him she is. Except I'm not playing a validation game, but expressing a way in which I identify. Men, especially gay men, put such high value on masculinity that they see men feminizing themselves as degrading. They think that telling me that they see me as masculine is the best compliment anyone could give me. Throughout my dating experience, I have never been complimented by these guys for being feminine. With these harsh social contrasts between masculinity and femininity in place, I had to become familiar with an etiquette that expected me to explain myself whenever I disclosed that I'm a drag queen as if I've done something wrong.

Once, when my boyfriend and I were watching RuPaul's Drag Race, I started reminiscing about something I would do as a drag performer. I began my next sentence with "If I were to become a full-time drag queen, I would..." Then my now ex-boyfriend cut me off by saying "No, you won't."

When I was taking a freshman speech course, the first speech we had to do was an informative one. I chose to give mine about internalized homophobia. In order to establish credibility on this topic, I chose to out myself at the beginning of the speech. When I was practicing my speech with my ex, he told me to be careful about coming out to my class and that I should reconsider that part of my speech. I knew that I ran somewhat of a risk in doing this in front of a class in Central Texas, regardless of how close San Marcos is to Austin and how "liberal-hippie-dippy" people think it is, but I knew that it wouldn't become that big of an ordeal. I mean, people must have already known that I was queer and I hadn't been gay bashed by that point, so I didn't have much to worry about, right?

As it turns out, my speech went well, and the instructional assistant for my class said she was studying and writing her thesis about the Westboro Baptist Church, which made us hit it off pretty well for the rest of the semester. It seems as though my ex was judging out of the fear of getting judged. I honestly didn't think anything would happen, and I would have welcomed any criticism if my instructional assistant or classmates had something to say, but they didn't.

About a year after taking that speech class, I decided to pursue a career as a secondary school speech teacher since I was already a communication studies major. I always dabbled in the idea of becoming a teacher because there are a lot of teachers and people who work in education in my family, and I actually liked communication studies enough to teach it. Also, since I was always an odd student (like one who decides to come out in a speech), I wanted to be a more accepting and understanding teacher for students like me, unlike most of the ones I had encountered in my secondary schooling. So I moved some things around in my degree plan in order to get certified to teach.

However, by the time I got to my last semester of regular classes, I decided that I did not want to teach anymore. Imagining myself taking teacher-prep classes at a high school that I would also be working at the following semester and then student-teaching the semester after that terrified me. Also, I began considering the potential

294

of going to grad school and doing something with education. I was formerly told by a disability counselor not to pursue teaching because I have Asperger's and something as highly social as teaching would not be suitable for me, even though I was a communication studies major.

Since I figured that becoming a technical writer would sustain me quite handsomely and it seemed like a field that would be suited for an introvert who likes to write, I thought about pursuing the Technical Communication program at Texas State. The following semester, I replaced my Curriculum and Instruction minor with English and took my last communication course in "training and development." It was during this semester that I discovered that I could study the rhetoric of drag in the Rhetoric and Composition program at Texas State. It came as a surprise to me, not so much that I *could* study it, but the fact that I did not reach that conclusion earlier or on my own. The more I thought about studying something that I'd been obsessed with, the more it reinvigorated my enthusiasm for grad school.

Throughout the semester, I worked on various portions of a training packet that I had to turn in at the end of the semester. In addition to turning in those packets, every group had to present a 30 minute portion of something from their packet. As an ice-breaking activity at the beginning of my group's presentation, I decided to use one that required a deck of cards where we designated larger numbers to royals as cards of "high status" and lower numbers and jokers as "low status." After drawing a card and holding it over their foreheads so they couldn't see what they got, my class was instructed to respond with negative nonverbal cues to whomever drew a "low status" card, and respond with nonverbal cues that showed deference to those who drew a "high status" card. After explaining the activity, one of my group members and I demonstrated in front of the class. My group member drew a 2, so I gave her a scowl and turned away from her with a hand on my hip while she bowed to me. When we finished the demonstration, my group member and I looked at our cards, and I noticed that I drew a queen.

I pretended to flip long hair I didn't have with long fingernails I also didn't have while saying "Ooh! I'm a queen!" as my immediate response to drawing that card. The room full of classmates all laughed. And it wasn't a laugh like they were laughing at me. I had given a genuine caught-in-the-moment kind of response, and they genuinely laughed. They respected me for the remainder of our presentation that day. At certain points during our presentation when it seemed like one of my group members was losing our audience, I would jump in to help her and the rest of the class would respond. When I would speak up, everybody's gaze would go from glazed-over to focused right on me with full attention. I had never experienced such a connection with a class that I presented to before. When our presentation was over, I got a lot of praise from my classmates and professor. This experience created quite a rush for me.

Among all the other things that were going through my head as I went home after my presentation, I thought about how what I said easily could have made a turn for the worse. They could have all laughed *at* me and refused to listen or take me seriously for the rest of the presentation. They could have not responded, which wouldn't have been that bad, except it wouldn't have led me to the epiphany I came to. Saying that "I'm a queen" encompassed everything that was going on with my life at the time because I already decided to study drag. That experience led me to want to become a professor as well because classroom management was one of the things I feared most about assisting a high school teacher before taking over my own class as a student-teacher. However, I then realized that I was able to show femininity by being collaborative and using flamboyance to be nurturing as well as humorous when the time was appropriate. I was able to show masculinity by being more directive when I needed the class to focus. This along with the fact that I would have the opportunity to research and study drag in great depth just made everything make sense to me for once in my life.

When I wanted to teach at the secondary level, I was really just humoring the idea of being a teacher and seeing how far I would actually take the challenge. I wanted to teach, but I knew that it was going to be a difficult position. As time progresses, more things are being expected of secondary teachers just so they can keep their jobs because school districts keep cutting down. Not to mention that speech is one of the subjects that is constantly on the chopping block with school boards. Plus my salary wouldn't have been very justifiable.

I believe that being a professor and a drag scholar would give me the opportunity to explore my research and academic interests, and let them drive how I teach and what I teach because I am aspiring to incorporate drag into pedagogy. I know that I am idealizing this career path right now, but it is the first career path that actually incorporates most of the things I value. When I learned that it was possible to have a career focused on drag without being a performer or living an artsy-performer lifestyle, I was living! Not only do I not have to learn how to dance or live the nightlife of treading to gigs at gay bars for tips while still needing a day job to sustain myself, but I also get to analyze and research drag, gender, and sexuality. The epiphany I had during that training session really gave me a drive that I haven't had before. Even though drag still might not be taken seriously, I have learned that not taking it very seriously is kind of the point of it. Drag is meant to be ridiculous because life, society, and constructions of gender are ridiculous, most of the time without being as self-aware.

Noticing that people are uncomfortable with it and pushing it further is part of the experience of drag performance because drag is meant to push certain boundaries in society. On the other hand, teaching and presenting are performative things that challenge me to push my own boundaries. My anxiety about being in front of people always seemed like it was going to defeat me, but I always managed to channel that nervous energy into something useful for the audience because it gives me the nervous Aspie-charisma that I am known for. Acknowledging and accepting what you have to work with and working with a little discomfort at times seems to be a useful strategy for making it through life. Whatever way you choose to connote being a *queen*, I am proud to say that *I am a queen*.

The Silencing Invisibility Cloak

Shane Bentley

I knew early in grade school there were things that made me different in ways that were Not Normal; there were reasons why I was always out of sync with my peers and often felt like a "freak," as I was sometimes called. But only in adulthood did I finally learn words for those things and understand them. Too-visible quiet and quiet invisibility were constants in my early life as an undiagnosed autistic and unacknowledged biracial agender person, as if a silencing invisibility cloak concealed my reality from even my own sight. This invisibility cloak was formed by a confluence of societal forces and compliant behaviors: systemic erasure and passing.

The ability to pass as white or as a cis person is like an invisibility cloak that automatically envelopes me unless I decide to take it off. It doesn't slide off easily like Harry Potter's, though; it's a heavy cloak that takes time and energy to remove. It's supposedly there to protect me. People can't hurt what they can't see, right? Except that isn't really how it works. They can still get to you—they just won't know they have. So it only prevents deliberate, targeted harms. This is no doubt an important function; I am much less likely to be assaulted or killed, for example, than someone who doesn't have these cloaks. Still, such a cloak protects others from the sight of you as much as it protects you from their sight. As long as you keep it on, they don't have to acknowledge your existence, much less any indirect harm they have done you.

The ability to pass as allistic or neurotypical is a different sort of invisibility cloak. It's function is the same, but it's a more unwieldy, layered garment. Putting it on and keeping it on is a constant effort. If I don't pay enough attention to it, the slippery layers can fall off without me even noticing. There's a clingy layer beneath them, though, which is noticeably different but still obscures my reality. Let's call it the erasure layer. This layer can be difficult if not impossible to remove, because it is knit from strands of ignorance and disbelief and reflects the viewer's assumptions back at them. The resilience of the erasure layer, then, is dependent on the strength and durability of the viewer's ignorance and preconceptions, and only the informed viewer who looks through a lens free of preconceptions can easily see through the layer. A key assumption perpetuating this erasure layer is that "autism is a white boys' thing."

The white and cis cloaks also have an erasure layer. The erasure layers of my cloaks mostly reflect these commonly held yet false preconceptions: "There are only two genders," "People with that body shape are women," and "People with that skin shade and eye shape are white." These pervasive ideas even clouded my perception of myself for years, until I acquired the education necessary to unlearn them.

**

I was aware of my Native ancestry as a child, but only in the most distant sense. I knew my paternal grandmother was Ojibwe, but didn't understand race well enough to know that meant she wasn't white or connect it to my own identity, and the connection was never really spoken of in my household. I inherited grandma's dark eyes and hair but my mother's light skin and general shape. I rarely wore Native cultural artifacts, as much as I loved the beaded jewelry grandma gave me. White people assumed I was one of them.

Eventually I became aware enough to realize "looking white" was not necessarily evidence of *being* white. I was a teenager by the time I encountered the word "biracial," and as alienated from my nonwhite heritage as I was, it took even longer to connect it to myself. I wasn't sure I even had a right to claim it—I felt I wasn't Native enough to count.

I started to rethink this in senior year, when I attended an event called Challenge Day, which was designed to break down barriers between students and foster friendlier educational environments. Participants were wrenched from our comfort zones with odd group activities, intimate chats with relative strangers, and enlightening demonstrations of difference and commonality. At one point, a moderator summoned all students with Native ancestry together. I perhaps shouldn't have been so surprised by the faces I found when I joined the group. They looked like me. Black-brown eyes, thick yet fine dark hair, and mostly light skin surrounded me. These were people like me, invisible part-Native biracial kids adrift in the sea of white culture, whose history was constantly erased. I would never have told them they weren't "Native enough" to count, and I was undeniably one of them, so I couldn't continue to tell myself that either.

***

In childhood and adolescence, I also assumed I must be a girl, and just not very good at it. At being a girl, that is. The idea didn't make much more sense to me then than it does now, but it was the best explanation I could come up with in the absence of other possibilities. Binarist definitions of gender were the only ones available to me for many years, and their logic dictated that because I wasn't a boy, I was a girl by default. It seemed a bit arbitrary even to child-me, and I had trouble grasping the fact that most people actually assigned significant meaning to these categories. For me it seemed like an empty label. I came to feel that I wasn't really a girl, but any mention of this was immediately dismissed——so I stopped mentioning it.

Then college happened. My first gender studies class thoroughly dismantled the essentialism and binaries I'd been taught and led me to reexamine my identity. When I learned that "trans" was really an umbrella term that included people who didn't fit into the false gender dichotomy, I thought, "That could be me!" However, I remained unsure of my gender identity for years, largely because I didn't understand what a gender felt like or how one would recognize it in oneself. How could I be certain I wasn't a woman, when I didn't know what it meant to be one?

Well, the answer seems obvious now: if I didn't feel like one and didn't know what it meant to be one, I couldn't have been one. It was easy to reach the same conclusion when thinking of how I knew I wasn't a man; why, then, did I need a higher standard of proof to accept that I wasn't a woman? The difference, of course, was that I had been told I was one my entire life. Overwriting this message was a slow process, especially when I didn't have a specific term to replace it with. Discovering an online community of nonbinary bloggers, reading their stories, and learning the words they use to describe themselves accelerated the process. Eventually I grew to embrace my genderlessness and find in it an incredible sense of freedom.

***

I could never seem to speak quite loudly enough. What apparently sounded in the normal range to others sounded too loud to me. I'd feel as if I was practically shouting just to be heard, which was unnatural and difficult to remember to do (and further complicated by the fact that I couldn't tell the difference between "normal" and "too loud," if I ever was too loud, because it all seemed too loud to me, and how was I to know where the line was for others?). Often, I didn't manage to speak at all.

My earliest coherent memory takes place at preschool, sometime before I turned five. There was a little blond boy named Max who I thought was cute, and for some reason Little Me decided to tell him so. But of course, she did so at a volume difficult for most humans to hear, and Little Max somehow misheard "I think you're cute" as "I hate you." His eyes grew suspiciously shiny, and Little Me was horrified—that was the exact opposite of what she was trying to communicate! She rushed to correct him, and it was all cleared up quite quickly; he probably forgot within days, but she never did.

In third grade, a girl my age moved into my neighborhood. We went to the same school, but because we weren't in the same class, I only saw her at recess. One recess, I noticed her idly sitting at an otherwise empty swing set, a bit slumped. She looked so lonely, it was painful to observe. Approaching another person without invitation was normally out of the question for me, but I had to do something. So I took a deep breath and walked slowly toward the swings. But when I sat next to her, my courage seemingly evaporated, and I couldn't find my voice. Fortunately, the act was enough to prompt her into beginning the conversation.

Countless moments such as these are woven into the fabric of my history, though most of them, especially when my age rose into double digits, did not end so happily. My trouble with speech became increasingly difficult to write off as shyness. The needs unquestioned at 10, such as having my mother speak for me at doctor's appointments, were much less acceptable at 20. Still, the word "autism" was not seriously mentioned in connection to me until depression finally drove me to a counselor at 23.

Over weeks of research and discussion, it became increasingly clear that I was in fact autistic. Inexplicable obstacles and behaviors suddenly made sense. My social anxiety was learned through years peppered with undesirable outcomes resulting from my inability to make myself understood and/or understand others, which I now knew were attributable to low cognitive empathy, differences in perception of sound, and being semiverbal. Autistic burnout shed new light on the pattern of recurring depression and regular dips in my GPA. My habit of pacing for hours on end, whether at school recesses or in my bedroom, instead of playing with toys or other children (or doing whatever it is ordinary adolescents do when I reached that age), I now recognized as stimming, a perfectly normal, healthy behavior for people like me. And there was an entire community of people like me who shared these traits and experiences.

The relief of finally learning I'm autistic is akin to the freedom I found in acknowledging myself as agender. In each case, the knowledge is both validating and liberating. It tells me I'm not a "freak"—there are lots of other people who are different in the same ways. I don't have to keep trying to meet societal expectations and pass as "normal," because there is nothing wrong with how I am. I can't always speak, but that doesn't mean I will be silenced. I am free to take off the invisibility cloak.

Litany Against Fear/Litany for Love

Kassiane A. Asasumasu

For the Love Not Fear flashblog. With thanks to Frank Herbert for the Litany Against Fear used here.

I must not fear.
Every time I have these conversations, the ones that devolve into hate, I remember: I am moved by love.

Fear is the mind-killer.
They are afraid and fear is turning to anger and anger is turning to hate, but I can be fierce with love for their kids, for Autistics present, past, future.

Fear is the little-death that brings total obliteration.
Standing strong in the face of the wall of dehumanizing hatred is an act of love. My love for my community is my shield and my strength, and it is tempered by ice and by fire.

I will face my fear.
I will stand with love. I am standing for love.

I will permit it to pass over me and through me.
This is for their children. This is for those who I will know in the future. Who I love without having met yet. For

those I know now, and love with such ferocity there are not words for it.

The anger and hate hurts, but it will not break me.

And when it has gone past me I will turn to see its path.
Change is coming. Change has started and more will come, like a wave or a landslide or even a waterfall.

Where the fear has gone there will be nothing...
Our efforts, our love, is not in vain. The children and adults we are fighting for will feel the ripples from our work, even if we never meet them.

Only I will remain.
At the end of the day, love will prevail.

Fierce, ferocious, fiery, protective, strong, squishy, gentle, love.

Internal Conflict

Fragmented Perfection (Cindy Facteau)

Sometimes, life's overwhelming
The future holds no certainty-
Sometimes, I feel like a dead woman walking
Time is of the essence for everyone but me-
Sometimes, it seems as if I'm drifting
On stagnant waters in some distant sea-
Sometimes, it's difficult to close my eyes
I'm afraid of the horrors that I might see-
Sometimes, I gaze into the mirror
Wondering, "Is it me? Is it me?"
Sometimes, I fear I ask too many questions
When I'm struggling just to "be"-
Sometimes, I emerge victorious and triumphant
But those times are few and far in between-
Sometimes, I think that I dream far too much
Searching in vain for something best left unseen-
Sometimes, I'm an icon and a goddess
To everyone except for the heart in me-
Sometimes, I just want to scream out loud
But I've been told that anger does not become me-
Sometimes, I sit in quiet introspect
Thinking, "Could've been, should've been"-
Sometimes, that's not so important to me
I'm a round hole trying to fit squares in-
Sometimes, I feel underprivileged and unlucky

Then I remember the homeless veteran with the noisy gut-
Sometimes, promiscuity seems more tangible than love
But I know it's not my style to be a slut-
Sometimes, my brain works in overdrive
Then the circuits short out and the motherboard's fried-
Sometimes, I wonder why I lived through this all
When so many other have died-
Sometimes, my soul can hear music
That I know nobody else can hear-
Sometimes, I long for emotional lucidity
A kindred soul to hold close and dear-
Sometimes, it doesn't seem worth it
Maybe my future wasn't meant to be bright-
Sometimes, I think that's an absurd, fleeting thought
As I tuck my son in for the night-
Sometimes, my inadequacies frighten me
I want to escape from it all and hide-
Sometimes, I remember that adversities come
To those who are strongest inside-
Sometimes, I am brutally honest
With everyone except for myself-
Sometimes, I settle for second best
When perfection's right there on the shelf-
Sometimes, I wish I had more money
When I see how very little I've got-
Sometimes, I value my life experiences more
Because there are some things that cannot be bought.

Vignettes

Stephan B.

I remember an old dirty window. I was five years old and not allowed outside. So I'd sit and read by the dirty old window surrounded by red bricks. My eyes would glide between the pages and occasionally glance outside. From that window you could see most of Casper Street. The kind of "view" was very subjective even though it seldom changed. The other kids would be running around playing at any given time of the day during those scorching Detroit summers. Our neighbor, an elderly gentlemen, would be sitting on his porch, still as a statue. He seemed oblivious and aloof to anything but his porch. Adults would walk through all the time. They never stopped. They never waved hello to anybody. They'd just keep walking, the kids would keep playing and the old man would keep sitting. I would keep reading. Whatever information could be gleaned through that window could never be processed more than one way. At least not by me, at least not back then. As far as my imagination could stretch, it could never distort the reality of the Casper Street I saw through that window. Still, I'd wondered why I wasn't allowed outside to play.

One day, the street did change though. Driving home, my family witnessed an explosion five houses down from ours. There was a huge blast. Rubble, hot glass and insulation fiber littered the street as smoke filled the sky.

The sound shocked me so much I had begun to cry and some of the car alarms in the neighborhood cried too while their owners were screaming. My mother did her first U-turn on a one way street that day. We moved shortly thereafter. I don't think the street was ever really the same.

My family had eventually moved to Dearborn. We lived in a big yellow house on Kentucky Street. It was a much nicer neighborhood than Casper Street. It was nice enough for me to go outside and I could even walk to school. It looked more spacious because it wasn't a one-way street. I lived there with my mom, a nurse, who always worked hard taking care of other people even though she had an array of medical problems herself. My stepdad Nidal, whom at that point I still thought was my biological father. My sister, Heather, who is the oldest and most maternal of my siblings. My older brother Michael, who despite being really mean back then always found a way to make everyone laugh. Lastly, my brother Anthony, who would get angry when I called him anything but Tony. My stepdad wanted to move there because he had a lot of family, friends and clients in Dearborn. He was also a devout Muslim and Dearborn had a lot of mosques. Most of the Arab community there really respected him, though I would come to learn that they didn't hold the rest of us in the same regard. By "us" I mean, my mother, a pale Puerto Rican Catholic who would not convert and her children from a previous marriage.

The sun was shining on Kentucky Street and I could see the kids across the street playing tag. I asked my mom if I could go outside to play with them and she actually said

311

yes. I was shocked and excited and I started to run for the door right away. She stopped me, though, with a strange look on her face. "Don't run, you'll trip and fall." "Stay in front of Kentucky Street." "Don't cross the street without looking both ways." "Be careful." "Don't play too rough." "Remember your manners." It felt like forever before I actually managed to step out of the door. I got to the other side of Kentucky Street and asked "Hey, can I play?" The kids looked at me and said, 'No."

I had been diagnosed when I was around 7. By then I had already been expelled from several daycares and elementary schools. The diagnosis came after concerns about how I spent weeks walking with my hands straight to my sides and when asked why I responded with, "I'm in a coffin." My great-grandmother had passed before then and looking back I was probably coping with that by mimicking her as I often did. The doctors and my family thought I was experiencing schizophrenic hallucinations. I don't know if my mother felt any relief from the MRI that told a different story.

Even though I wanted to walk, my mom drove me to school and had my older brother Tony walk me home every day. On the most beautiful days in fall when the leaves turned orange and a powerful breeze balanced out the hot temperature I would be saddest of all. The school was called McDonald. I only went there for those first few months of fall.

My teacher was a tall, skinny Arab woman with long black hair who dressed in all black. To me she seemed liked one of the nicest teachers in the whole school. Tony said when he went there in the fifth grade his teacher would walk around with a meter stick and smack your hands with it if you misbehaved. I didn't have to worry about that yet because I was only in the third grade. One day, I asked my teacher why she wore all black and she told me, "I'm in mourning." I knew what mourning was, but still didn't fully understand the concept. I asked her again "What does that have to do with what clothes you wear?"

Now she looked at me differently than the first time and said, "We have to wear black for forty days after someone dies in my religion." All the other kids in the class looked at me like I was an alien.

The half hour of recess we always got told same old story of rejection. The first day I could see a small group of my classmates on the woodchips talking. "Let's play hide and seek," one of them said. "Okay who's going to be it?" I trudged over the woodchips and raised my hand. "I'll be it." I said nervously and with a bland expression I always wore back then. They returned the usual look, which I hadn't yet understood. Then one of them started laughing. The rest followed his example. The first boy walked up to me and spit directly on my face. That had never happened to me before. I thought maybe it was normal so I spit right back keeping my same blank expression. The rest of them stopped and looked at us. Then he hit me. I may not have known what spitting meant, but I knew what a punch meant. I punched him right back so hard I must've knocked his teeth out. The other kids stood around staring at me while this boy had crumpled to ground crying, kicking, and screaming. Teachers ran over and one of them pulled me by the wrist to the principal's office.

I wasn't new to getting suspensions. I wasn't new to sitting in front of the principal, looking down towards my feet with blood on my knuckles waiting for my mother to leave work early to come pick me up. She'd scold me and say "Do you want me to lose my job?" I had a ton of "misunderstandings" with other kids at schools before. For some reason, though, this time seemed different. It was certainly the last time any of them tried to spit on me though.

Then I met Jacob. He lived down at the corner of Kentucky Street by the alleyway. He was in the third grade too, but he had a different teacher. I saw him one day at recess. There were three kids talking to him. When I noticed he was crying I walked over to that corner of the playground. One of the kids had pushed him down. I don't know why I wanted to help him. I just did. When I got there one of the kids spat on him just like he did to me. I stepped in between them and told them to stop. Their expressions changed to something unfamiliar and they walked away without saying another word. Then I noticed something. Jacob was white. Jacob was white and those kids were Arab and I didn't know what I was. I'd never thought about it before then. Jacob and I quickly became close friends. After that, we would always play in the alleyway by his house or alone at recess, and the Arab kids wouldn't bother us there. Even after I got expelled from McDonald we'd still play together every day.

Our time at the Kentucky house, which is what I came to refer to it as after we moved, was filled with strange events. A neighbor placed a dead bird on our porch with a candle. I never understood why they did that and I still don't. A boy from across the street came by one day while my brother Tony and I were sitting on the porch and he peed on the grass. He looked directly at us while he did it and walked away without a word when he was done. The boy that lived next door to Jacob tried to steal my bike. I went to the tire shop in the alley and rolled a tire to his house. He came outside and I don't think he was expecting me to pick up the tire and throw it at him. I knew what "surprised" looked like by then. I went into his backyard and rode my looney tunes bike back home. His older brother followed me and started yelling at me. "You crazy – look at what you did to my brother!" He pushed me off my bike and that when's my older sister came out. She beat him to a bloody pulp, screaming so loud and at such a high pitch, the obscenities actually became imperceptible. He ran into his house and his mom came out with her slippers in her hand. She was speaking in Arabic and neither I nor my sister knew what she was saying. Then all of sudden she started smacking my sister with her slipper. My sister snatched the slipper out of her hand and started smacking right back. She had the same look her son had earlier, a look of surprise. She went back inside, but that wasn't the end of it. That boy continually tried to mess with me and Jacob and it continually caused problems. Then one day Nidal talked to his dad and it stopped. I still don't know what he said.

One day my mom and Nidal got into a huge fight. "The kids hate it here blah blah blah!" "The kids are doing fine blah blah blah would you rather we moved back to blah blah." That's when they saw me and stopped. They went into their room to continue their conversation. We moved to a townhouse in the city of Taylor the next week. I thought it was really cool looking at the time. My older siblings went to the high school just across the street but I was going to school in a different city, Inkster, at the time. I quickly grew to hate it just as much at the townhouse, if not more. Yeah, I was allowed outside, but why would I want to go outside? Most of the kids wouldn't talk to me. I got into fights with them all the time. So I just stayed inside reading.

At night it was hard to sleep because you could hear fireworks. Well, back then I thought they were fireworks. In July, sometimes they actually were fireworks. Eventually, I saw my sister's friend crying from the living room one day. I never saw a boy that old cry before. His mom who had lived on the other side of the complex had been accidently shot and killed earlier that day. He and my older siblings stayed friends long after we moved out of Taylor, which wasn't too long after that day. My mom had told me before we moved to Taylor that it was a great place. I guess she had changed her mind though.

I was still going to the same school in Inkster though, they said they were going to "mainstream" me very soon. They said when I got mainstreamed they would throw me a party and I could have any food there I wanted and they would pay for it. Naturally, I was more concerned with going to a "normal" school than getting a going away party. I wanted access to an actual library, and that proved to be better incentive to get "mainstreamed" than the party. The teachers treated me like I was completely invalid until the very end.

My English teacher there, Ms. Colette, was different though. The other teachers talked to me like they did everyone else, but not Ms. Colette. I finished every worksheet she had in the first month of school. I completed her curriculum and even wrote her a thousand word essay about Michigan's state symbols. I'm sure it came as a surprise to her that a 4th grader would write an essay unbidden. She always seemed astonished by the level I was reading and writing at. After she was done giving the other kids their assignments and lecturing them, she would play Scrabble with me. She loved playing Scrabble with me. We could talk about words all day. She even bought me a dictionary for Christmas. English was easily my favorite subject back then. "Someday you'll make a great writer," she'd say. I'd write her short stories and always ask if there was anything more to learn about English. She decided to teach me about prepositions. She showed me a book called *Keys for Writers* and instructed me to try and remember as much of the page as I could. When I got home I thought back to it, and tried to remember all the words listed here. The next day I showed Ms. Colette the page and she almost fainted from shock as she called over her teaching assistant, Dan, to look at the paper and got out *Keys for Writers*. I had 100% accuracy. I had every preposition on the page written down in their exact order. She said she only expected me to remember a few. That was the day I found out what a photographic memory was. I definitely took it for granted back then.

When I graduated from that school in Inkster, I was the happiest I'd ever been up until that point. It was the first time I can remember smiling because I wanted to and not because some camera guy was forcing me to. The muscles in my face definitely were not used to that. I hated that school so much. The library was smaller than my bedroom. Most of the teachers treated me like I was autistic or something. Which I was, but I didn't know that at the time. I wasn't going to miss any of them. Except Ms. Collette and her assistant Dan. Ms. Collette actually cried at the party. She gave me another dictionary as a going away present. I forgot to say thank you. I had chosen White Castle for the food at the going away party. I certainly have a few regrets from my last day at that school.

When I got home that day and opened the dictionary Ms. Collette gave me I saw a message written inside of it "Dear Stephan, my most favorite Scrabble partner! You have so many gifts and talents but my favorite thing about you is your sense of humor. My best to you. -Collette." I remember feeling sad and thinking, "What sense of humor?"

I rarely laughed as a child. Most people say their favorite thing about me is my smile and back then I only really smiled when I laughed. People must've thought I was an ugly kid. I would watch SpongeBob and countless other cartoons and sit with a blank expression. Not that I never laughed. I had a very specific sense of humor back then. Members of my family, namely my sister and brother, were really the only ones who could get me to laugh. They were excellent storytellers. When they told a story I could have heard it a thousand times over and still laugh at it.

I went to a nearby elementary school for fifth grade. That's where the school in Inkster decided I'd be "mainstreamed." I got a bad feeling from that school. It reminded me of McDonald at first. I didn't want to be an outcast again. Livonia had a population of around 100,000. Just over 95,000 were Caucasian, only around 1,000 were black and the rest were from other races. However, nobody at that elementary school seemed to mind my darker skin tone. They didn't spit on me. I didn't have any "misunderstandings" like I did at the twelve previous schools I'd been expelled from. I liked it there because the work was a bit harder. Then I had another desire. To go to high school. The work still wasn't hard enough for me there.

At the end of the year, Livonia Public Schools went through some major changes and instead of entering the sixth grade at the same elementary school they would put me in a different elementary school instead because the current school would no longer have fifth or sixth grade any longer. I was only at the upper elementary school for one month before I got expelled. It was my last expulsion. Hurray. They sent me to an alternative school in Redford. I wasn't allowed back into Livonia Public Schools again until the eighth grade. I ended up skipping the sixth grade because of it.

While I had been diagnosed much earlier, I wasn't told about having Asperger's until I was around 11. When my mother and my psychiatrist dropped the bomb on me, I didn't take it very well. I thought of the representations of autistic people the media had fed to me and did what most people would do. I panicked. I denied it. I was ashamed. I already didn't fit in and I had no friends. I had prided myself on my grades and intelligence to make up for my lack of social anything. "Autistic" sounded like "retard" and at the time both words were thrown around as interchangeable insults amongst my peers, and even my family. I refused. I was already often the odd one out being a dark-skinned Puerto Rican boy in predominantly white schools and neighborhoods. I had both been a bully and been bullied. I always got stricter punishment than my white peers. In the 6th grade the school even went as far to call the police when I had a meltdown. An older white kid had a more serious meltdown a week earlier and never faced law enforcement. It definitely wasn't fair, and at the time it only seemed unusual. I know better now.

My mother had seen my autism as inconsequential. I had continued to ignore it. I wasn't fighting other kids anymore so we just stopped going to therapy. Either way, I still didn't really have any friends. I could talk to the neurotypical white kids I was surrounded by and every conversation seemed to go the same way. "You don't act black," or "You talk like a robot." My formal way of speaking and preference for higher-level vocabulary had not made me an effective communicator with my peers throughout school. When they called me a robot, I always shrugged it off in an effort to carve a friendship. I didn't succeed. A lot of the time, in the vey suburban city of Livonia, kids didn't see me, they only saw the sum of my stereotypes. They saw a black thug from the ghetto, and that intimidated them. They steered clear, and I didn't know how to approach them. Then when they'd hear me, they'd hear my monotone voice and hefty vocabulary and they'd change their minds. In their minds eye my skin color was no longer brown but something more ambiguous, and I was now worthy, and they were safe. It wasn't universal, not everybody was this horrible caricature of colorblindness, but it still remained a near daily experience until high school.

I remember freshman year, I was so excited to finally get to be in high school. I thought, "Finally, an environment where I can challenge myself." I determined not to speak with anyone and just focus on my academics. I wanted to work, not to blend in, but to remain completely invisible. I decided to take Spanish as my elective because I wanted to be able to understand my grandparents better when they spoke it and surprise them. My mother never taught me Spanish. She always said she didn't know how to speak it. It wasn't the first blatant lie she had told me and it wasn't the last either. My somewhat unique memory made it a breeze along with all the other classes. I would come to find out that it wasn't actually a photographic memory. I learned that some people with Asperger's Syndrome have what is called a filmographic memory. It's a little different in that it's kind of like recording a video in your head instead of taking a photograph.

I remember the first day I met Jackie. She was the giggliest and bubbliest teenage girl I have ever met in my life. That first day of class I came in late to my geometry class because I couldn't find it. I remember everyone staring at me while I scanned the room looking for an empty seat. I had this burning sensation inside of me. It was something akin to shame or embarrassment, I'm not sure though. It was my least favorite feeling. To make matters worse the seat was all the way in the corner. I could feel their eyes follow me as trudged to the back saying excuse me to each and every person in the aisle. Jackie was the only one of

321

them who was smiling. She even started to giggle a bit too.

She was one of the first people to talk to me at all. She was my first friend there. I wanted her to like me. I wanted to be like her. It wasn't uncommon for me to mimic other people I respected. This time was different though. Mimicking Jackie had changed me permanently. I hadn't changed into her but I did pick up some of her quirks. I was no longer afraid to talk to my peers. I started to laugh at things more often. I'd smile all the time. The way I talked, walked, and even dressed changed too. I was no longer this intimidating, timid black kid with Asperger's who sounded like a robot when he talked. By sophomore year I wasn't even recognizable as that timid kid. As a result, high school ended up being a lot of fun. I was in nearly every school club, I was in the performing arts program. I tried talking to everybody and hanging out with everybody I could. I participated in student government. I had so many fun and interesting experiences because of it.

My peers who were in the same position might have thought their childhoods were dull in comparison to the childhood I had. Though they'd be shocked to find out how much I truly treasured my mundane high school experience. Being who I was, where I was, I fit in like a puzzle piece. Sure, it would've been nice if the puzzle piece was part of the same puzzle, but life usually isn't like that. It's not that I regret my childhood, without all of the weird crazy stories I could tell, I'm certain I wouldn't be who I am today.

Nowadays, people are still quick to place their labels on me. I'm regularly told I don't seem autistic or that I'm not black. My acquaintances are under the impression that being black and being Puerto Rican are mutually exclusive. I still deal with being profiled. I have to explain to people what being autistic really means. I have to show them I'm not what they expect me to be, and that's okay. I worked so hard to overcome the social obstacles my diagnosis put forth. I worked hard to rebel against the labels placed on me, to be authentic. I am not a walking stereotype. Nor am I defined by diagnosis. I do not fit into the boxes others try to put me in.

Devout

Miss Fabien

Faith renew,
For the day is new.
Heart lift,
To play is a gift.
Stood gazing hand outstretched,
To the game of tangible strings and flirty things.
Tentative as always
For the strings could combust
Bust into hopes ashes
The temptation seems too much
For they gleam with a hot sticky lust, dance seductively
But reluctantly, I do not touch,
Right now.
Silly question but
Where do I stand?
We've gone from talking to holding hands.
Closely I watch
For a change in the mood
Vulnerable me just look
For my heart protrudes
And it's awkward
For my feelings elude
Or sound sense of reason
Treason, treason!!
I say to my heart:
How can you be serious?

The glue has not yet set
From the last ridiculous gamble and bet!
Why do this dance?
Why take this chance?
When in the end we'll part?
Red faced and ashamed or
Angry and lammed
Why?
Because I must!
I'm young, stupid and I give in to lust.
I trust too fast,
I fall too hard,
And every time of my heart I leave a shard
But jagged as it is
It beats
It pumps
It loves
And if by the end I walk alone
My faith in love is still devout.

Diagnosis Me

Louise Thundercloud-Hills

*Content/TW: Shock treatment (ECT), institutions,
medical/psychiatric violence against queer people.*

I was not diagnosed as a person with Aspergers until
2009. Whew! In my 50's. By then, I became aware that
many people of color, & sadly most women; are diagnosed
really late, if at all.

I suspected in the late 90's, that I might have some form
of autism. Also that I more than likely had some sort of
ADD thing going on, but I was not aware of how to find
out. A doctor confirmed all the diagnosis I thought I
might have, after they shoved me into the psych ward of
Howard University Hospital.

I have no issue with self identification, I have: Axis 1
Aspergers Syndrome, Obsessive Compulsive Disorder,
Post Traumatic Shock Syndrome. 2. Axis 2,
Claustrophobia & Clinical Depression.

The doctors also hung other diagnosis on me, that after
the thick cloud of psychotropics wore off, did not even
apply to me.

Paranoid schizophrenic (for which they liberally gave me
shots & grocery bags full of colorful pills). Bipolar was the

last diagnosis that fell by the wayside. The way they gave me all those colorful diagnosis, was to look in the DSM to see what kind of "illness" I had. No one could put their finger on what it might be. (I wonder how many folks have gotten diagnosis the same way).

I was still in South Carolina, Columbia the capital of South Carolina. "Oh well," my psych said, "we must diagnose you with something, we are not sure what it really is, will you go into the hospital? We can observe you better there."

"Of course," I said, "I know something is wrong, I make my parents mad all the time, I am always being picked on for being slow or stupid, going into the hospital was a welcome break, from the horror I was living. I did not feel that I belonged in any way to my family, I was sure I was the freak they told me I was in school."

In the hospital, I experienced a series of shock treatments, because I told another patient that I saw my grandmother & aunts & grandfather all the time. (They had all been dead for a long time, but I saw them all the time, for my family it was natural, it was part of our tribal & family culture). The hospital felt I needed shock treatments & lots of them too.

With each shock treatment (the doctor said it was a success after they zapped me the 8th time), I became more & more depressed & withdrawn. I had also become very fearful that they would do worse things to me. I stopped talking.

One day, in group therapy, I saw this cute blonde girl, & went over to talk to her. Nicole & I became lovers immediately & inseparable. Nicole always told me to be very careful, not to let anyone see us being romantic with each other. In South Carolina during the 80's, being a lesbian was punishable with hospitalization & shock treatments.

I remember sneaking in to the bathroom with Nicole, we kissed & then the kissing was deeper & both of us wanted more. God could Nicole kiss!, she slid her hands up & down my sides & back. I couldn't stand it anymore. I started to kiss her into the bathroom stall, when suddenly, here comes a nurse. She caught us kissing.

What happened next was so fast. The nurse yelled for staff. It was two big black guys who can in with 3 nurses. I could not believe any of this! Nicole got onto the floor & kicked anyone who came near her, she was crying & screaming, I cried too, this was turning bad, we only were being loving to one another. Nicole bit, kicked & spit. One of the guarded either slapped or punched her, then the nurse that came in with the other two, took a huge looking needle, & jammed it into Nicole's arm. Nicole wasn't moving at that point, they dragged her out. I watched her feet as they skidded across the floor.

I was standing there terrified & pinned to the wall by the guards. The last thing I remembered the words, shock series for this one.

Everyday after that, Nicole seemed to be in a fog all the time. It was hard for her to stay awake. What they hell had they done! No one told me anything, when I asked. Everytime I tried to get over to her chair, to rub her hands, the stupid guards were there to shove me down into the chair.

I later found out, South Carolina had a law on the books that allowed men to have their wives committed if they were lesbian. The law said they would be institutionalized in mental health facility for "sexual deviance".

Around that time I met Sarah. Sarah's husband had her committed for "sexual deviance" he also had her declared an unfit mother in court. She had not seen her boys in nearly a year. She was not allowed to see her boys.

Sarah had severe asthma. We were all in South Carolina State. That place was what I call a snake pit. We had cots on the floor. The nurses often did not want to have to do anything for any of us. The male staff were simply there to put strait jackets on us, silence us & immobilize us anyway they could.

I learned that since I voluntarily went to the Bull St hospital, that I could sign myself out AMA or against medical advice, & legally leave. Which is what I did eventually.

I returned 3 weeks later, to find that Nicole had been transferred to another facility. Sarah still was there, so I wanted to see her.

What happened to Sarah, was a very sad story. I walked down the long row of cots to Sarah's cot, I did not see her, but there was a lump in her bed I pulled back the sheets &

there she was dead. The woman in the cot next to her cot, told her that Sarah had been dead since yesterday afternoon. She told me Sarah died screaming that she couldn't breathe. The nurses didn't even leave the nurses station.

That angered me so much. Sarah was my friend, she was old that me & did not deserve to die. When I asked the nurses how Sarah died, they said that they have so many people to take care of, they can't rush to one, they were understaffed. Still pisses me off.

Stereotypes

S. Henderson

I'm not an actual hoarder, but I have had close relationships with people who are and I find the uninformed stereotypes and sense of superiority the average person gets when devaluing such people pathetic. I prefer "organized chaos." I know where everything is, and everything has its place. I believe the degree of executive functioning issues can create chaos that for some is not manageable in the way it is for some others so I have no right to judge people who can't manage. While hoarding can be destructive especially concerning animals and trash, some items are more difficult to write off as unnecessary, especially when some individuals have unique experiences that others would not understand. These could be cultural or personal. I have some difficulty getting rid of receipts, or paperwork this is not some arbitrary choice; as someone on the autism spectrum it has never occurred to me that some individuals can say something and not have to back it up with something concrete, that some people are given the benefit of the doubt, while others do not have such an advantage. As an autistic woman of color I like to have receipts to prove I did not steal, I have actually never stolen anything. I'm sure most people would not even believe that. I would prefer not to have an interaction with most white women that was not on paper that is sadly impossible but would make me feel more safe. White women make me feel unsafe, the insidious abuse and micro aggressions from them in my opinion are far worse than the more overtly negative experiences with males of any color and that is saying a lot I was once actually physically bullied for silently reading in public, it's harder to maintain moral superiority when you are being violent. White women have gone out of their self righteous way to harm me, and my character specifically while maintaining their image of moral superiority. FYI white women just because I don't resort to physical violence does not mean I can stand your passive aggressive condescending selves; it means I resent that I will have harsher consequences than you if I were to do so and that my actions as a woman of color would be deemed a problem of character rather than just a mistake that human beings make, like they are considered just mistakes when you do the worst of things.

As it became more evident to me that some individuals are deemed more credible than others simply by virtue of their class, race, gender, and so on it became more clear to me that I'm not part of any of the groups of people who are given consideration, as such I have a great fear of not being able to provide evidence of my encounters, especially against higher SES abusive cluster b personality disordered white women who are not held accountable for their abuse and racism due to having emotional problems, when women of color are criminalized for having emotional problems that go unacknowledged . So many people can't even conceive of how such seemingly "nice" individuals would flat out lie about others. Needless to say I try not to associate with white women and though my level of anger at them and compassion for their victims may not be noticed from the look on my face whenever I hear about incidences like the racist woman in Texarkana, lying about blacks assaulting her at Walmart, or the "emotionally disturbed" fan who accused Conor Oberst of rape and recanted, or the countless white women starting fights with black women then saying they were the victims, the feelings there and overwhelming. For someone like Conor Oberst even though he will likely be looked at as a potential threat, he will also likely continue to be successful, he is a white male celebrity, those of us who are already considered possible threats from the false narratives being pushed by societal bias including "the angry black woman," "the welfare queen," and many other damning images conjured up to reinforce the superiority of the average white American are downright harmful to those of us who don't get to start off with a clean slate of equal consideration. I know I have not committed any crimes but that doesn't stop me from being considered a criminal without a criminal record.

I understand double consciousness and I know how I'm perceived, and I know my disadvantage. These women are manipulators who regurgitate these very narratives to smear campaign and implicate those who they attack. I was recently slandered in a classist, racist, ableist smear campaign as a hoarding, psychotic, angry black woman stereotype by a white woman I've only met once, who is to me an unfortunate mixture of Sarah Palin, Nancy Grace, and a bro. A woman who was gossiping at me and my husband about my husband's mother being a hoarder and bragging about throwing her things away in a home she was not even invited by my husband's parents to live in, then preceded to ask me if I was a hoarder right out of thin air of superiority and assumption, no agenda there of course. She then went on gossiping at me, calling a young man I didn't even know a loser for living at home at 21 yrs old. She builds herself up by tearing others down, it's funny the volatile way that she described me, that person would have hit her in that one time disrespectful meeting. I saw her and her toxic family dynamics coming from a mile away but what about the ones that I don't see coming, my mind creates scenarios where my character is assassinated and I can't prove that the events did not occur the way that the superficially charming woman says they did and all anyone will say is we would expect that from this angry social misfit, as has already been the case for so many woman of color. I value my integrity and society does not even entertain the idea of people like me having it so I live in isolation as I do not know other autistic women of color. My dream is a little different from MLK's in that I dream of a world where the content of my character is not erased by implicit bias.

This is my cluttered living room. The majority of the items are things I made, painted or refurbished myself and most of my house is cluttered with my projects. I think if I were a rich white woman I would just be considered an "Artist."

Photo (S. Henderson): Color photograph of room full of furniture, tapestries, carpets, and ornaments, many with intricate patterned designs. The colors of the room are mostly warm reds.

Unpacking the
Diagnostic TARDIS

Dee Phair

Moving house is like stepping into a TARDIS. As you find all the stuff that's been crammed into your rooms, you start thinking that your house might very well be bigger on the inside. Also, finding papers and mementos from times long gone feels like stepping into a time machine.

Whoosh

In 2014, I started seriously wondering if I might be autistic. The thought had occurred to me before, but I thought that:

1. Autism can't be accurately diagnosed after a certain age.
2. If I were autistic, surely the multitude of therapists, psychiatrists, neurologists, psychologists, and social workers would have picked up on it sometime in my childhood.
3. Trying to use autism as an excuse for why I fail at life is deeply insulting to bona fide autistic people.

But what about that special nursery school I went to when I was a kid? I went back there last year, and there were definitely kids on the spectrum there.

I decided to ask my mother if the nursery had given me a diagnosis back then. My mother said that she was told I had "autistic traits." She mentioned that, while packing things up for the move, she came across some of my evaluations from that time.

I found the box in the garage.

Whoosh

Sometime in 1983, as preschool after preschool told my parents that I wasn't following orders like the other kids, it became obvious that I wasn't fitting in. It was at that point that my mother started taking me to all sorts of professionals—psychologists, neurologists, psychiatrists—to figure out what was "wrong" with me. Diagnoses and ideas for treatment were bandied about. ADHD. Aphasia. Semantic-pragmatic disorder (translation: hyperactivity, not speaking, early 1980's code word for autism).

Due to my mother's professional connections as a neurology nurse, I was able to attend a therapeutic nursery school, which, unbeknownst to any of us, specialized in autistic, and very bright, children. Whatever they did seemed to work, because a year later, my speech was advanced for my age. That's pretty much all I had ever been told.

Whoosh

I sent an email to one of the neurologists who evaluated me in 1983. She was affiliated with both the nursery and the hospital where my mother worked. I asked her if she remembered me, and what, in today's terms, my diagnosis would be. Autism? Asperger's Syndrome? Something else entirely?

I recall you were one of those children who have autism features when young who "recover" and do very well, although they may still have mild social or other behavioral issues....Indeed today you might have been labeled Asperger syndrome [sic] or high functioning autism, labels that no longer exist in the [DSM-V].

At the neurologist's suggestion, I posed the same question to the director of the nursery.

We felt at the time that you were on the autistic spectrum. You would not have been diagnosed with Asperger's because you had a delay in your [acquisition] of language and that didn't fit the diagnostic criteria... What made us feel that you were on the spectrum was not your language delay—that alone would have been considered a communication disorder. It was the way you used the language that you had socially... Also you didn't naturally pick up on how to engage and socialize [with others]—particularly with other children. This also involved picking up social cues and developing social reciprocity. Kids who are not on the spectrum, even if they are language impaired, pick up these social skills without needing to be taught directly.

All this leads me to wonder: why didn't my parents know all of this?

Whoosh

In 1985, we moved from Brooklyn to a sleepy suburban town within an hour of New York City; its main draw was the ease with which you could commute to the city. This meant I had to go to a new school. Because my original school wasn't accredited (something I didn't learn until recently), I had to repeat first grade. I already felt different because I was in suburbia, but now I was being held back! To make things worse, they were going over stuff I already knew! Sure, I didn't know how to tie my shoelaces, but I knew how to tell time on an analog clock, I could count up to 99 using my hands, I could read and write and do all the math that the other kids were just learning. In fact, there were things in second grade that I'd already learned in Brooklyn. On top of that, we were the only Black family in our neighborhood. There were other Black kids in our school, but they were bused in from the other side of town. And they thought that I spoke funny. My parents assured me it was because the other Black kids were American, while I had Jamaican and Nigerian parents.

Whoosh

Back to the director of the nursery:

You did a lot of "scripting" or repeating short chunks of language that you heard from people, from TV, from books, etc. ...You also had "prosody" which was not typical. That is, the "melody" of language. This is difficult to describe unless I imitate it for you. It's a kind of sing-song quality, which by the way, you don't have any more.

Could it be that kids thought I spoke funny because... I actually did speak funny? I learned to speak by repeating what I heard on TV, on the radio, and from other people. I often didn't fully know the meaning of what I was saying. But hey, Mom and Dad know best, right? Since I was the only one that didn't fit in, and I was the only one who was half-Jamaican, half-Nigerian, and all Brooklyn, surely those must have been the reasons why I was so different.

Director again:

You also had a lot of anxiety and had difficulty regulating this. Some of this was due to the difficult home situation, mainly involving your dad. I remember being told by your mom that when your father would beat your brother, you would wait outside to give him a tissue, in an effort to make him feel better. This kind of stress would be difficult for any child, whether or not he or she were on the spectrum.

So, while being neurologically different from my peers, this was happening. As I got older, I started getting beatings as well. Notice that I say beatings, not spankings. I got spanked as well, if, for example, I stole my father's coins to buy candy at the stationery store. But I'm talking about whipping out (pardon the pun) a belt or a piece of baseboard molding and hitting wherever my father could reach. I'm talking about riding in the car with him and suddenly getting popped in the mouth for not answering a math question correctly, or quickly enough. Or forgetting my homework. Or forgetting many a thing. I remember my father standing over me as I practiced playing a song on the organ, and him hitting me if he thought I was getting sloppy, making too many mistakes. Never mind that we'd been sitting there for hours on end. Or if my handwriting wasn't perfect. A letter might be too large, or it might have gone below the line on the paper. I've ruined composition books because the force of his hit caused my pen to cut through multiple pages. Of course, that was reason for the beatings to continue.

And if I didn't like something, and dared to complain, or show anything other than blankness? The beatings would continue until my morale *appeared to* improve.

At this point you might be wondering, "Why didn't you ask for help?" I did, many a time. I cried for help so many times that I learned not to bother anymore, because nobody would listen. When it came to the word of a child with known behavior problems versus a respectable-looking professional upper middle class gentleman, well, I wasn't believed. At one point, the police threatened to arrest me if I called them one more time. Sometimes, I regret not making the call, not begging them to put me in jail. My father would threaten to have me put in a mental institution. After a while, I asked him to please put me there, as I couldn't imagine being in a worse situation. He told me that I'd end up in a foster home and get sexually abused, and at least he didn't drink, use drugs, or sexually abuse me.

No, he didn't. That would have left physical evidence. My father was many things, but he wasn't stupid. He was also very careful to make sure he didn't leave any lasting marks, though I had many a busted lip when I wore braces. Except for the time he knifed me in the back, because I accidentally cut the leather of the organ bench. I still have that scar, but by the time I realized that what he did was so incredibly twisted, it was too late to do

341

anything about it. CPS asked me questions and took pictures of it, but nothing ever came of it. My father probably explained that away as well. Emotionally disturbed child and all.

I never got a break. I took abuse from my peers in school, and abuse from my father when I got home. My mother worked at nights, so she didn't know the half of it. Her days off were spent either sleeping or arguing with my father. My brother got the hell out of Dodge once he went off to college. Dad tried his hand at manipulating him from afar, even going so far as to make sure my brother had no money for textbooks. After that, my brother couldn't take it anymore, and kept his distance for a few years. My father tried to convince us that my brother didn't come back home because he'd joined a cult.

Whoosh

Eventually, my emotional disturbances landed me in therapy. None of the therapists or evaluators seemed to suspect autism. At least, not that they told me. Instead, they all tried to patiently explain that, due to the cultural and generation gap between me and my parents, I had to learn how to deal with the hand I'd been given.

My parents even got family friends to evaluate me to figure out what why I was so "emotionally disturbed," why I wasn't a "good little girl," and... nothing. I spoke to one, a school psychologist, recently, and he said that I showed signs of depression and hyperactivity, but he would have been extremely reluctant to label me autistic, because he didn't think labels were really that useful.

I've noticed that a lot. Professionals seem to want to decide for me whether or not I'd find a label useful.

During college, I had a full evaluation done, because I suspected I had ADD (with or without the hyperactivity component). The psychologist said that I didn't have ADD, I just needed to be motivated. She said my IQ was "above average," but she wouldn't tell me the score, because she didn't want me bragging about it. At the time, I was flunking out of college and suicidal. In my mind, I had absolutely nothing to brag about.

Whoosh

Last week. I looked up local therapists who claimed to specialize in autism, and went for an initial visit. I told the therapist a bit about my childhood, and how I'd felt ostracized and isolated. Her first reaction was that "African-Americans tend to keep to themselves."

I then had to explain that my parents were immigrants, and that both Jamaicans and Nigerians generally value community and familial bonds.

Once again, a therapist had tried to explain away my difficulties with the color of my skin.

I hear that both women and people of color are underrepresented in the autistic community. I have to wonder how much of this is due to professionals making assumptions about race and gender, and what we can do about it.

At least I've figured out the first step: to make sure people know we exist.

Hi, I'm Dee. I'm Black. I'm a woman. I'm the child of immigrants. I'm a mother. I'm autistic. And I know there are more people like me somewhere.

Try not to be afraid; you're probably not as alone as you think you are. Regardless of whether we're good at being quiet and submissive, we keep getting talked or shouted over. It's okay to shout back.

The Undiscussed Pain of Racial Oppression, and the Quest for White Privilege by a Multiply Diverse Female

Rhonda G.

I put off writing this article until the last possible moment. This story opens a deep, rusty box; the kind with a spring-hinged lid that snaps back when you try to open it. The intersection of multiple diversities within one woman. It is a story of abuse.

It has been really hard for me to dissect my diversity, and in fact, at forty-eight years old, I am really still parsing the bits of information and ruminating about my identity.

One of my earliest memories is of my mother's father, swinging me around and around on the beach in Florida. His head was blocking out the sun and he was silhouetted against it. When I looked up, the sun was so bright, and it caused me to look down at the sea shells bleached white.

From a very young age, I loved to spin things. I would find a particular necklace that I had, and swing it around in a circle, faster and faster, watching the centrifugal force generate a pattern in the chain. I remember doing this for hours sometimes. I also remember people walking up to me to touch me to get my attention, and the feel of their tapping jolting me out of a semi-conscious whir of sounds and sights. I used to like to burn things and watch them be consumed by the fire.

In school, hearing for me was difficult, and looking people in the eyes painful. I could either look or hear, but I could not do both together unless I focused very hard, and doing that took a tremendous amount of effort. My teachers frequently yelled at me for not paying attention or daydreaming, but I could never figure out to what it was that I was supposed to be paying attention.

It seemed to me that everyone else had access to information that they were not telling me. How did they know what was "appropriate" and okay to do? Where did they learn this and why could I not figure out their codes? My inability to do this was also starting to be noticed by my classmates and teachers, both of whom would take every opportunity for criticism and insult. Later, restraints and physical violence would follow.

In school, though, I also found reprieve in world of art, music, reading and writing stories. I was given a rare distinction in elementary school by having my story chosen for the young writer's club and a drawing being hung on the wall. For me, these were rare, golden moments.

346

Elementary school was also where I started learning about my Native American heritage. Growing up, my mother and father would tell us of my father's Cherokee blood. My grandfather was a sharecropper, half-Cherokee and worked non-stop from the time he was eight-years old after his father passed. He and his mother supported his many brothers and sisters in Alabama during the depression.

When I was in elementary school, the federal government had a program that Native American children could take to learn indigenous culture. My younger brothers and I learned native dance, beading, songs, and history, and socialized with other Native American children. I immersed myself in the culture as we went to "Indian Day Camp" and in classes during and after school.

The indigenous cultural environment really suited me. There were not "right ways" and "appropriate behavior", but strong, personal examples from elders who let you do your own bead designs or dance steps, but would show you how they did it too.

After a few years of being involved, government funding tightened up and so did the rules for qualification for the program. You had to produce documentable evidence of tribal affiliation, and we had nothing to show our connection to this heritage that was so evident in our faces and bodies and family lore. As a poor family who had traveled around following work, everything related to our cultural heritage was lost except vague whispers of stories, such as losing our possessions on the Trail of Tears.

Assimilation was survival. Our family clearly survived much, because there was nothing but poor southern dirt farmer left.

The rending of this program away from my fifth grade self was devastating, and for a year after I culturally appropriated "Chinese," as much as any ten year old in Flint, Michigan could. I would only eat with chopsticks and insisted my mother make rice. My hair was long and dark, and my dark eyes, and full body was being more and more violently targeted in my white, working-class school district.

In middle school, not a day went by it seems, that I did not hear N-lips or N-hips, and a barrage of abuse about my opposite-of-waspish physique. There were fistfights and threats of fistfights, and being chased by rock-throwing classmates. Teachers looked the other way, or participated in the mocking. A few teachers, a Spanish teacher, a Journalism instructor, gave me just enough encouragement to keep me from dropping out of school all together. The corporeal punishment had diminished from elementary school, in which paddling, being restrained and taped to my chair, and grabbed by the chin was a common occurrence. Mental abuse and isolation densely populated my middle-school and high-school years.

Flint, Michigan in the 1970s and early 1980s was an interesting place in which to grow-up. In my family, everyone worked either directly for General Motors, or for some industry driven by the automakers, like the trucking industry, or building radios at AC Delco. They were the blue collars that helped to build this county's wealth from

348

the natural resources dug up from our grounds. They also built unions that fought for every cent and benefit that these workers depended upon to lift them out of the fate of the dirt farmer. I later watched that ripped away as the union was crushed, jobs were shipped overseas, and the factories that once fueled the American Dream of Flint families and the U.S. working class were destroyed.

Schooling in Flint, and in many other working class communities across the United States, was focused on conformity and compliance. Teachers crushed independent thinking and children became their handmaidens, enforcing uniformity. Women's liberation and the civil rights movement were paid scant attention. Native Americans were sad-eyed marchers on the Trail of Tears, sentenced to reservations.

Flint is a mid-sized city in the Midwest, and the insular nature of a working class community, the enforced conformity of mannerisms, dress, appearance and physique created an unyielding foil for my unusual thoughts, behaviors and darkness. The most dangerous manifestation of this tension was someone trying to run me over in a car while calling me a "fag" and an "n*****", sending me diving into a ditch. Twice.

Working class children were to be seen and not heard. You were to make yourself small and quiet. I took up a lot of space. Outside of school, church became the enforcer, and so every dimension of my life was issuing rules that I could not understand. This was always interpreted as willful disobedience, followed by punishment.

Fast-forward thirty years and I am now working in academia. I am still an outsider. I identify as Autistic, but only to close friends and people that I trust. The Flint girl inside me feels economically vulnerable, and as a closeted Autistic, I have heard more than shades of racism and ableism in stories about hiring, tenure, and promotion. My racial identity was never recovered, and I am still untethered, a collectivist in an individualist world.

Having just recently left a fulltime administrative position in academia, I am now in the role of adjunct faculty without health insurance. Getting a diagnosis of autism is low on my list because of the expense. I also cannot afford to get my DNA tested. The ownership of my "legitimated" identity still lies outside of myself. Though an outsider in nearly every dimension, I am now inside a space of self-acknowledgement, able to affirm to myself my diversities.

"Where do you come from?"—beyond the white neurodivergent conceptualisation of "Difference"

Ebru Çelik

Introduction

I am writing this only a few months after I received my diagnosis. I have been processing it ever since. What does "autism" actually mean? There are a number of different theories that attempt to explain the origin of the cognitive differences between autistic and allistic people and thus each theory defines autism differently: Empathising-Systemising theory, Intense World Theory, Social Motivation theory, Excitation-Inhibition imbalance and possibly many others. Donna Williams describes her autism as an "assemblage", and as a biologist this term interests me in many ways. Autism is "polygenic" meaning that multiple genes of small effect additively or multiplicatively contribute to its etiology. The genotypes underlying autism for different individuals may also be different, and so I have my own unique "neural assemblage" of endophenotypes which together give rise to a set of behaviours which meet the diagnostic criteria for "autism". It has been difficult to give this account as I find myself resisting an "essentialist" view of autism. Whatever may be at the root of this neurodevelopmental trajectory, it is widely agreed that every autistic person will have some sort of social communication and language difficulty combined with a set of markedly repetitive behaviours.

The mainstream discourse surrounding autism is one that emphasizes "social difference" and this includes the described self-image of many a/Autistic people. Autistic people commonly report that they have felt "different to others" from a young age, or possibly "from another planet". During my assessment my mother was questioned on the behaviour characterising the early developmental periods of my life (with a focus on ages 4 and 5). Her answers contributed a large part to my diagnosis. I have since felt compelled to reflect on my childhood years and the inner life and self-image I had then. This essay is not about the full extent of how I have struggled with autism and how I experience it per se, but rather how factors other than "autism" may interact with "neurodivergence" and contribute to an overall feeling of "difference". The content here is based on both research and experience.

Describing the feeling of "difference"

If someone had asked me as a child whether I had felt different from others, I would have probably answered yes. The reason for this, however, remains speculative. When reflecting on this feeling as an adult it seems distinctly ineffable and mysterious and I am still unsure as to whether it is unique to "autism". To verbalise it would be to make a very normalized and familiar feeling sound suddenly strange and foreign. Many of my life-long feelings sound like this to me when I verbalise them. My grapheme-colour and personification synesthesia is an example of this. "I feel subjective about the visual quality of numbers and letters. Some of them are more likeable than others. Partly because of their colours but also their personalities." When I discovered that very few people related to that it was revelatory. My synaesthesia may also extend to misophonia as certain sounds trigger anxiety or extreme discomfort akin to 'pain' whilst other people seem not to respond at all. I am about to take the same risk when attempting to describe the way this "difference" felt when I was a child. My older sister is also neurodivergent and whilst she has been diagnosed with a number of conditions that are often comorbid with autism, she has not actually been diagnosed with autism itself and I am not in a position to suggest that she is on the spectrum. When I was a child I felt that somehow my sister and I were both so different that it surprised me when people could recognize that we were girls and not mistake us for "aliens". It would surprise me that people considered me to be a person just like them. I can recall the memory of absent-mindedly standing in the bathroom (possibly my life-long safe place) when I was 9 years old and saying to myself out loud: "I'm not a real person...I'm a pretend person...like an alien". I considered the possibility that everyone felt estranged and unreal like this. "Yes, the truth is, we are all pretending" I thought.

I grew up in a migrant working class area of the city and my primary school was multiethnic, so I was not the only

Turkish child let alone the only ethnic minority. It seemed I had no reason to feel like I really stuck out. There was no overt racism that I could sense at that age between the anglo-white children and the black and ethnic minority (BME) children. What I did notice however, was that whenever I met anyone new, one of the first questions I would get asked was "where do you come from?" Hearing this question so many times growing up, shaped my self-image such that I believed I was conspicuously different looking, and so followed the feeling that I was perhaps not even recognizable as "human". This is clearly not the most rational conclusion, but my diagnosis suggests that I was a child perhaps prone to 'atypical' ways of constructing narratives from what I observed. Either way, I will never really know.

There were many ethnic minority communities within my neighbourhood that somehow shielded these children from the effect of being othered by white English children. I had befriended a group of Greek Cypriot girls on the first day of school. They seemed like the first children I had met who were welcoming towards me. I noticed this after I approached a blonde blue-eyed English girl standing by the art display. We were surrounded by paintbrush filled pots and watercolour paintings and the wall paper was a mauve blue. I was 4 years old but I remember it clearly and I remember the colours that surrounded us, since my diagnosis I have read that autistic people tend to retain their long-term memories in more detail than allistic people. This has led to many awkward conversations with life-long friends who cannot remember nearly as many events from our childhood and teen years as I can. I approached her with what I now remember as a loud affected tone and her response was to physically push me away almost without a word. I had had similar experiences with other children I had approached and I had by this point realized that meeting new children was harder than I thought it would be. However I was not entirely dispirited, as I had not yet identified myself as the problem. Making friends with the group of Greek Cypriot girls was very simple. I sat next to the girl in assembly who would later become my best friend. I mechanically said "hello". She said "hi" back. That was all it took and I joined her friendship group of other Greek Cypriot girls.

Now as an adult it retrospectively feels as though the frequent micro-aggressions that functioned to other me as a child had an almost violent effect on my self-image, mutilating it such that I felt inherently different to "human" altogether, but why would I feel like this when I grew up around other ethnic minority children? I come from a refugee family who never intended to stay in the UK as long as they did. Whilst they were part of migrant communities in the 80s, over time they began to progressively feel more and more isolated. Did I maybe internalize this narrative of isolation from my parents? Was it maybe something else very different? I have also known from a very young age that I am queer although I had no name for it at the time. I now ask myself whether my autistic perspective also had a large part to play in the construction of this self-image.

Could autism explain why I only had one substantial friendship during those several years I spent in primary school? Could it explain why the Greek Cypriot girls I invited to my first slumber party ignored me the entire time in my own home whilst I never really knew why? Did it explain why I would often be given the "talk" by the group of girls explaining their distance or silence around me, because I had said yet another 'strange' or 'rude' thing? Maybe it explained why the Turkish girls in my class did not care that I was Turkish like them, and did not wish to spend too much time with me. Maybe it also explained why I ultimately did not really mind, because activities or pursuits other than friendship (reading, drawing, learning facts, playing computer games, listening to music etc.) interested me just as much if not more.

Before my diagnosis my only thoughts about my childhood were that I was privileged to have grown up in a loving, accepting and supportive family environment. Furthermore, retrospectively I accepted that school was generally stressful for everyone as children are often cruel. I would go on to experience the transition between primary school and secondary school that many autistic people experience, where their quirks or differences are no longer charming, merely "eccentric" or cause for a slight discomfort in others, but a reason for their peers to ostracize them completely. It is only when I reflect on my teen years that my autistic traits begin to appear more obvious to me.

Autistic black and ethnic minority people

Since my diagnosis, I have constantly asked myself, does this language of "difference" that is often used by autistic people, apply to me? It is difficult to assess, as I may have conflated the effects of being othered from a young age as a queer ethnic minority with the possible feeling of estrangement that characterizes autism. When autism has such a white and cismale face in the media and in terms of who is often diagnosed, it may be difficult to entirely relate to the idea of "difference" in the way many white autistic people have conceptualized it. Whilst there is a need to improve awareness of autism in people assigned female at birth, the recent emergence of research in this area implicitly focuses on white assigned female at birth people and cis "females", just as the labels "girls" and "women" hegemonically refer to *white* assigned female at birth people and cis girls and women, erasing the intersection with BME, trans and nonbinary identities. There is also an underdiagnosis of autism in ethnic minorities (Begeer et al., 2009; Mandell et al., 2009). I once came across an online pamphlet on this issue that tried to ascribe this underdiagnosis to the lack of awareness within these communities, however ethnic minority children are specifically less likely to be referred to a specialist autism clinic even after seeing a general practitioner (Begeer et al., 2009).

My sister has received many different diagnoses in her lifetime, some of these contested or questioned by successive doctors. I have wondered whether her difficulties were innate or due to the early life event of being separated from our parents for a few months when they left Turkey as political refugees. I have since learnt that Turkish refugee children born in the late 70s, before their activist parents were beginning to flee the military coup of 1980, often develop new psychiatric disabilities as adults. I am not sure how widespread a trend this is, but a few of my parents' friends have had children with similar difficulties. Migrant and ethnic minority individuals have complex histories and experiences that are outside the

357

white imaginary. There is a tendency for white people to attribute every social or communication difference to our ethnic background, no matter how well we speak English. I have seen this myself when working in schools. A staff member very vaguely explained the social behaviour of a Middle Eastern pupil as being due to "possible cultural differences" even when these frictions occurred between that pupil and other children of similar cultural backgrounds. Furthermore, it is perhaps worth mentioning that as a toddler my parents took me to a speech and language therapist because they were concerned about my speech and language abnormalities. The speech and language therapist reassured them that this was due to my growing up in a bilingual household and that this caused "confusion". There is now wide consensus that bilingualism does not lead to abnormalities or delays in speech and language development.

I believe the under- or misdiagnosis of BME (black and/or minority ethnic) individuals is due to certain types of marginalization being normalized or accepted as long as it does not result in "criminal" behaviour. When such behaviours are criminalized they may result in the diagnosis of "conduct disorder" (Mandell et al., 2007). This often results from racial profiling as many black autistic children and teenagers have been targets of police brutality. Marcus Abrams (2015) 17 years old was approached by police and baselessly accused of being intoxicated before being attacked and consequently suffering a seizure. Kayleb Moon-Robinson (2015), 11 years old was arrested and manhandled by a police officer and charged with 'disorderly conduct' after kicking a trashcan in response to being scolded for disobeying a rule. Troy Canales (2015) 18 years old, was body slammed and punched in the face by three cops after hanging out outside his own home, after his mother cried out that he was autistic, he was still handcuffed by the police. A black 10 year old autistic girl (2015) whose name was not disclosed, was slammed to the ground, crying out that she could not breathe as her face was crushed, and handcuffed after climbing on school desks and up a tree. Neli Latson (2011), 18 years old, was waiting one morning for his local library to open when someone reported him as a "suspicious person...possibly in possession of a gun" but after harassment and a police search, no weapon was found. He was still later placed in isolation.

White cismale individuals have a more valued existence in society and so must be successfully integrated so as to fully benefit from their privileges. Furthermore migrant or refugee status is inherently "pathologised", not in the medical sense but socially. Any aberrations in development I suspect are largely attributed to migrant and refugee status and the knowledge of this status clouds the assessment of any "innate" differences.

References

Begeer S, Bouk SE, Boussaid W, Terwogt MM, Kokot HM (2009) Underdiagnosis and Referral Bias of Autism in Ethnic Minorities. J Autism Dev Disord. 39: 142-148.

Jack Kahn. 2015. DIS Magazine: Donna Williams on Neurodiversity (interview) [ONLINE] Available at: http://dismagazine.com/blog/78778/dismiss-donna-williams-on-neurodiversity/.

Lauren Lowry. 2011. Bilingualism in Young Children: Separating Fact from Fiction http://www.hanen.org/Helpful-Info/Articles/Bilingualism-in-Young-Children--Separating-Fact-fr.aspx.

Mandell DS, Wiggins LD, Carpenter LA et al. (2009) Racial/Ethnic Disparities in the identification of Children with Autism Spectrum Disorders. American Journal of Public Health. 99: 493-498

Mandell DS, Ittenbach RF, Levy SE, Pinto-Martin JA (2007) Disparities in diagnoses received prior to a diagnosis of autism spectrum disorder. J Autism Dev Disord 2007; 37: 1795-1802

How to Create a Diamond

Angel McCorkle

Author's note: Disorders, emotional or otherwise, can feel like a battlefield, and trauma can take away your defenses. Here's the worst way I've learned to arm myself so far.

When you wake up, don't scream.

Realize that the bubble in your chest is just panic—your organs are not actually trying to crawl out of your mouth in order to escape the rising swell of tension in your body. Try to breathe, and don't worry about choking the first time. It means you're awake, and that you're on your way to something resembling *okay*—but first, you have to drag yourself up through layers of ash and smoking embers until you start to see the sun.

Pull air into your lungs until you feel the film and fluff surrounding your brain start to break away. Don't think about getting up; just do it quickly, before your body realizes what's happening. That way you're over the toilet bowl by the time the panic turns your blood to acid and you start heaving for the first time. You can even make a game to see how quiet you can be; everyone gets good after their first few years.

Take your first deep breath of the morning. Sometimes you get lucky and that's as far as you get—genuflecting pitifully before a tarnished porcelain stand—but luck doesn't live with you anymore.

Brace yourself. Wonder if what you ate last night has had a chance to fully digest.

Heave.

Heave.

Wipe your mouth.

Heave.

Suppress the urge to heave more as you realize that no, the food hasn't completely digested.

Cry on the floor for ten minutes and think about ending your life. It doesn't have to be the way you're actually going to do it—it's better if it isn't because once it's real it's a plan and a plan becomes ideation. Ideation means you have to tell your doctor and your doctor makes you tell your partner and your partner cries and makes you promise not to do it and to always talk to someone about it periodically because—and they won't say it then, because maybe they don't even know it themselves yet—in six months they aren't going to be around to stop you from trying. Promise them anything they ask because you think you need them around more than you need to be alone.

Know (somewhere deep down) that you're too much for everyone in your life to handle—but don't see it. Never see it. Don't bring it to the front of your mind. Feel it in your bones and know that you can't do anything about it and swear to hate yourself for it for the rest of your life.

Wait for your muscles to soften and hope you feel like showering. If you don't, that's ok—because you're not leaving the house anyway and no one will say anything if you don't leave your room for another day.

Probably.

Spend a few hours thinking about everything they might be saying about you. Make sure to let it paralyze you while you're sitting on the floor in your underwear, staring at the stretchmarks on your body and wondering how many more times you can push yourself to the point of tearing before you finally start splitting apart.

Dodge calls. Dodge texts. Dodge messages and visits from people trying to help in the wrong ways (but still the only people trying to help). When your body starts breaking down, tell yourself it's for the best. You were going to die anyway; now your family will be able to cash in on your insurance policy. Tell yourself that committing suicide has always been about the insurance policy.

Make bad choices. Tell yourself you're making them for good reasons: because you need money, because you can't borrow, because you only have a few marketable skills. Don't think about morals or safety or statistics. Don't read the warning signs spelled out in bright letters and printed on enormous crimson flags. Don't react. Don't do anything about your gut instinct because you need to prove yourself more than you need to recover right now—and proving yourself means pushing your nose so close to the grindstone that you're still standing when you pass out.

When things start going wrong around you and your plan falls to pieces, leave. Leave with whomever came with you, even if her protection isn't there yet, no matter what payout is promised. You don't have to fight this fight—either of you. Don't stay around for what happens next.

Don't.

Or do. Because you can't leave without transportation and you can't bear to leave someone else like *you* alone if they might be in danger—and so you both stay.

And you promise you'll be ok and that you'll wait with them and if something goes wrong, you'll at least be there. And you *will* both be ok—you promise—because safety comes in numbers. Women and people like you protect each other. And you'll have each other if—gods forbid—the worst happens.

Though—and you should know by now—the worst always happens. So when it does happen—and you see you have no other paths to take—and you see yourself folding before it even starts—

Go through it.

Go through it, shut yourself off, take it and shove it down so deep inside you that you can pretend it didn't even happen for a while. Know that you won't be able to go back to that city anymore without feeling like a pressure cooker as you ride through, thinking about everything that you let get taken from you there.

Don't tell anyone anything. Not your best friend, not your other best friend, not your mom, not even your partner as they're shoving you out the door. Hold it inside until you're not sure it happened anymore, but at least no one will look at you differently ever again. Don't think about it in the shower or while you're watching your favorite show or while you're playing with your dog or when you're trying to roast vegetables. Push it down. It will come up when it's time; know this from experience. Add it to the list of things wrong with you that will never be right. Cut out all the people in your life that remind you that you're a victim, and that will always see you that way. Don't see yourself as a victim...but don't see yourself as a person either.

Every few months, reach around inside and see how it's doing—the little pocket between the curvature of your ribcage where you condensed all your darkness and rage and vulnerability about being seized, violated, and tossed away like so much rancid garbage. Don't worry if it's hardened, sharpened, and it shines—that's what it's supposed to become.

It's you; it's your very own diamond of hatred.

It's huge and heavy and stronger than almost every part of you, and it hurts to grasp—but it's yours.

Never let that diamond go. Put it back inside you where it can rattle around and slice through the muscle and fat and kill everything inside that's been trying to grow. Try not to mind. You're doing fine. You're still alive, still walking around, still surviving—but now it's different: now you have something as real and as hazardous as you are when the next person comes to try to take you down. Know that the edges will most likely slice into your palms and bleed you dry even as you strike them down, but don't focus on that. Know you may go down again. Try not to care.

But make sure to take them down with you, too.

Redirection

Fragmented Perfection (Cindy Facteau)

Sitting outside in the December night cold
Thirty-two years young, yet feeling so old
Chilled to the bone, but I can't go inside
I've escaped from the chaos and come here to hide.
I   look   to   the   rooftop,   lined   with   icicle
lights
A strand is burnt out
So am I.
Fighting the fight at a break-necking speed
Checking each box, fulfilling each need
Preparing each meal with diligence and care
And still somehow finding some laughter to share.
I look to the stars, twinkling in the moonlight
They all shine so bright
So do I.
Thoughts cross my mind of how far we've come
The miles we've covered, the distance we've run
It is time to come in from my thoughts in the cold
The hour is late...and I've got two boys to hold.
I look to the sea, waves majestic in the night
The sun shall rise again
So will I.

Teratophilia: A Journey Towards Monstrous Self-Love

M.D.

This is a story about things that only happen to Other People.

I've been Other People all my life. As I write this, the entirety of society is lined up around the block to tell me I should have known, I should have made different choices, and all of the things I could have and should have done to prevent the situations I've endured. Some would say I should have died rather than suffer such indignity, but what use have mentally ill, autistic, multiply disabled, queer women of color for dignity? Because I did *not* do those things, because I have failed to die, because I made the choices and the "choices" that I made, I am a monster.

I still believe them. I know I am a monster who has always deserved *everything*; all of it: every bruise, every word, every moment when I knew I embodied the essence of *thinghood*.

I choose to *love* that monster.

For that, I am a freak, a pervert, a teratophile.

And you should be extremely afraid of me.

Westminster, California
1988

"*They* hate me", I replied, and my mother's eyes darted to the corners of the room as if they held the key to understanding her darkly recalcitrant progeny. "Why would you think they hate you?" she coaxed, and I felt my chin grow stubborn; surely my mother knew better than to ignore facts.

"They *hate* me", I said slowly, carefully, as I scratched the back of my hair. Her eyes locked onto the motion, and her hand followed, finding the mats the bristle brush hadn't touched. With an exasperated sigh, she reached for the blue safety razor that would cut away the clumped strands and leave a more natural looking edge than scissors; I gazed defiantly at the rattail comb she'd abandoned hope of years before.

"It's not a popularity contest", she muttered, and I felt the prickles as each hair grew taut under the razor and then released itself from its parasitic drag on my scalp. I shuddered, and gooseflesh ran from neck to knee. "You're there to *learn*. Just listen to the teacher and tell her if they pick on you too much".

I decided to take her advice, and the next morning as Ms. Joaquin shook my arm and my eyes filled with hot tears, I knew she was right. Ms. Joaquin hadn't read the books I had, she didn't know that one morning soon I would wake up with pure white skin and hair, even better than the teased blonde mane that she was so proud of. She might have watery blue eyes that showed her purity, so different from the "dirty southern italians" she made sure we knew she shared no common ancestors with-I would have inscrutable *amethyst* eyes.

(I'm not a mistake)

I knew they would be inscrutable, I'd picked that word right away during the test to see if I had "learning problems" like Ms. Joaquin said. She finally let me go, and I took my homework to do in the first grade classroom, since I was too stupid to be allowed to sit with the second graders and nauseate them with the cat pee smell of my ratty clothes. I hunched in the corner and drew pictures of Princess Amalthea from The Last Unicorn video I made my mom rent over and over. I knew it would be easy to turn into a princess; if a unicorn could do it, I knew it was only a matter of time before I awoke washed clean, sparkling white and magical.

Months later, I overheard my mother telling her friends, "I grabbed that bitch by the hair and drug her all the way down to that useless principal's office! And I said, to him, I said...and they were all staring! I said, 'somebody better call the cops, cos I'm gonna slit this bitch's *throat!*'"

Listening to her ugly laughter, I thought back to that earlier day when my mother had dry-wiped her face with a trembling hand. "Why didn't you *say* anything?" she whispered, her throat clicking dryly as her eyes darted for answers again. I echoed the gesture and brought my hand to my own face, where it still held the ghost of soreness where the basketball had made impact, the boy screaming and laughing while I made stupid Donald Duck sounds in my throat.

"Why didn't you...why didn't you *tell* me?" I stared at her in confusion, then sympathy. She'd been at school earlier that day; the boys and Ms. Joaquin had probably been mean to her too, and I knew why. "They hate *me*," I informed her sadly, and held her shaking hand until it stopped.

California, 1992: La Madrugada

I pressed my face to the washing machine, panting hoarsely, hoping they'd given up, gone away, that the hammering of my heart and the hammering on the door would finally cease. Dingy morning light, *la madrugada*, squeezed through the tiny, barely aboveground window in the downstairs laundry room, spidery and flecked with dust. Just as my harpstring muscles started to loosen, I heard someone trying the back door, the one I'd forgotten about. Too many doors, perforating a place that should be safe.

The door opened and I heard feet tramping toward the laundry room.

I burst from my bolt-hole, and tore through the downstairs living room, up the stairs, through the upstairs living room, all the ridiculous rooms in this new, huge, nonsensical house, and out onto the balcony. At bay, I turned to face the pallid, hateful, frightened faces of my pursuers. "We...we're here to take you to school...remember?" the big one said. The small one hid behind her. I remembered going to her house at my mother's insistence; I'd brought a weighty volume to bide the time there. That house made even less sense than this one. The kitchen full of terrifying and esoteric appliances that shot beams of light into my eyes; that single room in their house was bigger than our old apartment. My nostrils flared and I screamed, "I'd rather *die!*"

I turned away towards the view from the balcony, the one that sold my mother on this house. The hill, the town, and far in the distance, the ocean. I wished I was there, I *should* be there. I was drowning, but no one could see the water filling my lungs. "I'd rather *jump!*" My tormenters backed up and left me there; I heard the phone dialing and quiet talking, far away now.

I slid down the parapet and kept my eyes on the horizon where light twinkled at the strip of water. I remembered when I used to run outside in the sun barefoot, the juice of mangoes bought from the ice cream man's truck running down to my elbows, the sidewalk shining with broken glass and relentless heat. My mother used to pick the glass from my feet, oh so carefully, tweezers searching in the lacerated flesh, the foam and burn of peroxide.

As *la madrugada* fled and the air grew heavy and warm, I heard the sliding glass door to the balcony open and my mother's Sunflowers perfume roll out of the air-conditioned house. My mouth flooded with nauseous saliva. "What the *hell* is wrong with you?" The horizon blurred and the water seemed to glow with fiery immolation, specks jittering and blending back into the watery sun's fury. I listened to her sit down.

"I thought things would be better now. I always wanted to give you kids everything. I can finally afford it, and you don't even want any of it. What do you want? What the hell do you want?" I thought of The Little Mermaid, watching the sea and the white glare upon it. I thought about turning into foam and walking on knives with every step. "I want to go home", I whispered.

New York, 2012: Patient Presents as Academic and Upset

I've been an artist since I was about two years old. I was making art before I learned to walk. I have drawings I did when I was a child, a teenager, a young adult, and all the drawing I've done since then. I worked as an untrained, freelance graphic designer for about a decade, stupid shit like tattoo and web design. I may or may not have had some shows.

My REAL art is all in boxes in closets in my house. The pieces that survive.

You will probably never see any of it.

I have boxes and boxes of drawings and paintings.

I have two decade's worth of... "illustrated poetry" might be the best term for it.

I have tens of thousands of words of creative writing, short stories, et cetera.

I *loathe* it.

Because my very best moments are born of dehumanizing, unendurable pain. *My* pain, pain so grotesque it breaks language, suffering so exquisite it shatters into pigment particles and stains everything.

Everything I create is a facet of myself trying to somehow cope with what I have seen and experienced. My experience with writing is trying to force that dynamic into words that don't break, language that conveys, language that *wounds*.

I want language that leaves marks on people. I want language that is a vehicle for change, healing and reintegration. For the surgical extraction of things that no human soul can bear to live with. Words build the strawman and the stuffy-guy; words name it and words burn it so that we can let it go again, and again, as many times as we need to.

I want to decolonize my written word; I want to elevate my verbal world.

I want language that takes the stone off my back and returns it to its sender.

I ended countless friendships with people who told me my art was beautiful, pretty, something nice to hang in their house. It sounds the same to me as "you're cute when you're angry."

I've burned pieces that people liked, just because they liked them.

I want someday to have enough faith in humanity to trust that seeing my pain will irrevocably scorch the viewer. Enough faith to trust that people will respect the person I have built on the ashes of what was destroyed.

Until then, I'm not here to brighten your day or amuse you with my funny insults.

That is not why I am here.

California, 1993: The End

Flip on the light and the roaches skitter away. In the kitchen, get the pickles, cheddar cheese, bread and milk. Pour. Cut into tiny, tiny squares. Make a huge cup of caffeinated, milky tea in the travel mug. But I'm not going anywhere. I never do.

I wake at 7pm and wait until everyone goes to bed. Pick up my books, creep about the silent household. Read, read, read for eleven, twelve hours. Go to bed as the first light hits the sky...the bottom dropping out of my stomach when I hear my mother's alarm clock going off. Pull the covers over my head. She doesn't bother to come in here anymore. Her Sunflowers perfume might creep under the door and grab me by the throat, shake awake the morning terrors. Creep, sleep, repeat. Cut the cheese and pickles into tiny squares. Wake up at noon to the silent house, pick wild fennel in the backyard. Cackle at the sky.

I'm 12 years old, and my life is over.

Go back to bed.

Pennsylvania, 1983: White

White isn't a color. White is a texture. White has curling edges that pick at the corners of my vision; white falls into my eyes and melts in fat, cold tears. They run down the sides of my face, into my ears and I shriek with laughter. A tugging at my feet, and off we go.

My mother glances back at me, a shape seen through white flecks picking, picking at my lashes. She begins to sing.

You are my sunshine
My only sunshine
You make me happy
When skies are grey...

My bootlaces are clutched in her competent fist as she hauls me along, her breathless singing in time with her long strides. The sky is grey, grey and releasing gouts of the snow, the same snow that rushes beneath my head with a shushhh, shushhhh noise. I throw my arms over my head and my wool-encased fingers feel the first needles of the wet cold of the world that tries to invade the layers of my wooly carapace. Along the side of the blanketed road, the dark shape of the mailbox slowly emerges from the White.

We have arrived at Onclejohn and Ontee's house.

I squeal as my mother scoops me up so quickly I feel a fluttering sensation inside, laughing and hollering.

"John! John, we're here!"

A burble of voices and rush of hot air swirls us inside, and she plops me down in the nest of pillows and toys in the corner. My mother clops gaily into the kitchen and the welcoming murmurs of Ontee and Onclejohn and the sharp scent of coffee form a safe cocoon of familiarity as I paw through the pile for my favorite things: the wooden cylinders. Almost immediately I have them lined up and begin rolling my hand over them, back and forth, rolling them under my hand hard until my palm tingles. Onclejohn's voice thread separates from the murky underwater kitchen noises.

"...I don't think you *do*, Nees."

Ontee.

"Now, John, if she hadn't helped...nevermind the *beans*....on time."

Using both hands now, I roll the cylinders with all my might, my upper body rocking back and forth with the effort.

My mother voice grows high, impatient.

Ontee's clary sage shadow creeps past my vision, shuffling down the hallway. Her eyes are darting black chips that flash and disappear as she slips behind the door leading to

377

the rest of the creaking house. As she goes, my finger slips between two of the rolling cylinders and a bright starburst of pain shocks up my arm. It tastes like blackberries.

California, 2001: Smudges

"It's SAGE," I cried desperately, holding up the burned, crumbled leaf-ends up to their cold eyes. "From the garden! Look, right out there, it's sage that we grow *right here*!"

"You know we don't allow drugs in this house. You've been smoking pot in here, and that's just unacceptable. You're going to have to leave. You're an adult, you both are. You need to learn how to take care of yourselves."

"…both of us?"

"We built this place for him; we never had *you* in mind. He can go with you, if that's what he decides to do."

The slamming door sounds like the lid to a coffin. I think of Lestat. "It's *your* coffin, my dear. Enjoy it. Most of us never get to know what it feels like."

I finger my barked shin, wishing I'd looked into those eyes a week earlier, as I crawled out of the bedroom window screaming, clutching the styrofoam container of food to my chest. After the fire inspection, they had had the door between the main house and the new addition walled over. Is this me, crawling out the window, hot tears and snot (blood?) dribbling down my face, slithering through the garden and the sliding glass door into the main house and onto the chair in the dining room? I watch their feet

378

arrive and duck my head under the hot weight of disgust. "I just wanted to eat!" I wailed, mouth full, trying not to choke. My hands shake, and I sob open-mouthed like a toddler who doesn't know that other people have thoughts, that everyone has private places in their minds that can take an ugly snapshot of you and make you stay that way, twisting and foaming forever. A toddler who doesn't know that pictures of brown people are pictures of criminals, druggies, lazy people trying to *get* something from everyone, get one over on someone, and get away with something.

But I just want to get away.

White sage is growing endangered. I never understood why they call it "smudging"; cleaning up the thick stench of my own terror and despair is both right and necessary for proper housekeeping. I am growing; I am endangered. I am growing, in danger.

I turn to stare at the door, waiting for it to open and preparing my defense for why once again, I Have Ruined Everything.

California, 1995: The Devil You Know

She is punctual and I appreciate this. I open the door and there she is, marshmallow face and eyes that disappear when she grins. "Can I do clay with you?" she asks, peering around me to see if everything is arranged: bones, jewelry, figurines, plastic barrettes; she can see the drawings that paper the entirety of the walls and even the ceiling. The finger paintings that we had done when I showed her how to make pigments from crushed bricks or charcoal and mixed them with Crisco. We rubbed and rubbed the fatty mess into the paper to make art like transparent wounds, me smiling my not-smile as I explained that this was how prehistoric peoples had colored and waterproofed leather. Kind of. It's Sunday night, and everything is ready.

I nod tersely, and point at the floor, where the plastic bags full of clay we dug together sits between two books I have covered with sheets of paper. She gets the Atlas, which is bigger. Kids need more room. I remember when they dug up the vacant lot, and we had gone together to explore the intermediate and cavernous eyesore like a missing tooth between the bracketing houses. Scooching down a hill of dirt on my butt and back up on all fours, just like I navigated the stairs at home, I stopped and reached out to touch a particular lump. I knew, but I still smelled it to make sure. "Come here, come *here* and look what I found!" I squeaked breathlessly. She came running over another dirt-mountain, and pulled up on her heels and squatted, rocking. "Is it dirt?" she puffed, sweating her weird child-sweat. "It's clay," I replied, my voice quiet with excitement. "*Real* clay, from the ground. We're going to make stuff out of it." Her eyes disappeared as she grinned.

Now her face is solemn, but her eyes jitter with anticipation. As I turn and click on the Sunday Night Reggae music programming, she plops down in front of our makeshift Altar of Creation and wiggles up to her assigned book-station. I use one of my broken guitar strings that I had saved, and deftly wind it around between two pencils to lop off two lumps of clay I've carefully worked most of the stones out of, get my fingers wet, and let my mind drift. This is as happy as I get anymore. Even getting a new book or a gift just makes me feel scared and sick, my heart pounding irrationally. I don't think about last Christmas, where I got so many presents I cried until I threw up, much to my horrified mother's chagrin.

If you know your history,
Then you would know where you coming from,
Then you wouldn't have to ask me,
Who the 'eck do I think I am.

I lean back once to turn up "Buffalo Soldier", leaving a clot of Earth's blood on my radio. I bitterly resent that the four and a half years between our births has recently widened into the almost uncrossable abyss between nine years old and fourteen years old. I bitterly resent almost everything, however, including how even the merest murmurs of human voices through my bedroom door grind into my eyes like sandpaper. *This*, at least, can be ameliorated with ceremony, with verbal silence, with reverence, with pleasant company spent in purposeful worship.

Buffalo Soldier troddin' through the land, wo-ho-ooh!
Said he wanna ran, then you wanna hand,
Troddin' through the land, yea-hea, yea-ea.

My heart soars as I think about how, after we are done, I will spend several days brushing the figures with water, and leave them out to bake in the bright, hard sun. I have never known my father and don't care; she has never known her father and feels the loss keenly, a hole in her life that I hope is soothed the same way I am soothed, knowing I was born on the Earth I shape in my hands as my ancestors did, and the ones who came before them, and the ones before them. My bones know I need no kiln, and I don't have one anyways. This house sits on the ruins of cities built with earthen bricks baked in the sun. So were the Missions that stole our/their/my history. Torn from the ground that birthed them, the figures we make can and will bear the weight of their existence.

I shut the music off, so my sister knows that talking is now Allowed. She's created various blobs with smaller blobs attached(ish) to them, a maybe-snake, a dented blob that might be a bowl of some kind, but my eyes latch onto a tall and skeletal humanoid... something... that towers over the terrible mess like the King of Blobs. Two twisted horns top a grossly misshapen and oversized head, and its face is mostly taken up by the massive hole of a mouth, yawning in terror and despair over two barely visible punched-in eyes. The body is lumpy-spindly, armless, and a concave ribcage teeters like a gaunt pendulum, keeping the whole unnerving horror more or less upright. "That's the Devil," she informs me with a satisfied nod.

I press my lips together and prepare to pass judgement. "That is the most fucking awesome thing I have ever seen in my life."

She seems confused but very pleased. I add, "Can I paint it black if that's okay with you." She agrees, but the irritation is already coming back. I shift and sigh heavily. "Okay, well, we're done then." She whines a bit, which increases my irritation. She doesn't want to go. "Can I sleep with you tonight?"

My nostrils flare. "You know the answer is no. Ask mom."

"Mom's working."

"Then ask Grandma."

We yell at each other for a while and after she leaves, I sit across from the figurines we have made. I've shaped my usual human figures curled up into balls, some with arms over each other, hiding and crawling away from the light. But I'm transfixed by The Devil. Unlike my figures, who are just trying to escape something unknowable, something unbearable, trying to escape *themselves*, The Devil stands there proudly broken, screaming his pain and rage at the world. I try to see what she sees; I try to know what the Devil knows. But I can't, all I can do is stare and wonder how much pain wet clay can feel.

This is what The Devil knows. One night just a few short months from now, my sister will wake up from one of her famous and lifelong night terrors, and run through the house. No one is home. Something is Wrong. She will run into my empty room, looking for something, anything to prove she isn't still having a nightmare, something to make her wake up, someone to tell her everything is okay. She will see the radio covered in our clay fingerprints, see the cassette tape stopped and that is when she will also see the blood, *my* blood, mixed with the dried clots of the earth's blood. My room is empty, and my blood is everywhere. And that is when her eyes will disappear into barely visible gouges, her mouth open wider and wider in horror, at first soundlessly gasping in denial, no, *no.*

The Devil knows why my sister is screaming, and he knows it is my fault.

New York, 2014: The Alchemist's Daughter and the Iron Maiden

One thing that never changes is how my everyday interactions are affected by the fact that others can't accept my disability and my personhood at the same time.

Like, the fact that well into my twenties I had the same amount of autonomy a child does. Less than some children. That it *wasn't up to me* what I ate, what I put in my body, whether or not I was allowed to have a bank account, or was allowed to leave the house. I've been drugged without my permission or consent; I've had people *switch my medications out for illegal drugs* because they thought it was funny, they wanted to see what would happen, and they thought it would "teach me a lesson". It's *okay* to do that to *retards*, you know. And guess what? No one cares. That happened, and worse things. No one ever "did anything" about it. There is no magical system in place that prevents that from happening, there's no justice for that. We cannot be trusted and *what we say doesn't matter*.

Getting *complimented* for modes of behavior I've learned to survive, to behave like a person to whom it is NOT okay to do that to, is grotesque to me. I've learned to hide the parts of my brain that don't work, or just don't exist. There are aspects of my disability I will never be discussing with anyone. Even my closest loved ones. I can be happy, and I *am*, but I can never be *safe*. Luckily, most people can't even imagine *not* being able to do certain things. People see what they expect to see, in the context you present it to them.

It's so much easier for them to pretend I'm a big fake, that I'm making it up, than to confront the reality that these things happened to me. It's much easier and more comfortable to live in a world where bad things only happen to people who deserve it. Who would want to live in a world where someone with a college degree, who has a respectable job helping disabled people, who lives in a house with a partner and some cats, can be the same person who ten years earlier, could be beaten publicly in a car for ordering the "wrong" food? Who could be kicked out of that car and told to *walk* home?

One of those people is a monster, because only monsters deserve to be treated that way. One of them is a respected and loveable human being. One of them is Real, and the other is not. Can't be.

I almost broke myself earning these prizes: degree, bank account, college job, academic awards and recognition….so that I would be the kind of Person who mattered, so it would *matter that those things happened to me.*

I didn't realize that the only way for this Person to live, the one with degree-job-house-autonomy-respect, was that the other, that Other had to die. Has to hide, to be shoved down and made imaginary. The bawling, suffering, terrifying, terrified, abused *monster* has to die so this Person can live.

Are you ashamed of that poor, battered Thing? Will you slit its throat on the altar of respectability? Or did your innate knack for alchemy create a suit of armor to house its soiled flesh, its bruised pomegranate heart, and *will you keep it safe?*

Will you press your twisted face to the cold steel at night and whisper

I love you
I love you.

Florida, 2007: Paradise and the Phoenix

Every year in Southern California, babies die because their caretakers leave them in the car. It doesn't matter if the car is dark or light, or if you crack the windows; the internal temperature reaches over 130 degrees Fahrenheit in five minutes. For each baby that dies, about 150 pets go, and several elderly people left in hot cars, or sealed in small rooms without air conditioning. Most of the latter are written off as "natural causes". Public Service Announcements grace every commercial break from May until November, but pets and people die like clockwork.

In September, the hot winds blow up from Santa Ana and the chaparral dehydrates and twists skeletal plantfingers in supplication. Then, around back-to-school time, everything from the sea to the Cojon Pass, from the Grapevine to Encinitas *burns*. Every afternoon sun shines a choking orange, and the chaparral releases its oily seeds to be watered in the spring, when houses slide off the hills and rich people weep on the news.

To this day, I can't catch a whiff of even a campfire without thinking of the huge, cartoonish grade school calendars turned to September: the peach-colored cartoon kids with their old-fashioned bookstraps, the air and the ground plastered with the orange, red, and yellow leaves that I had childishly mistook for flames; I thought they, too, were on *fire*.

Florida was the greenest place I had ever seen. My mom had picked up and moved there with the whole "fan damily" when I was eighteen. The air felt like breathing water; I needed a shower from the exertion of taking a shower. My mother made broken jokes about the alligators who would sun themselves in the ditches, and at night I watched armies of armadillos run across the lawn in the moonlight while I nervously smoked cigarettes on the "lanai", a kind of screened-in porch that was necessary in the insect-laden Floridian air.

I spent long hours talking on that porch with my mother and sister. They both wanted answers, they wanted to know "what happened". They had been under the impression that my life was perfect, or close enough. Getting through the last decade had taken enough of their energy and attention; I never gave them a reason to worry. I spent at least a month just trying to get used to the climate, the wildlife, the absolute chaos of occupying a rather small house with my mother, two of my sisters, brother-in-law, and my three-year-old nephew, whose room I shared for the time being.

The first month, Mom was so glad to see me that she would spend whole paychecks on fancy deli cheeses, fresh cherries, imported dates, and arcane lotions with cocoa butter. My no longer fat-cheeked sister would spend hours preparing special meals that were consumed in nanoseconds and left the kitchen a total wreck. No one was really sure if I was visiting, or if I was coming to live there, or if I was just "taking a break". I couldn't help since I didn't know either; I was just so glad that they were happy to see me.

The day Chris Benoit murdered his wife and son and then committed suicide was the day I decided I was never going back. It seemed symbolically apt; Benoit had been my husband's favorite pro wrestler. I chain-smoked and drank coffee, the humid air wrapped around me like a fur coat. The sky was grey and pregnant with the promise of torrential rain that flattened the overgrown lawn every day from 3 to 3:30 pm, and again at 7pm. I felt cored like an apple. The last decade of my life seemed from this vantage point like a derailment; a detour from whatever life I was supposed to have been living during that time. For all intent and purposes, I was 17 again, not 27. It had been so long since I'd thought about who *I* was, what *I* wanted, instead of twisting myself into whatever shape was required to survive.

I heard the screen door bang shut behind me, and I tilted my face up to the sky and watched a silver cloud burst forth silver rays, although the sun itself remained hidden. Another bang, this time of thunder, and the afternoon storm drenched me to the skin. I felt like the chaparral that must burn to live; burn itself from stem to root in order to release those tiny seeds. Nourished by my own ashes and running down that hill, I knew that the life inside me that had been watching and waiting could finally green.

PART FIVE:

CULTURAL WORK & MOVEMENT BUILDING

Time Wars Tales: Legends of the Order "Her Sister's Keeper"

Bijhan Valibeigi

Olympic Peninsula, September of 1852

Eve had run for weeks. Perhaps, she thought, even months. The family who imprisoned her and killed her mother had taken her on a journey, across the mountains. Then, as soon as the family who claimed to own her had their backs turned, she simply ran away. Eve had no idea where she was going, or how she was supposed to get there. All she knew was that she could not wait around to be killed, like her mother. Only nine years old, Eve knew that, because of her dark skin, she was supposed to be valued less than those who were pale. They called her "slave", although she didn't know what that word was supposed to mean. She knew, deep down inside, that she valued her own life. Eve ran because she didn't want to die.

It was confusing for Eve to feel good and proud while sliding around cold mountain mud with an empty stomach and aching joints. She had nothing but pain in her body, coldness down into her bones. No shelter, very little food, and nothing but dirty water. Yet somehow she felt more

Human than she had ever felt before. No one was telling her where to go or what to do. She obeyed no one. And she felt good. She felt free.

Now, however, Eve was running out of energy. The life was ebbing from her. Her knees were weak, and it took effort to breathe. Eve had never been this exhausted, nor gone this long without food and water. Without help, Eve knew she would die. But she didn't know who she could trust.

Peering through the mists, ferns, and evergreen trees, Eve saw a Human-shaped silhouette. She couldn't tell anything else about the person, however. For a moment, her mind was filled with images of being dragged back to the family who killed her mother. Then, in another moment, her mind was filled with images of her death at the hands of hunger and exposure. The next moment after that was spent grappling with weighing the two against each other.

Finally, the fear of the latter death won out, and Eve cried out, "Help! Help me!"

The figure turned and began moving towards her. Eve's heart sank as she prayed that she had not made a fatal error. Her heart sank further when she realized the figure who approached her was cloaked in black from head to toe. Fabric flowed around them, making it difficult to tell where they ended and the clothing began.

As the six-foot tall figure drew very close, Eve realized that if this figure was not benevolent, she would not have the energy to flee.

"Mah sa Allah," the voice which came from the figure was feminine and flowery. Eve did not recognize the words, and assumed it was a foreign language. The voice continued in a strange accent, "Are you unhealthy, young person?"

Eve realized that she was looking at a woman who was wearing a cowl-like cloth, fixed to her head and flowing down her shoulders to just above her toes. The cloth covered her whole face except for a slit from which her striking purple eyes peered out. As the woman drew closer, Eve saw that underneath the flowing cloth, the woman was also wearing black pants, shirt, boots, and gloves. Other than the small tan folds around her eyes, she showed no skin. The only hairs Eve could see on the woman were her obsidian eyelashes.

"No," Eve responded, "I'm not healthy, Ma'am."

"Come with me," the woman said, extending a black-gloved hand to her. Eve looked into the warm purple eyes and at the hand extended to her, and decided to take a chance. As Eve grasped the hand, she noted that it was warm and soft.

"My name is Manijheh," the woman said as she led Eve down a fresh path, "What is your name?"

"Eve," she responded, "My name is Eve."

"Howdy, Eve," Manijheh said, her eyes twinkling, and her unusual accent making the word 'howdy' sound strange.

"Howdy, Meni...Manja..." Eve struggled to pronounce the name she had just heard.

Manijheh giggled, "You can just call me Mani."

The ferns became more sparse and the trees parted as Eve and Manijheh entered a misty clearing. In the middle of the clearing stood a simple cloth tent, in the style of teepee, surrounded by laundry, water buckets, and various other objects which Eve could not identify.

With Manijheh explaining and asking permission each step of the way, the adult took the child's clothes, washed the mud off her skin, set the dirty clothes to soak, and wrapped Eve in a thick woollen blanket to get dry and keep warm. After leading Eve into the tent, Manijheh began taking off her gloves and long clothing so that she could set a fire. Eve noticed that Manijheh had hairy knuckles and wide shoulders.

"Where are you from?" Manijheh asked.

"The Jones family," Eve said.

"No, where are you from?" Manijheh asked again, confused.

Eve furrowed her brow, "I... I don't know. Far away."

"Me, too," Manijheh said, "I'm not like most people from here. I was raised alone, by my grandfather. He was from even further away. I have never crossed an ocean, but he crossed many to get here."

"Why do you have such an accent?" Eve asked.

"I... uh..." Manijheh said, her eyes misting as she became lost in thought, "I did not learn to speak this language until I was an adult. Not until my grandfather passed away in the fire that destroyed our home, and I had to approach other people so that I could survive," she seemed to snap out of her memories, returning to her previous cheer, "I also speak Salish, but I was right to guess that you speak English."

As the fire began to burn hot, Manijheh continued to take articles of clothing off, revealing her face, arms, and hair for the first time. Eve gasped as she saw silky black hair cascade down broad, muscular shoulders, and around a neatly trimmed and styled black goatee. Eve scanned Manijheh's body, realizing that Manijheh had no breasts.

"I thought you were a woman!" Eve said.

Manijheh looked confused, "I am a woman."

It was Eve's turn to be confused. She looked down at her own body.

"How do I know if I'm a girl or a boy?" Eve asked.

"Are you a girl or a boy?" Manijheh asked.

"I'm a girl," Eve said without thinking.

"Then you are a girl," Manijheh said without blinking.

Eve was no longer confused.

Suddenly, they both heard shouting coming from outside the tent.

"Muslim! We found you, Muslim!" The voice Eve heard reminded her of the man who killed her mother, and who used to call Eve his slave. Her blood went cold. She knew it was not the same voice, but it carried the same timbre... and the same threat.

Manijheh began putting her clothing back on, spitting the mild curse "Khak," as she picked up a cloth roll from the corner, "Stay in here, child. They do not know that you are here," Manijheh looked into Eve's eyes and said, "No matter what happens, do not make a sound."

As Manijheh strode out of the tent, again shrouded from head to toe in black cloth, obscuring her silhouette, Eve peeped from behind the flap of the tent. Manijheh held the roll of fabric aloft, like a weapon, as she faced three strange men who wore dirty and burned animal pelts. One of the men was holding a shotgun, another a knife, and the third held an oil lamp.

The one with the lamp spoke: "Give up, Muslim. You can't take us all on. Not now."

"Kooft-e maan," Manijheh said, then clucked her tongue in disappointment, "Will you never learn? I killed your men in Ohio. I destroyed your fortress in Vancouver. As long as you pursue me, I will ravage everything you care about."

"I don't pursue you!" As the man spoke, his face twisted and fangs burst from the roof of his mouth, "I pursue the sword! Give it to me!"

"Never," Manijheh clenched her jaw.

"Shoot her!" He said.

Eve's scream of terror was masked by the sound of the shotgun's mighty blast. The buckshot tore through the air, propelled by the gunpowder explosion. When the shots hit Manijheh, her body heaved. But the shots do not go through her body. Instead, they fell to the ground at her feet.

As Eve blinked through tears, holding her breath, she realized that Manijheh's body had resisted the shotgun blast. Purple light was flowing from her eyes, swallowing her up in a protective cocoon.

The men did not seem surprised. Instead, they seemed chagrined. "I thought we robbed you of that trick," the man with the lantern said through grit teeth.

"I wanted you to think that," Manijheh said grimly. The purple light flowing from her eyes changed direction, ebbing back into her and filling her body with a brilliant luminescence. The place just below her heart glowed from inside her chest. She unfurled the cloth roll she held, and revealed inside a wickedly curved scimitar which shimmered bronze, green, and rose.

"You want this sword?" Manijheh taunted, her smirk evident in spite of her covered face, "I'll give it to you. Here."

Manijheh launched herself at the men. The sword was imbued with the glow of her body. As she swung the scimitar, the light reached out like the licking tendrils of a flame, then coalesced into a disk of purple energy. Like an arrow, the disk was sent through the air and towards its target. The man who held the shotgun was split in two as the purple energy moved through him and into the forest beyond, parting the cold autumn mist like a whisper through silence.

First the smaller portion of the defeated man's corpse hit the floor; then the second, larger portion. The man who had held the knife met a quick, and almost identical, fate.

When the purple disks of light came for the man who had held the lantern, they dissipated instead. Eve saw orange light begin to flow from the man's eyes, and his chest glow with orange light. Whatever power Manijheh had, it appeared this man possessed some version of it.

"This ends now," the orange-glowing monster said, his fangs squirming in his mouth like pointed maggots.

"You have no idea how true that is," Manijheh said.

As Manijheh swung the scimitar at the orange beast, he evaded the blade and brought both fists down on Manijheh's ribs. She withstood the blow, trying to bring the scimitar back to bare, but found the orange beast was swift enough to be behind her now. After he landed more blows to her back, he swept her feet out from underneath her.

When Eve saw Manijheh land on her face, her mind brought her back to the moment her mother had been killed before her very eyes. Eve resented being made helpless then. She would not be helpless now.

Eve left the tent and threw a stone at the beast whose eyes glowed orange. It winced, but it seemed otherwise unhurt.

As the monster's glowing eyes moved to fixate on Eve, the small girl screamed, "Leave her alone! Let her be!"

While the monster was looking at Eve, and not at Manijheh, she thrust the scimitar upward and into his gut.

"Kooft-e maan, when will you learn?" Manijheh asked breathlessly, "Never turn your back on me. Not even when I'm on my back."

Blood dripped down her sword and over her hands. The orange glow in the monster's eyes faded as the life ebbed from him. He slowly collapsed to the ground. She used her boot to push the corpse off of her blade.

"What is he?" Eve asked, "What are you?"

The purple light faded from the woman's body, and Manijheh was she was when Eve had first met her.

"All three of these men were Vampires," Manijheh said, "Dusty and I... we are something else..." She said this last sentence with the same faraway tone which she had used to describe the death of her grandfather.

This filled Eve with more questions than she could keep in her head at once. She had heard stories of Vampires: fanged demons who sucked blood to sustain themselves, and bit victims to make turn them into more of their kind. But she had never ever heard of people who had colored light ebbing and flowing from their eyes, giving them incredible powers.

Before Eve could ask if Manijheh was some kind of a magician or witch, she saw that Manijheh's eyes were filled with tears. Eve decided that even if Manijheh was some kind of user of magic, that she was still at least a Human being. When Eve realized that she wanted to be hugged, she realized that Manijheh—who had just fought monsters and risked her life—probably wanted to be hugged as well. Eve ran over and threw her arms around her new friend. Dropping the scimitar to the ground, Manijheh threw her arms around Eve in return.

They cried until they laughed. They laughed until they felt better. They packed up and left as soon as they felt better. And they stayed together.

Haikus

Maanu Alexander

Sorrow
Dead puppies are Stiff
The cold bites into their skin
Only two days old

Hope
Hopefully one lives
Innocent yet nearly dead
Sometimes life's not fair

The Phoenix
From ash comes new life
The Phoenix rises from death
The fire of life BURNS!

Dragon
The Terran beast flies
Releasing Flames of vengeance
'Till charred earth remains.

On the Disability Hierarchy

G.A.

Dear folks with physical disabilities,

Just a friendly reminder that each time you act like a massive a*****e towards people with invisible disabilities such as mental health issues, learning disabilities, brain injuries, etc., you are perpetuating what is known as the Disability Hierarchy and basically sending out a message to able-bodied, neurotypical people that its ok to keep mistreating and stigmatizing us all.

Cut that s*** out.

Person A: "Diagnosed disability, physical or mental or not, we all need to realize everyone is fighting their own struggles"

Me: "Doesn't give people the right to take out their crap on others. If I have to keep my own stuff under control due to the double standards I pointed out, so should everyone else" (4 people liked this)

Person A: "I totally agree G, and from personal experience how can I not? I was trying to put things in perspective for both sides. Don't want to cause more offense but awareness on FB."

Me: "I know you were trying to be neutral, but I wrote this in a fit of anger though and this was me just being restrained. Trust me though, spend some time in disability activism and you'd be appalled to see some hypocrisy and double standards. It makes me wonder if thats the reason legislation is so delayed because people are too busy tearing each other and competing in the "my disability is so much worse than yours" Olympics."

Person A: "Well said G"

<u>What sparked the post:</u>

I wrote this Facebook status on my personal account some time ago after an incident involving a student-run disability rights organization that I used to be a part of, where an accessibility issue took place at an event where my organization was one of the co-sponsors. I cannot reveal much of what exactly happened due to privacy issues, but road construction in that part of the campus at the time affected the accessibility of the event. For instance, the directions to the event were hard to understand due to the construction blocking the pathways, especially the ones accessible to wheelchair users. Although no one foresaw the particular incident occurring, my group apologized and did their best to fix it the moment they were notified. However, while checking the group's Facebook account for updates, an attendee affected by these barriers took to Facebook complaining, while at the same time, making statements that implied the board of directors (of which I was a part) was able-bodied and "only cared about our ally cookies". This triggered and angered me to the point where I had to sign off in order to avoid making a public-relations mistake in my rage. Fortunately, someone else from the board signed in and spoke to the person, but for me, the damage was done.

This incident provoked such a strong reaction from me because it brought back memories of other incidents where my accessibility needs were questioned or policed because I look so "normal and healthy" despite being autistic. Besides being on the spectrum, I also have other diagnoses such as ADHD and anxiety. In addition to neurotypicals' disbelief and comments such as how I don't look autistic, I often feel like a minority-within-a-minority as most of the other autistic people I interact with on a daily basis are white and male. While I have been fortunate in that my autistic friends and acquaintances have been understanding as best as they can be in terms of how their challenges differ from mine, it does feel isolating at times not knowing other autistic people of color.

That said, I have become used to neurotypical or able-bodied people not believing me when I disclose my diagnoses. What hurts me more, though, is that my issues are also not taken seriously by other disabled people when they themselves know what it's like to experience discrimination. It was another example of the Disability Hierarchy, in which some disabled people are considered "more disabled than others". I have seen it happening in subtle ways in my own experience, from a blind student questioning why learning disabilities should be accommodated because "those students took resources from her" to being shamed by a passenger with a cane on a streetcar once for daring to use a seat (I am prone to sensory overload during rush hour and was at risk of losing my balance). In a sense, it reminded me of unspoken issues affecting other communities such as:

- Anti-racism activism still maintaining racial hierarchies through the preference of lighter-skinned activists.

- Animal welfare advocates, especially in the West, in their push for stronger legislation against cruelty perpetuate racist stereotypes of certain countries.

- White feminists ignoring the importance of intersectionality

All these incidents and micro-aggressions aside, other autistic people have told me their own stories of similar treatment. I'm sorry to say, but as much as I care about accessibility and fighting ableism, I have left the disability rights movement since then due to the infighting, the double standards, and some people's unwillingness to admit that they may have contributed to ableism even if they themselves have a disability. I refuse to fight for my rights with people who forget that even if they lack able-bodied privilege, they can still engage in neuro-supremacy without knowing it, whether they call those with learning disabilities freeloaders or they do not speak out against stigma associated with mental illness. Dealing with ableism is already exhausting from neurotypicals, but seeing it within disability communities themselves truly feels like a betrayal.

I, too, am racialized.

Lydia X. Z. Brown

Content/TW: Brief discussions of violence and ableism, detailed discussions of racism and racist microaggressions.

I, too, am racialized.

I am constantly expanding my understanding of myself, my identity, my life, and my experiences as a racialized subject—what I mean by this is how I am made to have a race in my society and culture. I am Han and was born in China. I appear to be East Asian. Yet while I identify as a person of color, I am also transethnic. I am a transracial, transnational adoptee. My parents are white Americans of European descent. I was raised in a culturally white neighborhood in a city that is over 96% white. When I was a child and usually physically accompanied by my parents, I experienced the benefits of white privilege through my white parents. It is really only since coming to college and being physically separated and thus, dissociated, from my parents that I have increasingly experienced the violence of racism against me (especially in everyday racial microaggressions). Yet I have also become keenly aware of how I still benefit from the intersections of class (middle-class-ish) privilege, education privilege (I attend an elite four-year university), light-skinned privilege, and sometimes still white privilege (as when people assume from my name only that I am white, as it is not a stereotypically Black or Asian or Latin@ or Native/Indigenous name) and socialization as white.

For example, other people often assume that because my speech/writing patterns come across as articulate or eloquent, I must be educated (in my case, I am), and therefore, must also be upper-class/money-rich (in my case, I am not), and therefore, must also be white (and in my case, am also not).

In another example, I have frequently gone to check-in or registration desks at events or conferences and given my name so the staff person could check me off the list, only to receive confused comments about my not being white because my name was assumed to belong to a white person.

Yet I also had an encounter a year ago with the DC Metropolitan Police Department that at the time left me floored and shocked, but now comes as no surprise to me. After speaking to a white officer for about half an hour (including answering his questions), he excused himself for fifteen minutes and returned with an East Asian officer who spoke to me in Mandarin (a language I don't know or understand). When I said that I don't speak Mandarin, the East Asian officer gave the white officer an annoyed expression and said, "Dude, she speaks English." The white officer actually replied with, "How is that even possible?" I was standing less than a few feet away from them during this entire time.

(Sometimes people who appear East Asian, and probably are also Chinese, approach me and speak to me in

Mandarin, but that presumption on their part doesn't carry the same baggage as when non-Chinese people—though especially white people—assume that I speak Mandarin or any other East Asian language, or that I don't speak English.)

***

Since then, I have also had innumerable incidents during which complete strangers or acquaintances whom I'd met maybe a few minutes beforehand have intrusively and repeatedly asked about my ethnicity, ethnic background, national heritage, national origin, real place of birth, ancestral heritage, etc. This is even after I politely deflected. The presumptions behind these interrogations are that a) I must not be from the U.S., b) they are entitled to this information despite being perfect strangers, or that c) of course, I have a race and ethnicity, but they are just "normal" or "regular" Americans. White people also frequently compliment me on my accent when I speak English, whereas most people who appear to be white would never be complimented on their accent when speaking English without an obviously foreign accent.

Perhaps this is only quasi-related, but I also distinctly remember an experience when a South Asian friend (who is darker than me but also relatively light-skinned compared to many darker-skinned people of color) casually referred to me as a "white girl." The tone and context suggested that this was an offhand comment made as an observation of fact. Essentially, this person used the same tone someone might use to introduce me as their activist friend, rather than a tone that someone would use for an insult or sarcastic comment. This brief incident also made me more conscious of the fact that I definitely benefit from residual white privilege from my upbringing and socialization as white.

In another example of how I continue to benefit from conditional white-passing privilege, when I called the police to tell them that I would be leading a protest in their jurisdiction, my articulate, unaccented English combined with my name probably led them to assume that I was white, money-rich/upper-class, and educated—and therefore not violent and not dangerous and not a threat. If on the other hand, I had an accent on my English, a stereotypically Black or Latin@ (or maybe even Middle Eastern or South Asian) name, or did not sound as articulate when I speak, I might not have had such a cordial conversation with the police. They may have turned out in larger numbers to intimidate us the next day. They might have treated us as security threats either explicitly or implicitly. Even though there were darker-skinned people of color at the protest in question, because there were several white and light-skinned people (and more of them than dark-skinned people of color), and because I was the person who called in advance, we were probably not interpreted as a potential threat. (There may have been other factors in this presumption, but these were certainly part of it.)

***

I am also aware that as an Asian American novelist, if and when my novels are published, I may become the subject of dismissive criticism or extremely surprised acclaim among mainstream reviewers for writing about characters from Serbia, Pakistan, Iran, Yemen, Israel, and Germany on the basis that I am Chinese. Yet white authors who write about characters of races and ethnicities other than their own generally only receive similar, substantive criticisms from people of color, but often receive praise for realistic portrayals of their characters' cultural backgrounds and identities in mainstream media and similarly are assumed to be able to write from a "universal" perspective.

I am constantly learning and growing in my desire to be a better ally to darker-skinned people of color and to all the POC groups to which I don't belong (of which there are very many) in our quest for racial justice. At the same time, I am continually learning about the many ways in which my intersected experiences of privilege and marginalization have shaped me as a transethnic, transracially and transnationally adopted, Han Chinese American, East Asian person of color. I frequently learn where I have done wrong by my darker-skinned people of color friends and fellow activists and colleagues, and am trying to learn how to hold myself accountable for my participation in racist and white supremacist structures.

For example, in an older post on Autistic Hoya, I referred to Black people/African Americans/Africans as "blacks" (I think while also referring to white people as "whites"), and more recently, a Black friend of mine corrected me. I learned that using the term "blacks" to refer to Black people is dehumanizing and carries racist, white supremacist baggage. Because I am not Black or darker-skinned, I benefited from the privilege of never having had to learn this. In fact, if I hadn't changed my language and acknowledged the fuck-up, I would have faced minimal to no social or legal consequences.

411

My experiences have been complicated by the fact that while I am visibly East Asian/person of color, I have been socialized as white and therefore have benefited frequently from residual white privilege or conditional white-passing privilege, but also experience the reality of white supremacy and racism in my life. Living in the United States definitely impacts my experiences. For example, I know that my ethnic group, Chinese people, remains one of very few specific ethnic groups to have had a law specifically banning us from entering the United States, along with Japanese people, because of racism (and the myth of "yellow peril"). But in another example, I am also keenly aware that the form of white supremacy prevalent in the United States has historically and currently displayed its most overtly violent racism toward Black people/African Americans/Africans, Indigenous and Native peoples, and more recently, Latin@/Hispanic people. Right now, I am studying abroad in Jordan, where the racial and ethnic demographics and politics are radically different from those in the United States. Being a U.S. citizen also means that I must learn how to become accountable for my role (passive, inadvertent, unwanted, or otherwise) in perpetuating U.S. imperialism, especially in majority-POC parts of the world.

Most people who know me are familiar with my work for disability justice and civil rights. Sometimes, I experience the reductionism that happens when people hyper-simplify my identity and work to disability-only. But in the wake of continued racism (systemic and in microaggressions) in the disability communities, it is imperative for me to emphasize that I am not

412

merely *disabled* but also *racialized*. It is impossible for me to separate my experiences as autistic and disabled from my experiences as East Asian, Chinese, Asian American, and person of color.

This is why I am frustrated and disappointed when much of the visible leadership of the disability rights community is white (or if not white, able to pass consistently for white). That includes many high-level state and federal government appointees, board members and executives in disability rights organizations, high-profile activists and public speakers with disabilities, and disabled scholars, theorists, researchers, and professors of disability studies. This is also true of the autistic rights/neurodiversity movements as well as the disability rights movement at large.

This is also why I am frustrated and disappointed, as well as profoundly saddened, when cases of violence, abuse, and murder with disabled white victims receive significantly more attention than those where the victims are disabled people of color. Don't get me wrong—I am happy that over 150,000 people signed the petition demanding accountability after Chris Baker (who is autistic and white) was punished by being put inside a bag and left in a hallway. But how many people in the disability community paid attention to the case of Reginald "Neli" Latson (who is autistic and Black) when he was wrongfully tased, beaten, arrested, and imprisoned? His case received notice, to be sure, but at least a good majority of the people of whom I know attempting to publicize his case were also people of color.

413

This is also why I am frustrated and disappointed when disability activists speak about racism as though it's over, or dismiss racism as irrelevant to ableism, as well as when organizers for racial justice are completely ignorant to disability issues, or dismiss ableism as simply non-existent or unconnected to racial oppression and white supremacy. Just as I cannot separate my *disabled* identity and experiences from my *racialized* identity and experiences, I cannot recognize ableism without recognizing how it is affected by racism, or recognize racism without recognizing how it is affected by ableism. I frequently center my work on disability justice, but the struggle for racial justice is my struggle too.

AWN & WMDSC Joint Statement on Justice for Michael Brown

Deeply saddened and outraged by the refusal to indict Darren Wilson for Michael Brown's murder, the Autism Women's Network and the Washington Metro Disabled Students Collective have issued a joint statement calling for justice for Michael Brown.

November 25, 2014

On August 9, 2014, a police officer shot and killed Michael Brown, a young Black man, in Ferguson, Missouri. He was unarmed, but Darren Wilson shot him six times. Once dead, Michael Brown's body was left in the middle of the street for four hours. After three months of protests, community teach-ins, and actions nationwide, the St. Louis County prosecutor announced last night that the officer will not be indicted. The announcement comes without surprise to Black, Brown, and Indigenous communities that have long been victimized by police brutality. Officers responsible for the killings of unarmed people of color rarely face any real consequences for their actions.

Last year, George Zimmerman was acquitted of murder in his trial for killing Trayvon Martin, another unarmed Black man. In February, police shot and killed Yvette Smith, a Black woman, as she opened her own front door. Only days after Michael Brown's death, Los Angeles police shot and killed Ezell Ford, a Black man with psychiatric disabilities. In September, Provo police shot and killed Darrien Hunt, a Black man who was cosplaying a fictitious character. This past week, Marissa Alexander, a Black woman, pleaded guilty to charges filed against her for firing a warning shot at her abusive husband. Last week, Brooklyn police shot and killed Akai Gurley, another unarmed Black man. This past weekend, while the grand jury's decision in Michael Brown's death was still pending, Cleveland police shot and killed Tamir Rice, a 12-year-old Black boy.

Right now, Eisha Love, a Black trans woman, is facing attempted murder charges for defending herself against four men who attacked her. Neli Latson, a Black autistic man, is currently in solitary confinement stemming from repeated encounters with police and an original 10.5 year prison sentence after being profiled as suspicious and arrested while waiting outside his library in 2010.

State-sanctioned violence is rampant against people of color, especially those who experience multiple forms of oppression. Hundreds of unarmed Black people, trans women of color, and disabled people of color—many from low-income communities—are murdered with brutal, vicious violence every year. White privilege cannot be clearer than the benefit of the doubt extended to white people who claim they feared for their lives when encountering Black and Brown people, while Black and Brown people defending themselves from actual violence are charged and imprisoned without considering the circumstances.

Every year, the disability community holds vigils nationwide to honor disabled people who were murdered by family members or caregivers. Of the hundreds of victims on the lists that grow each year, the ones that receive most of the attention in the disability community tend to be white. Of the untold numbers of disabled people who experience police brutality, those whose cases are brought to public attention are typically white. This clear racial disparity is a replication of white-centric attitudes in larger society. The Washington Metro Disabled Students Collective and the Autism Women's Network believe that it is our moral responsibility to show solidarity for the low-income Black and Brown communities targeted by the vast majority of police brutality and Black and Brown activists and organizations leading the charge in the fight for racial justice.

While many members of the autistic and broader disabled communities are also racialized and low-income, it is imperative that _all_ of us recognize the necessity of supporting our Black and Brown friends, neighbors, and colleagues. We advocate not for vengeance or retribution, but for an end to the systematic violence of structural racism. We call for our community to show support for the families and communities of people who have been murdered by racist police violence and those who continue to face denial of any genuine justice. For those of us who are not impacted directly by police violence or anti-Black racism, we raise our voices—both metaphorical and literal— in support of yours. It is not enough simply to demand justice for disabled people or to be outraged when police kill _disabled_ people of color. Justice is for all, not "just us." The struggle for disabled liberation will never be complete without racial justice.

Black Lives Matter.

Lydia Brown, *President*
Nai Damato, *Board Chair*
Washington Metro Disabled Students Collective (WMDSC)

Sharon daVanport, *President*
Autism Women's Network (AWN)

This statement authored by WMDSC co-founder and AWN board member Lydia Brown.

Washington Metro Disabled Students Collective

Photo: Board Chair Nai Damato, President Lydia Brown, and member Allie Cannington attend CODEPINK's rally at the Department of Justice for Michael Brown, and the town hall afterward at Busboys and Poets. (August 2014). One sign has a drawing of a police officer with riot baton and says, "End the

War on Black, Poor Communities! Justice for Mike Brown!"
Another sign has a drawing of Mike Brown with hands up and
says, "Shooting an unarmed man with hands up 6 times is
murder. We all deserve better." Another sign says, "Wash. Metro
Disabled Students Collective in Solidarity with Ferguson.
#BlackLivesMatter." The last sign says, "We will not sit idly by.
#DisabilitySolidarity for Mike Brown."

How does it feel to be a neurodivergent heart?

Mikael Lee

How does it feel to be a neurodivergent heart?
Nebulaic star dust energy
Connecting familiar through the air waves
Our existence erased yet we find each other
Our thoughts labeled false by fabricated power though
we know truths carried forward by shamanic ancestors
Dangerous creators, causing revolutionary revelations
Madness labeled and locked away as wounded healers
and magic makers
Non-linear music, language beyond words
We come to each other
Again and again
Paint brush fingers poised to unlock our expansiveness
Coursing through time spilling out of chests into the
streets so strong
We begin again
How does it feel in our neurodivergent heart?
A song undirected surrendering to divine beauty
unraveled raw rhythm
of Home.

Undoing Racism & Anti-Blackness in Disability Justice

Lydia X. Z. Brown

Content/TW: Anti-Blackness, racism, police brutality, ableism, descriptions of violence

The post below the picture/fold appeared in shortened form as "Tackling Ableism and Racism in the Criminal Justice System" in the ENDependence Center of Northern Virginia's April 2015 newsletter for a special issue on intersectionality. In the wake of the unfolding catastrophe with Kayleb Moon-Robinson, an eleven-year-old Black Autistic student from Virginia convicted of virtually fabricated felony charges for an incident stemming from *kicking a trash can* and now facing potential time in juvenile detention, it seems especially relevant to share in its full, original version (with one small correction).

Not only Virginia, but nationally, we face a continued crisis of centuries of surveillance and policing of racialized bodies. Indigenous, Black, Latinx, and Brown people have always been the targets of state violence and the violence of structural racism. When combined with ableism, those at the intersections live in fear of constant violence

421

without any hope of justice. It's long past time that our movements, our organizations, our activists in the disability community start addressing our replication of white-centric structures and start challenging racism—and anti-blackness in particular.

Here's a start: Morénike Giwa-Onaiwu's petition for Kayleb & the ASAN statement on his case.

#BlackLivesMatter #JusticeForKayleb

Photo (Charlie Archambault): Kayleb, a young Black kid with glasses, wearing a gray hoodie, standing outside in a snowy driveway.

In February 2010, a passerby saw a young Black man outside a middle school library in Virginia and called the police to report a suspicious black male, possibly armed. After police arrived, an officer approached him, demanding identification. The young man outside the library appeared obviously agitated and distressed, and attempted to walk away calmly several times. By the end

422

of the encounter, eighteen year old Reginald "Neli" Latson and the officer had a violent altercation, and Neli was facing over ten years in prison for the crime of going to the library while Black and Autistic.

In 2009, two police officers approached a young South Asian man sleeping on the sidewalk. One officer claimed the young man pulled out a knife, which his partner later denied ever occurred. The officer fired four shots, murdering Mohammad Usman Chaudhry for the crime of sleeping outdoors while Brown and Autistic. The internal affairs review of the shooting found the use of lethal force had been within the scope of department policy.

Over the past six years, however, the largest autistic rights organizations led by autistic people have only occasionally addressed police brutality against disabled people. Only recently have our organizations issued public statements in such cases, demanding real justice for members of our community impacted by the violence of our criminal injustice system. It is no coincidence that most disability rights organizations, with relatively few exceptions, are led entirely or mostly by white people with disabilities. While police brutality certainly impacts white disabled people, such as eleven year old Emily Holcomb, arrested and removed from her school in handcuffs after defending herself against violent physical restraint, disabled people of color are particularly vulnerable to state violence.

Many activists within the autistic community will describe ignorance borne of ableism as the root cause for police violence against autistic and other disabled people. They will urge better outreach to police and prosecutors and training on developmental disabilities as the solutions. Yet they will rarely, if ever, acknowledge the equally insidious impact of structural racism not merely on which of us are most vulnerable but also on how our community responds. Police training is important and useful, but no amount of awareness training will erase unconscious ableism and racism. Outreach can lead to better outcomes for some, but those of us who experience multiple layers of marginality cannot rely on police as an institution to protect or serve us. Before they hear our presentation on respectful interaction with autistic people, they see Black and Brown faces and project racialized criminality onto neurodivergent bodies marked doubly by race and disability.

This is what intersectionality means: to practice social justice in ways that grapple with the complex impacts of multiple systems of structural oppression (or systemic injustice, if you will). For those of us who are non-Black autistic activists, that means recognizing that behavioral compliance, indistinguishability, and conditionally passing as neurotypical can be tools of survival for Black autistic people. Resistance to arbitrary norms of abled and neurotypical existence can take multiple forms. Survival and resilience can mean navigating complicated tensions between out and proud autistic existence and safety from racialized violence. Intersectionality demands complexity without easy answers or simple slogans, because the real lives of everyone in the movement are infinitely more complicated than single-issue politics can recognize. Intersectionality requires thoughtful organizing and intense labor if we truly seek to build more just and equitable communities.

we autistics, we villages, we humanoids

Jen Meunier (Gzhibaeassigaekwe)

Thirteen was the year of the shapeshifter.

Some pinhole of awareness broke through in my mind and my body realized the deep-down survival response that I needed to squeeze through the cracks in the small white town where I was born, to leave and not look back. Oriented in the direction of home, I observed and imitated white neurotypical mannerisms and like my mother and her grandmother, shape shifted into passing whiteness. Like her and hers, I wrapped it all in a bundle and placed it high in a tree where it would not be disturbed.

Because the people I come from believe in shapeshifters. The people I come from place their hearts in tall trees.

I left a world that was magically woven in colour and sound and light, a socratic melody of natural light where reality and abstraction moved together in waves, people were named in my language and my language was sound, shape and movement. Words lived on pages and gave rise to worlds that became more real than asphalt-desk-white-face-white-face. What I saw, when looking out the tall windows of my world, was chaos and unpredictability and it held so little meaning and anyway, was so unkind.

No doctor or psychologist diagnosed me with autism as a child or young adult. It's hard to describe other humanoids who lived in the same time-space because my perceptions were still my own then and took shape from what was important to me. A girl I called Herkimer after a carved swan I read about in a book. She had broad shoulders and thick blond hair and let me jump on her back and carried me. The solid firmness of my babysitter Cary's thighs pumping her bicycle pedals when she took me out for a bike ride. I saw other humanoids then as I see them now, in pieces and impressions whose matterness balances on the nature of their interactivity with my body, mind and spirit.

So I think, but can't be sure, that I was the only Native child and the only child-Autistic in the small white town north of Toronto where I was raised. I don't think that felt lonely then. It became lonelier as gender became that thing upon which all social meaning pivoted ever more sharply to a pointed edge I could not control. The edges of my femaleness were blurred and gave too easily into tree-climbing and ball-kicking and lone-schoolyard-wandering and I would not stay still to be painted or plucked.

As I grew older and tried to shave down my body into something acceptably feminine and white-'passing', the more my bones were stretched into a painful loneliness to fit the shape of an assimilated 'normal' body. I needed compassion, understanding and support. I needed to learn how to understand myself and be allowed to apply my understanding of the world reciprocally in an environment of safety and creativity. For so many of us, that was not what happened.

I knew one other Autistic adult, a woman my parents (who were foster parents) looked after for several years. She was of the generation whom Kanner theorized were victims of 'frigid mothers' and was taken from her family to a large, sterile institution where she lived from childhood to early adulthood. She was placed with my parents when I was about six. They spoke of her as though she was not there and made her eat alone. She used to rock and I loved her rocking. She soothed herself so well and when she cried, her powerful voice rocked the hateful house. She made the movements my body was paralyzed from and could not be quieted. I named animals after her and I loved her. In secret, I learned to bounce lovingly from toe to toe like she did and my shero's stims kept me alive. There were two times as a child that I slipped and rocked when I was not alone: on a long family car trip and at a friend's house. Both times the response was painful ridicule. Lock, lock buckle went my body into a still-stone shapeshifter. It's been twenty years since I have seen my sister.

I almost can't even re-read that it hurts so much. It is still hard to accept my own parents' reduction of disability down to acute unlovability. It is hardest to accept my own internalization of those cruel beliefs.

My white father sat me down and explained to me one day that his opinion was worth a dollar, that my mother's was worth a quarter and that mine and my brother's were a nickel and a penny. I asked, what about Ruth?* He said she 'didn't count' and that was how I came to realize that my value as a human would disappear if I ever let the still-stone down.

Talk, talk I must. Smile, smile I must.

'Oh, she is so articulate', they would always say. Little lifelines thrown from a gleaming white boat that would never permit me onboard. 'Oh, she is so articulate' and the disappeared-end would soundlessly grin 'for a retarded kid' and later I understood it to also mean 'for a Native'.

Thirteen was not a border where the line was crossed. The line was being crossed all the time. The days I stood on a line we drew on a dirt road and would not let the white men come and dig a landfill on an aquifer, or a whites-only suburb on treaty land, sacred ground. The nights we stood shivering in the headlights of their trucks and stared down dead-eyed cops in the morning. Those were days and nights when my autistic body and autistic mind began bursting with colour and light again because this body is sacred and made of dirt and water and old women's tobacco ties. This body is a lifelong love affair from childhood onwards, capable of deep relational insight. My body naturally demonstrates an essential and often forgotten principle of life on earth: reliance on the village of each other for a full and meaningful life.

My way of being in the world was something that nobody in the world around me had any knowledge or familiarity and this was more than a gap in the academic literature or the fact that Hans Asperger' treatise on Asperger Syndrome had not yet been translated into English.

This is an element they tried to disappear when villages were burned, when ships came and dead-eyed lies were told to us and promises were broken. This is colonialism brain-drain and what environmentalists might call a drastic reduction in biodiversity culminating in a dangerous reliance on destructive production. That is how they laid waste to the land and water; how they laid waste to we symbiotic creatures who live here and whose minds and spirits are created joyfully and powerfully neurodiverse. Autism Speaks spell neurodiversity like this: M-o-n-s-a-n-t-o.

I know Words now that I didn't know then, language that's been dug up and applied to the way my brain and body move and Be:

visual processing
why people and objects seemed to whizz by at impossibly
high speeds and lose their meaning

face blindness
why people become unrecognizable strangers when they
change context, clothes or hair

sensory processing
the reason why barking and clapping are so hand-press-ear
painful

dyspraxia
falling and tripping into doors and walls, why stairs
require such intense concentration,
why holding a pencil is so hard,
why my body tilts at an angle, why balls are so hard to
catch

429

and why my hands can make big moves but not small
ones.

echolalia
a language all its own, meaning understood in echoed
mirrors whose lean toward each other reflects the
common interdependence of living and unliving beings on
each other.

stims
emotion as movement, movement as emotion. body
expressiveness in a language broader and deeper than the
linear word can convey; ceremony;
a means of calm and a physical translation of joy.

*There is a protecting place in the orange chimney. Gym time at
school, when bodies careen past mine and threaten with danger, my
body stealthily makes its way to the orange stage curtains and
carefully wraps itself inside with a crack for my eyes. Years after
when needing relief, my hand draws thick orange borders around a
thin middle line of chaotic pain.*

We protect the places that protect us, and we are the
shelter of places that shelter us. We stand over our
mothers' bodies and sing them into their passing and we
stand on the treeline and sing down the loggers and
mines. At thirteen, I learned to protect the places that
protected me and though my language describes them as
external to my self, it was really me protecting me. Now at
thirty-two I am recovering body as nest and skin as
ceremony. I am finding acceptance for my needs within
myself and learning to communicate them to those who
love me.

My children will be wrapped in the love my body has taught me.

***

Now the task is to recover: language and memory, movement and making. The language of words that were stolen or forced into unsaid-ness. I must climb tall trees and take down the bundles that hung there in suspended imagination: words that come to life again that were of my own making and words that fell like leaves from my ancestors' mouths. Memories of a people who were never lost or are reborn under other names: we autistic, we two spirited, we disabled, we queers. We are humanoids whose value will not be quantified like coins or qualified as measurable units of exploitable lovability. Movement that more than just signifies meaning but moves spirit and energy, words as sound and movement—sound and movement as language with no colonial demands for standardization.

We will be raised and live in the village, loved and wanted because we are. Because we are We.

In his recent documentary, *White People,* Jose Antonio Vargas interviews young American people of color and white people about race and racism. When I watched his film, it made me realize how tightly privilege is bound up with fear. I hear white people talk about feeling 'victimized' by the very presence of non-white people. White police officers talk about Black and Brown men as though *they* are under siege. People of color bear the brunt of poverty, incarceration and violence so that white people can maintain material wealth, privilege in the criminal

431

legal system and can choose to do violence if their power is threatened, on an individual and a global scale.

Autism Speaks not only caters to this systemic fear-privilege, but suppresses the reality of systemic violence against Black and Brown autistic humanoids and silences our voices because we do not fit neatly inside the victimized-white image that makes autistic and disabled bodies marketable within a capitalist system. Even the idea of a 'cure' is inherently racialized because the "cured" body is white. The fear-privilege narrative of Autism Speaks hinges on perfecting the white male body and a powerful counter to that narrative hinges on autistics of color speaking in the forefront of that resistance and strongly centering queer and women-identified autistics.

***

Why are we the ones who are suddenly deficient because our brains are neurologically wired not to be so readily adaptable to social systems which are so uncritically accepted as normal? Why not put that normalcy to the test, instead of subjecting us to a constant battery of investigation that demands a cure for our nonconforming brains? What is it about autistic brains, and specifically our immunity to social conventions, that is so threatening that it demands 'therapies' that are designed solely to make us conform to white western norms? It's rare in the 'culture of cure' for these torturous practices to even be questioned, much more so to be named as violence. But we must question and name more deeply the violence of *what is being prescribed as normal* when it is itself so steeped in narratives of violence and racism.

I've heard that what it is about Indigenous bodies that provokes the violence of *windigos* and *wasichus* is our relationship to the earth, which is only 'unique' if you're living on another planet. It's not just Indigenous people whose 'way of life depends on the natural world'. All life on earth depends on the natural world and the gobbling-up exploitation that has been made 'normal' has created the delusion that violence: against the earth and against each other, can continue in perpetuity. The realities of an unfreezing Arctic, imminent flooding of coastal regions and the comfort of wealthy nations whose privilege is bought by slavery, war and genocide, say otherwise.

Much more is revealed in the narrative of resistance by autistic people than can be contained by any one movement. In the disability rights movement, we talk about disability as constructed: that we are disabled by a world that was not built for us. But the reality is that the industrialized world we have come to accept as 'normal' was not built to sustain life at all, only to consume it. Neurodiversity is part of a new scope of sight that needs to reach even deeper than social models of disability which retain the white colonial privilege of that delusion. Autistics of colour are among those who fall first and hardest to the violence against us that punctuates that delusion, and so our voices need to be heard across the movements that are rising today as we resist the final solution of 'curing' biodiversity. There is one common human disability that we all share and is not socially constructed: without air, without water, without land and without each other, our bodies, without exception, will die.

There's a doctor on the reserve who grew up here and she practices western medicine and traditional medicine in a two bedroom house across from the gas station. You take your shoes off and there's a basket of slippers and the waiting room has a kitchen where you can make yourself a cup of tea before you go in to see the doctor. No wonder the words rang so true when I read them: the feeling I get in that little house of healing has been called into meaning through the words the doctor has framed on her wall. You can see the poster when you walk in:

> "After Indigenous people become strong, have clear understanding of traditional values, and the ways and means to express such within the modern world, no longer living in fear of outdated genocidal policies and legislation, we will then start the process of 'Psychological Revillagization.' The people will have the frame of mind as our ancestors did while they were living in villages. Peace, power, righteousness will be an expectation of each member of this group. This will counter the current oppressed peoples survival tactics associated with lateral violence."

> (*Art of Peace*, Elizabeth Doxtater, 2014)

On Fancy Glass Doors and Slowly Dying

Ylanne So

They promised something—some*place*—safe and welcoming and warm. The first time she stood on the doorstep, waiting to be called inside, she wanted to start bouncing and spinning and flapping, and even though she knew that there were other people like *her* in the office on the other side of the glass door, she forced her body to stay still.

The glass was clean and polished, allowing her to see her reflection there, hesitance in her shoulders' tension, trepidation in the lips she chewed. Once the door swung open, inviting her in, she found herself at once an intruder in an unfamiliar environment where copy machines hummed and coffee gurgled in its pot and fluorescent lights buzzed faintly overhead. But for all the drudgery of modern office space, there hung the posters emblazoned with calls to action, with faces of people familiar to her from late night internet trawling and the occasional conference she'd dared enter.

The woman in the office, with a silk necktie and neatly combed blonde hair, probably not more than a few years older than her, rose to greet her, not quite making eye contact. "It's so great to meet you!"

But she didn't hear the niceties over the cheering inside her head as Meghan became real, as activism somehow moved from something that she only watched from the sidelines in comments section fights and online petitions, as she stopped forcing her hands to remain stiff and let her fingers unfurl to flap.

***

They promised a commitment to diversity, and the first through twentieth times she heard that, she believed it meant something. Especially before she started commuting off-campus to work a Real Job in advocacy when she wasn't spending her mornings in the stiflingly hot classrooms on the east side of the academic hall.

"We believe that we are made stronger not *in spite of* our differences, but *because* of them," said the white man with the red tie to polite applause, the one young student whooping quickly shushed with pointed looks.

"Students of color thrive here because of this community's vibrant diversity and emphasis on inclusion," said the only professor of color the administration had managed to pull away from a half dozen committee meetings scheduled during the same four hour block.

She could turn her head in the auditorium and find herself overwhelmed by a sea of white faces excitedly chattering about the most diverse environment they'd ever been in their whole lives. She sinks in her chair, imagining she's suddenly turned invisible, but she feels the stares on the back of her head even without turning around.

***

436

Being with Meghan is dizzying. And she learns that, from their murmured chats snuggled against each other under worn fleece blankets on their fifth or maybe seventh out-of-state conference together, from nearly tripping over her newly bought heels trying to keep up with Meghan's breakneck speed through the Senate halls. It's an emotional ride too. She notices changes in how other people *act* when she enters the room now that they know she's one of Meghan's people, when before she'd come here, they ignored her after "hi." She'd never known what it was like to be admired and addressed as Ms. before, especially from white people, and now—now, she has people asking her what does she do and does she have a card.

Meghan tells her she's made it. Meghan tells her she is Someone.

"You remind me of myself at your age."

When Meghan says that, warm shivers creep over her, and she tries to keep the flapping in, but then remembers that Meghan won't mind.

"I'm glad to know you," she says, beer in one hand, Meghan's hand in the other. "As a person. Not just ... not just an idea of a leader."

"You know, it's easy for people to forget that—to forget the human side of activists. But we have to remember that in the end, we're people too, or else we'll focus too much on *what we do* instead of *who we are*." Meghan smiles, knowingly, leaning against her, and she knows that tomorrow, it will start again with coffee at 8 and meetings starting at 9, that it won't end after the dinner reception, that, fuck, they'll miss the last showing of whatever that new movie was she'd heard Meghan talking about.

***

"Underrepresentation of students of color is a serious problem, and we should be encouraging more diverse applicants."

But there she sat, with the pale faces of administrators and admissions officers and student ambassadors around her, nodding eagerly at each restatement of the same problem, and by the time two hours passed, they'd succeeded only in reminding her that she needed to participate in these weekly rituals of self-righteous self-abasement if she really wanted to boost the numbers. If she really wanted to see faces like hers passing to the other side of the double glass doors with the university seal.

"Minorities are coddled here. Whites are afraid to speak their minds because if we do, we'll be shouted down with accusations of privilege."

But there she sat, trying to keep her hand steady on her phone as the messages scrolled down her feed, reminding her that she didn't belong, that she was only a manipulative liar, that she was not qualified and should never have been admitted in the first place. Pretending that she wasn't crying in the student commons, and inventing a socially acceptable excuse in the event someone stopped to ask if she was okay, and knowing that if she opened her mouth, the various configurations of words she'd arranged would remain interesting thought experiments and she would start bawling instead.

"And my family had to choose between rent and meals. What kind of privilege do you think I could possibly have, really?"

But she couldn't find the words to explain to this white man that she'd watched her white mother carefully counting change to make sure every penny went to the most efficient possible use, even while her some-kind-of-asian father took home six figures, because you could take the poor kid out of the shabby side of town, but you couldn't take the poor out of that kid. She couldn't explain how her father with three degrees to his name had to wait in the welfare lines when he started looking for work before he Made It, or how when he first met her mother, she assumed he was looking for a hooker and after the security officer walked over, he thought the man with the squinty eyes couldn't speak English even though he was from Here. She couldn't figure out a Socially Acceptable Way to explain why she wore her student ID around her neck in a desperate attempt to stop new frat pledges and construction workers alike from asking her "how much" (but remembered her mom had once turned tricks a few blocks away from home) and she wasn't sure she wanted to unmask that part of herself to him either. She had no way to explain to this white man, who had once railed against the supposed trendiness of AD/HD and Asperger's diagnoses, how or why the white disability counselor wouldn't believe her when she said she had dyscalculia and couldn't complete the math core requirement, and so ended up gracing her first semester transcript with a D and lying to her parents about how good her grades were.

So she looked at her hands and shrugged and didn't say anything.

***

From conference call to boardroom to hallowed government halls and fashionable evening galas with warm hors d'oeuvres with names she can't pronounce served on polished white plates by the only other yellow and brown and black faces in the crowd—Meghan is in her element.

But *she* is barely hanging onto the edge of her fancy spinning swivel chair, stuck trying to memorize the speckled pattern in the office carpet to keep herself grounded. When Meghan talks, she sounds like the Real Fucking Deal. In that confident, go-getter voice, with her pearl necklace and demure little earrings, Meghan is a secret radical in Executive Director's clothing. Meghan is everything she wants to be.

"We are happy to work with the Migrant Rights Alliance in pushing your issues, maybe putting out a statement on your legislative priorities or other campaigns."

She tenses, puts her hands over her ears, head down, screaming inside her head. She knows it's coming even though she prays she'll be proven wrong.

"But we would expect, of course, that you would do the same for our issues as well."

She swallows the lump in her throat and an hour later, writes an email with hands shaking so badly she has to try four times to spell Meghan's name:

Dear Meghan,

I wanted to share my discomfort at today's conversation with the immigration group. I don't think it's a good idea to treat disability rights and immigration rights as two separate sets of issues, since there are also definitely disabled people who are also immigrants. I think we can do much better at trying to practice intersectionality.

S —

She reads the same words until her vision goes blurry, finger hovering over the send button. In the end, she closes the window, email left unsent and saved in the drafts folder.

Later, she sits beside Meghan at their favorite sushi take-out counter, and when Meghan asks her how she thinks the call went, she finds a smile from somewhere to plaster on her face, and says she thinks it was great while Meghan reminds her they need to maintain an acceptable public face if they want the movement to remain credible and relevant for community stakeholders and major donors. (When she goes home, she has to google "return on investment" because she was too embarrassed to ask.)

And when the waiter with a face like hers has made it a safe distance away, where she knows she won't be heard, she asks Meghan again about why their fellowship cohort is still so white, and as soon as the words come out of her mouth, her heart starts beating faster because she can *see* Meghan's face stiffen. So much for that autistics-can't-read-nonverbals bullshit. She just barely stops herself from apologizing for asking, and tries not to squirm too much when Meghan says, well, they're trying. But hey, she should be happy because most of the fellows have disabilities, and that's a Big Deal because so many disabled people are shut out of civic engagement and public policy and whatever else they're doing these days. Unemployment rates and all that. There's never enough focus on disability, Meghan reminds her, and disabled people, well, we're a minority too.

Meghan politely pretends not to notice when she starts biting herself.

In the morning, she looks at the fellows' yawning faces as they come in for the day's seminar and counts the three of thirty who aren't as pale as Meghan. She counts them again and again, one, two, three, as if those numbers are the only things still keeping her in this world, and maybe they are.

***

They promised a place where she would excel, where others would value her unique perspective and contributions to the academic community.

But she knows better now.

The uncomfortable stares, the hurried glances, the sudden shift from chatter to silence when she passes in the halls; the slower, drawn out tones when they speak to her; the empty seats between her and the next student over; the occasional mocking giggle, the eye roll, the backs turning when she starts to speak; the invitations to happy hours and coffee chats and weekend parties that never come; the whispers about "special treatment," the constant commentary about her immaturity and lack of professionalism; the uptick in vocal register when they talk *to* her—like minuscule shards of glass, they cut, they cut, they cut.

They snicker when they see her coming.

Fuck.

And she knows—she *knows* how much privilege she's gained, how her friends back home have never ended up in places like this, will never get the fancy parchment paper with Latin and ostentatious signatures, but, she's lucky if she doesn't slice her arm open at the end of the week.

They promised a place where she could work from her passions, where people like her would be central to the conversation and the advocacy community.

But she knows better now.

She's seen five or six new faces in the office since she started there, and watched them come in bright and eager, some flapping and jumping the way she wanted to when she first arrived, only to watch them slink out the back door while Meghan shook her head in disapproval at their lack of professionalism and inability to fulfill their core job responsibilities. She's listened to Meghan laughing about how insufferable their state guy in Oklahoma is, and sat in the corner like a trophy when the all-white board came traipsing in for their annual meeting, and pretended she was capable of ignoring the sinister text messages and emails from back home telling her she's a sellout. (Meghan told her not to respond and fuel the flames.) She's learned how to spin broadcloth into something shiny and disguise bullshit as gourmet chocolate for the sake of their funders and the Public Image that Meghan keeps talking about.

She's learned to mimic their scripts, to keep her flapping behind closed doors, to have crisp, fresh business cards and a firm handshake at the ready. But they know her, they fucking *know* her, and she knows too that she does not belong here, that her mask is too transparent, that her can't be Acceptably Queer or Quietly Disabled, that her face is an inconvenient reminder that "community" can't mean "white community."

They nod and smile when she talks, but when she leaves, they throw her papers in the rubbish. Fuck.

She comes home to an empty house and kitchen table covered in a thin layer of dust, and screams, and throws things, hoping they'll break, to the floor—coffee mug, last night's papers, the pens from the last conference hotel where she's been.

Meghan tells her she's okay. Meghan tells her to breathe. Meghan tells her she belongs. Meghan tells her she'll come out of this alive. Meghan tells her she is important and valued.

She looks at her pay stub and sees she made $800 the last month (after Meghan gave her a raise) and can't figure out if she'll have enough for rent, or whether she'll make it through another few years before she might have a degree printed on fancy paper to bullshit her way to a salary and her own polished glass door or whether she'll be banging to be let in after hours in the hopes of finding someone with only one face instead of a dozen or more different ones, a hero whose shadow wouldn't give her chills— or whether, if she tears down the walls and she's lucky, she might find some hope of home there.

Meghan hugs her, squeezing tightly, then has to rush to catch a flight. "I've always got something to do for the movement," Meghan says with a rueful smile.

She sinks to the floor, email pinging every few minutes, ceramic shards scattered over the tiles, no degree in sight, not sure how she'll make it through the glass doors the next morning, not sure how she'll see well enough through the liquid rising in her eyes to put something on the stove. All she knows is, they made promises she's not sure they could have ever kept, and she's here sobbing in the kitchen, with a knife in one hand, slowly dying.

PART SIX:

AUTISTRY

Taiyo Brown

Closed Toe Sandals

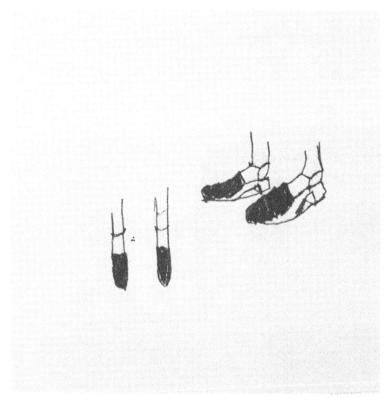

Photo: Drawing of two views (side and top views) of Jennifer Lawrence's closed toe sandals. Black ink on white paper.

Brooke Candy

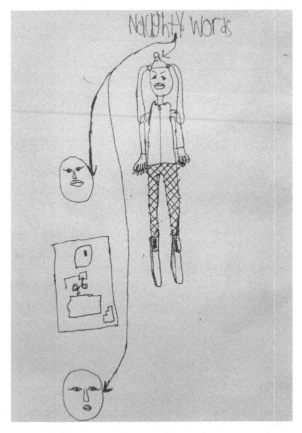

Photo: Drawing of rapper Brooke Candy. She's dressed in fishnet stockings and 12-inch platform shoes and a zip-up jacket. She has two long pigtails, and two bubbles on top of her head. Her face has sharp dark eyebrows and full lips. The drawing has two arrows to show her face two more times. The faces show "Brooke Candy's potty mouth." There is also a small rectangle drawing in the lower left side of the Kahler Apache Hotel Waterpark. Black ink on white paper.

Taiyo Brown

Abstract Painting

Photo: Painting of a fish, Abstract painting. Bold crossing lines with thick brush strokes. Thick lines are mostly black, with some bright green, blue, yellow, and red mixed in. Watercolor on white paper.

Yvonne Christian

The Wild Side

Artist's note: I did this one on a Saturday night in October 2013 with a few other paintings while watching a horror movie on TV. I ended up calling this "The Wild Side" because I had heard that singer Lou Reed had died. I always liked his song "A Walk on the Wild Side." Some of my paintings are named after rock songs. I was using my acrylic paints and working with bright and dark colors with this one.

Deion Hawkins

Cat

Photo: Cat - Loving animal

Deion Hawkins

Lion

Photo: Lion - Strong and fierce

Deion Hawkins

Swimming lion

Photo: Swimming lion - New experience

Mikael Lee

Music Open Body

Photo: A guitar surrounded by bird anatomy embryos and wings.

Mikael Lee

Flight Containment

Photo: A collection of bird wings in various shapes and sizes centered with a small box. The idea behind it is flight that is stronger than containment.

Mikael Lee

Flight of Sound

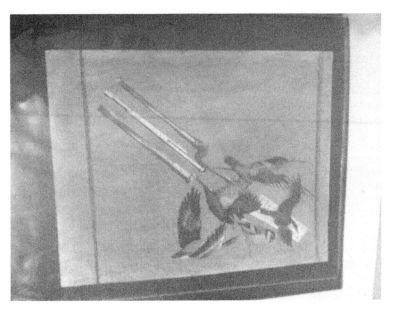

Photo: A variety of wind instruments with various birds coming out of the end pieces. Idea behind it: The connection of music to the natural world, flying through sound.

Rikki Katherine Lee Moses

Blues

Photo: "Blues." I felt happy because it reminds me of "Blues Clues."

Rikki Katherine Lee Moses

Light

Photo: "Light." I felt the colors represent different shades of light.

Story by Vivie Bella Papaleo
Illustrated by Monica Mangano

KOOKYMAKA

I am Vivie, and this story is a real life experience for me at age 3, and I gave the neologistic onomatopoeia title of "Kookymaka" to the sound my tummy makes when it burps at nighttime. My cat Bubble is my accomplice in making food choices. Writing/telling life lesson stories is my passion.

Summary:
"Kookymaka" is what a little girl calls her tummy burping at nighttime. The sound occurs because she is a picky eater. The sound only disappears when she makes healthy substantial food choice throughout the day instead of wrong food choices in being her favorite grape jelly and frosting.

Below are the 2 storyboards and the story text of 12 pages:

Page 1:
My name is Vivie. I am a precocious toddler. Do you see this awesome looking chocolate frosting jar on mommy's countertop? I do and it looks yummy! I am about to get on the bus for school, maybe I could take it with me in my backpack. Mommy won't know...

Page 2:
Ah! Genius! I will put the frosting in my blingy jewelry jar and then mommy will think it is a show 'n' tell day. Off the school!

Page 3:
At school my friends at lunchtime are perplexed by my eating from a jar instead of a sandwich. But here's the thing: I do not like regular lunches. I am different, and chocolate frosting makes my princess powers stronger!

Page 4:
It's my bedtime...uh oh my tummy is burping. That burping hurts and rumbles. I call it KOOKYMAKA. What do I do? Mommy will be upset if she knew I only ate my favorite best frosting in the world for lunch.

Page 5:
I cannot take the KOOKYMAKA any longer... "Mommmmyyyy!!!" My cat Bubble snickers while cuddled on my bed. She knew this would happen, she encouraged me to do it! No time for the blame game, must resolve this now.

461

Page 6:
Mommy came into my room and it's like she already knew what was going on. Well, she noticed the empty frosting can in the garbage. She wanted to teach me a lesson. "Vivie you cannot live on just eating chocolate frosting!" she said with a smirky smile. "I made you some healthy chicken soup and I hope you will make better food choices from now on. You are a big girl now Vivie." I sweetly said, "yes mommy, I will, I promise!" I ate the soup and my KOOKYMAKA disappeared.

Page 7:
The next morning I woke up feeling much better. It was breakfast time. Bubble stood next to me and gave me a mischievous look as we gazed up at my other favorite thing to eat...grape jelly. I could eat that whole jar!

Page 8:
The craving was there and was in full gear. I grabbed the grape jelly!

Page 9:
I ate the grape jelly so fast before mommy woke up and it was heavenly! I was in my glory and could feel the sugar, oops, I mean my super princess powers about to kick in...

Page 10:
And then it happened, the KOOKYMAKA returned! Argh...

Page 11:
I begrudgingly looked up at the apple and banana on the left on the shelf and knew that the only way to make my tummy burping go away was to eat something healthy.

Page 12:
So I did. I ate the banana. It worked. Bananas make me feel better and I still have great energy eating healthy. Mommy was right and I will eat better from now on.

FINIS

Emma Rosenthal

L.A. Paradise Chimera: The Toxic Landscape

The Toxic Landscape consists of 4 photos within the larger, work: Los Angeles Paradise Chimera which is a photo-poetic series comprised of distinct thematic chapters of photography. Each photograph includes one or two short poems the length of a social media "tweet" of 140 characters or less. The image and text convey the photographer's dialogue with the city, exploring themes of economic inequities, alienation, discrimination, race, culture, dis-ability, convergence, the environment, connection, disconnection and community.

The images in The Toxic Landscape are shot with medium format color slide film and processed in a negative color wet lab and cross processing to challenge assumptions and expectations of color, taking a situation that is color predictable to create images that appear surreal and counterintuitive to illicit a contradictory feeling of toxicity and beauty in a disconnected landscape.

Using a plastic camera, the images are soft with light leaks that produce unexpected shots of color and the absence of photographic data within the image.

Format: Medium Format
Camera: Diana F+

Film: Crossbird 400 or Fuji Slide film 400
Number of Prints: 4
Paper: luster
Size of Print: 8x10

#1 **View from 55th Street: Alameda Corridor, Los Angeles, CA**

hope is a dangerous emotion promising beyond what it can deliver.
this mass of freeway & distance stole my heart & dreams so very long ago.

Text: hope is a dangerous emotion promising beyond what it can deliver. this mass of freeway & distance stole my heart & dreams so very long ago.

#2 Industrial Studio Drive by and Self-portrait: Alameda Corridor, Vernon, CA

windows open north, bathing the room in diffused light. will we create truth or delusion? can shelter be found in imagery & verse?

hidden in the mirror of photo static memory; a drive by conspiracy of lens & car & eye. i capture you in a micro-second of frozen time.

Text: windows open north, bathing the room in diffused light. will we create truth or delusion? can shelter be found in imagery & verse?

hidden in the mirror of photo static memory; a drive by conspiracy of lens & car & eye. i capture you in a micro-second of frozen time.

#3 L. A. River, Skyline and Jail, Los Angeles, CA

women die in here, behind steel bars. these are tall buildings that
hide what we do not want to see. a concrete basin guides the river past.

Text: women die in here, behind steel bars. these are tall
buildings that hide what we do not want to see.   a
concrete basin guides the river past.

#4 Public Utility Plant: State Street, Pasadena, CA

the vines promise to redeem the earth of all the abominations of
capital & greed. there is a path, a roadway, a rail to take us away.

Text: the vines promise to redeem the earth of all the
abominations of capital & greed. there is a path, a
roadway, a rail to take us away.

Emma Rosenthal

L.A. Paradise Chimera: Postcards from the Nether World

Postcards from the Nether World consists of 4 photos within the larger work: Los Angeles Paradise Chimera which is a photo-poetic series comprised of distinct thematic chapters of photography. Each photograph includes one or two short poems the length of a social media "tweet" of 140 characters or less. The image and text convey the photographer's dialogue with the city, exploring themes of economic inequities, alienation, discrimination, race, culture, dis-ability, convergence, the environment, connection, disconnection and community.

Cross processed photographs to be scanned and printed in the size and format of a postcard.

The images in Postcards from the Netherlands are shot with a 35mm camera using color slide film and cross processing to challenge assumptions and expectations of color, taking a situation that is color predictable to create images that through cross processing, appear surreal and counterintuitive.

Using a plastic camera, the images are soft with light leaks that produce unexpected shots of color and the absence of photographic data within the image.

Format: Panorama sprocket 35mm
Camera: Diana F+
Film: Crossbird 400 or Fuji Slide film 400
Number of Prints: 15
Paper: lustre
Size of Print: 4x6

#1 Alley-Cyan, Alameda Corridor, Los Angeles, CA.

twists and turns, take me from the street to the spaces hidden from sight. will he find me or will i die here in the shadows?

Text: twists and turns, take me from the street to the spaces hidden from sight. will he find me or will i die here in the shadows?

this industrial landscape is a maze of intricate tools of mass destruction. the viaduct to our precious way of life.

Text: this industrial landscape is a maze of intricate tools of mass destruction. the viaduct to our precious way of life.

it is this, our delicate dance with the machines of death hoping they will illuminate the dawn.

Text: it is this, our delicate dance with the machines of death hoping they will illuminate the dawn.

#4 Water Tower-Yellow, Alameda Corridor, Los Angeles, CA

the water tank holds sustenance high above. on hot days we serve
tea right out of the vessel. let us have a party under industrial skies.

Text: the water tank holds sustenance high above. on
hot days we serve tea right out of the vessel. let us have a
party under industrial skies.

#5 Water Tower- Cyan, Alameda Corridor, Los Angeles, CA

the availability of potable water is not universal. i reach up to the stolen drink. it is always here when i have thirst to quench.

Text: the availability of potable water is not universal. i reach up to the stolen drink. it is always here when i have thirst to quench.

475

Contributors

Amanda Filteau is a biracial person, currently a law student. They spend a lot of time thinking about what racial identity means when you look racially ambiguous.

Angel A. McCorkle. Born and raised in sunny San Bernardino, California, Angel is a black freelance writer, film/ TV production major, and comedian for pretend. They spend most of their time playing with dogs, writing, and thinking of a third item when listing things. She has been known to switch pronouns, but prefers "they" if you're not close.

Anmei He exists with her husband, their pets and not enough book space. She speaks three languages, reads two and has a foul mouth in one. It is her hope to one day speak and write with an ideal level of skill and sarcasm.

Bijhan Valibeigi is the creator of Time Wars Universe, the free role playing game of time travelling espionage Strike Team, and the world's first deck-stacking game Supreme Command; she has also written the Time Wars Tales series, which includes the book Beginning of a Bizarre Friendship and the action adventure fiction blog Legends of the Order. When Bijhan is not pwning newbs in every kind of game ever made, hating on TNG for being objectively worse than Star Trek, or cheering for the BC Lions, she spends time at home with her partner RaeRae, three lovely cats Reza, Kya, and Jasper, and old cranky dog Elsa. For more Time Wars: Legends of the Order, visit TimeWarsUniverse.Wordpress.com. To explore the Time Wars Universe through games, novels, and more, visit TimeWarsUniverse.com.

Cindy Facteau (Fragmented Perfection) has served on the board of directors of the Autism Society San Diego since 2009, and is the current President. She is also a member of the Autistic Self Advocacy Network (ASAN). She is an autistic mother of two autistic children, ages 18 and 8. Married and divorced before age 20, she has been happily remarried to a 13-year Marine Corps veteran since 2002, and served on the commanding general's advisory committee for the Exceptional Family Member Program while living on Camp Pendleton.

Cindy is a child abuse, rape, and domestic abuse survivor. She was homeless as a teenager until placed in a group home after a drug overdose, making her a ward of the State of California. She challenged out of high school, began college at 17, and successfully fought against being conserved. She moved out of the group home before her 18th birthday, and has lived independently ever since.

Cindy identifies as a bisexual human being of mixed ethnic blood that secretly wishes she were a Time Lord instead...because she also strongly identifies as a nerd. Her more earthly interests include writing, music (listening to and playing), and frightening conservatives everywhere with her ethos and appearance.

Christopher Tucker has been a Social Media Ambassador for BreMobile Inc. since June of 2015. Before that he has held a number of jobs in different fields, including a stint at E-structors Inc. / Sims Recycling Solutions for one year and seven months as a Material Sorter. He has also done volunteer work such as his work with the UMD Campus Food Pantry in the Spring 2015 semester. He graduated from Howard Community College in 2011 with a degree in General Studies. He currently attends the University of Maryland College Park pursuing a degree in American Studies which he started in 2013.

Confessions of a Black Rhapsodic Aspie (COBRA) is a twenty-something-year-old Black Aspie male whose special interests span from instrumental music to card games, video games and anime. If you wish to know more about him, follow his blog at https://confessionsofablackrhapsodicaspie.wordpress.com!

Daniel Au Valencia is an actor—by life, not by trade—which he loves to remind people of because they often think of "autistic actor" as a contradiction like blind painter or deaf musician, even though blind painters and deaf musicians exist also. Strangers almost always perceive him as a white, neurotypical man, when really he is Jewish, Cuban, Autistic, and probably doesn't have a gender. Daniel's special interests include acting (what a surprise), sign language, and Autistic culture. His favorite stim is tap dance. Daniel Au Valencia blogs under the name **Acting NT**— http://ActingNT.blogspot.com.

D. **Campbell Williams** is a married public health graduate student, coffee addict and autism advocate. In addition to being Aunt to 7 nieces and nephews, she enjoys writing, travelling, and learning about social justice issues, particularly as they relate to the black community.

Dee Phair (sometimesdee) is of African and Caribbean descent, and discovered her autism diagnosis in her mid-thirties. She is currently focusing on raising her two bi-racial sons, and spends what little spare time she has singing in choirs, playing video games, and joining online political debates.

Deion Hawkins is a handsome, Black male, age 21 with autism. He is verbal, has challenges with attention and expressive language. He takes a private art class at Art Works Now in Mt. Rainier, MD he started in late 2013. With challenges in fine motor skills, he began using tracings. With expertise and compassion of his instructors, today he is drawing free hand and loves the art.

Ebru Çelik is a queer second generation Turkish immigrant and scientist from the UK. Her interests are: neuroscience, mental health, the social roles of psychiatry and diagnosis, far left politics: namely both structural and interpersonal power relations; other people's life stories, sexuality, music and literature.

Eliora Smith is a white-passing Ashkenazi Jewish person. They spend most of their time thinking about time travel and wishing they were a dragon. While they do that they also write, tweet, make jewelry, and cuddle with their cats.

Elly Wong is a student at Syracuse University. They are Chinese-American and a child of refugees. Elly likes magical realism and disability, two things which they do not think are unrelated. They are interested in disability policy, democracy and disability, and fictional characters with strange brains and strange genders.

Emily Pate is an autistic TV/sketch writer, actress and mother to a fabulous autistic boy. They live in San Diego. Think DIEHARD, but with a single mom living in California. Just kidding, she's never seen DIEHARD. Is the main character a single mom? Because she might watch that. Emily spends her days working, devouring film; tv; and internet articles, going on adventures with her kiddo, writing, and procrastinating writing. It's really more like FRANCES HA, but if she had a kid, and it wasn't set in New York. She runs a spoof blog and is working on a dramedy series. You can read her funnies at ameliaflor.wordpress.com and connect with her on twitter @msemilymarie.

Emma Rosenthal is an artist, writer, educator, urban farmer, human rights activist, and award winning emerging photographer, living in Southern California. Her work combines art, activism, education and grassroots mobilization and is impassioned, sensual, political, life affirming and powerful. She explores the use of art and literary expression to elicit an ethos more compelling than dogma and ideological discourse, providing new paradigms for community, communion, connection and human transformation. As a person with a disability she is confined, not by her disability but by the narrow and marginalizing attitudes and structures of the society at large.

She has been a featured poet and speaker throughout Southern California at a variety of venues and programs including; The Arab-American Festival, Highways Performance Space, The Autry Museum, Barnes and Nobel, Poetic License, Borders/Pasadena, Beyond Baroque, Freedom Fries Follies (a fundraiser for The Center for the Study of Political Graphics), KPFK, Arts in Action, Chafey College, UC Irvine, Pasadena City College and Hyperpoets.

Her work has appeared in several publications including Lilith Magazine, The Pasadena Star News, The San Gabriel Tribune, The San Gabriel Valley Quarterly, LoudMouth Magazine (CSLA), Muse Apprentice Guild and the following anthologies: Spectrum: An Anthology of Southern California Poets (Spectrum Publishing 2015), Dreaming in Public, Building the Occupy Movement (World Changing Press, 2012), Shifting Sands, Jewish-American Women Speak Out Against the Occupation (CreateSpace Independent Publishing PlatformS2015), Coloring Book; An Eclectic Anthology of Multicultural Writers (Rattlecat Press, 2003). Her work has shown in several galleries in the Southern California area, including 135 A Collective Exhibition, the Galleries at Whittier College (Light Among Shadows: Human Rights Heroes), and Pasadena City College, as well as Beans and Leaves Coffeehouse in Covina, CA.

Emmalia Harrington is a multiracial cisgendered non cissexual autistic woman. She's still surprised that she's an adult, which isn't as scary as others have said.

She's making forays into being a published author and is happy to contribute to this book.

Miss Fabien is a British and Afro Caribbean singer and songwriter who enjoys spoken word, anime watching, and Xbox playing. She is also a support worker.

Finn Gardiner is a queer, black, autistic community activist of West Indian and Black American descent. He holds a degree in sociology from Tufts University, and has extensive experience with community advocacy, peer education, and activism, primarily in the disability and LGBTQ+ rights sphere. His work is primarily focused on social inequality, the achievement gap, and working toward an intersectional view of disability rights. Finn currently works for the Autistic Self Advocacy Network as the Boston Community Coordinator and the Institute for Community Inclusion as the 2015–2016 Barbara Wilensky Gopen Fellow, and serves on the Massachusetts Attorney General's Disability Advisory Committee. He lives just outside Boston with a black cat and an excessive number of books.

G.A. is a university student, of Latina (ethnically Mestiza) origin, from Toronto. She struggled academically and socially in school during her childhood, being bullied and abused by peers and teachers in the process, due to beginning school not understanding English, as well as not learning quick enough for neurotypical standards. Despite this, G.A. managed to eventually enter university through a bridging program after a disastrous attempt at college, where she was finally assessed and diagnosed with several disabilities, of which autism is among them. In addition to rediscovering a love of learning on her own terms, G.A. is also a nerd with interests such as reading, Star Wars, neuroscience, NASA missions, chocolate, memes, and chilling with her cat.

HarkenSlasher is a Filipino Software Engineer working in one of the top earning BPO companies in the Philippines. He went to a university somewhere in Manila majoring in Information Technology. While not geeking it out with the computers, he enjoys most of his day daydreaming, wiki walking and figuring out how the social cogs of love and relationships turn. You can find more about him through his site at neuroblending.wordpress.com.

Helene Fischer is a Sequential Art student at Savannah College of Art and Design. They grew up with a Cuban mother and a White father, and were diagnosed with autism at the late age of 18. Helene frequently advocates on their campus for the inclusion of and accessibility for disabled students, especially those with neurological disorders. Their comic "Monster Girl" (coloring by **Krissy Baxter**, another autistic student) was a project intended to heighten awareness of the struggles autistic people experience while interacting with neurotypical individuals.

Jane Strauss was autistic without portfolio for most of her life, being diagnosed in middle adulthood. She has always lived on the margins. Her identity is and has been as a middle eastern person who is not even welcome in parts of the middle east. She attempted to fit into majority culture and found that discrimination was alive and well, so she stopped that game. She is a lapsed thespian and techie, attorney in remission, parent, writer, activist and photographic artist.

Jen Meunier (Gzhibaeassigaekwe) is a two spirited, Algonquin, Autistic and disabled human and all those names give her feelings of fierce pride and gratitude. She is currently completing her second degree (in adult education) and has a long history of resistance within land defense and environmental/social justice movements. Her life work is writing, caring for people through hard times and creating spaces for healing. Current hand-flappy-worthy interests are coppicing, mournful folk music and Star Trek. She lives with two cats, a little dog and a LaForge-like human. Text is her first language, speaking is a distant second and Jen communicates best using AAC. You can write to her at thesheelephant@yahoo.com.

Jennifer Msumba is a 39 year old bi-racial autistic adult. Her father is from Malawi, Africa and her mother is Italian. She grew up in a mostly white suburb of Boston, MA. She is a survivor of years institutional abuse, growing up in facilities since the age of 15. Besides writing and speaking about her experiences, she is a professional pianist and enjoys her family, friends, animals, Pez collecting, Lego/Nanoblock building and being outside.

Jessa Sturgeon originally planned to major in physics and computer science but quickly fell in love with philosophy after taking a seminar in the philosophy of chemistry during her first semester of college. Her favorite areas of philosophy are language, cognition, perception, and science. She is particularly interested in the effects of many philosophers in these fields either failing to consider how disabilities relate to their arguments and models, or else explicitly rejecting them as irrelevant outliers. Jessa was diagnosed with autism and other disabilities as a child. She is mixed race but primarily identifies as Korean-American. Currently studying law, she recently celebrated her first anniversary with her also autistic husband.

Joseph "Joey" Juarez was diagnosed with Autism Spectrum Disorder (ASD) at the age of three years old at UCLA NPI currently the UCLA Semel Institute for Neuroscience and Human Behavior. Joseph was Nonverbal until the age of 10 years old. His early education included attendance in public education: Kindergarten-Special Education Program. Joseph attended Public Education (1st through 12th grade)—In a Full Inclusion Program, with the support of a one-on-one instructional aide with academic accommodations. He received the Academic All American Award, USA Water polo in 2006, Waterpolo Student Athlete of the year 2007 for Commerce Aquatics; graduated Whittier High School with honors and 4.25 GPA in 2008, earned UCLA Bachelor's Degree -BA major in Sociology- in 2013, UCLA MA Graduate Student admitted in 2014 with a focus on Human Development and Psychology (HDP) Major/Autism Research. Department of Education, Projected Master's degree/graduation: June 2016 and currently member of the Master's Waterpolo team, West Hollywood Aquatics.

Kaijaii Gomez Wick is a poet, amateur mathematician, and crochet enthusiast living on the East Coast of the US. They are mixed-race, ethnically quarter-Venezuelan, and are working to become fluent in

German. They appreciate cats, logic, mathematics, poetry, media, social improvement, and soft synthetic yarns. They are seeking a Bachelor's in German and Mathematics, and intend to become a poet as a career.

Kassiane A. Asasumasu is a vintage 1982 autistic & epileptic activist who has been active this whole century. K is also Hapa, though people like to forget that until they're called on being awful. Life goals include spending more time with cats and dragging neuroscience kicking & screaming into the neurodiversity paradigm.

Keara Farnan is an aspiring writer from Vancouver who primarily focuses on poetry, essays and short fiction. She has been a writer for the past eleven years, and only wishes to continue pursuing writing by publishing a novel, which she first starting writing at age fourteen. In Keara's spare time she likes to hangout with friends, play guitar and bake.

Kelly Bron Johnson (@KBronJohn, @OneQuarterMama) is a Barbadian-French-Canadian (and dual citizen) who lives in Montreal, QC, Canada with her husband and son. She is an Autistic self-advocate and is working to educate workplaces on accommodations for Autistic adults, as well as trying to create a community of female Autistics working to break down barriers to female diagnosis. She works full time as a social media manager and you can find her on the Internet at almost any hour.

//kiran foster is 148 centimetres of mixed-race intersex qtpoc survivor disabled sex worker migrant liminal everything. an indian/chinese singaporean, a prison abolitionist and intersex activist in the context of sex-based imprisonment in aotearoa new zealand, and a very unsuccessful undergrad, they spend most of their time turning tricks to fund the trans safehouse they run, looking after their cats, and trying to sell their abrasive autobio zines.

Kristy Y. loves to draw and write, loves good food (BBQ is their favorite!) and cares about human rights and social justice issues. In their spare time they practice writing short stories and they draw pictures.

Legacy Onaiwu is seven years old. She is sepia, which is a different type of brown that is reddish and a bit lighter than brown. She lives in America but her family comes from West Africa. Legacy wants you to know that God made her gifted and autistic. It's hard to explain, but she will try. God is the one who created the Heavens and the Earth. You can look for a book called the Bible to read and find out more or you can look the Bible up online. Gifted means you understand things faster and easier than other people do. Autistic is a disability that means you think, speak, and move differently than other people. Legacy's favorite colors are purple and pink and she likes Roblox and Minecraft, books, toys, and creating stories and videos on her iPad. When she grows up she wants to make movies and video games. Her best friend is her younger brother Lukas, who is also gifted and autistic.

leylah is 15 a hoh lesbian neutrois girl who is iranian and white (mixed race!). leyla loves cats and social justice as well as a good meme.

Louise Thundercloud-Hills is a 59 year old mixed African/ indigenous pre-american woman, who is a guerrilla poet as well as a frontline activist with many issues. She is proudly autistic & differently abled. The anarchists she works with all are Aspies. Louise is ethnically as well as racially mixed. Calling herself native American implies that she somewhat identifies as that nebulous term American, which she does not. Her nations are Lahota/Tsalagi/Siksika/Coast Salish. She is also tribal African Ibo.

Lucas Vizeu is an Animator/Writer from New York City. He is a first generation American born to Latin@ parents (Brazilian and Dominican), and identifies as Autistic and Afro Latino. Lucas grew up in Chelsea and Brazil, and went to Macaulay Honors College At Lehman College as a computer graphics and imaging major and a Japanese minor. Lucas has been involved in disability, immigration, and anti-gentrification activism in multiple capacities. He is an Alumni of the first Autism Campus Inclusion project by ASAN. He currently runs the animation startup Abstract Fish Co, making humorous and weird cartoons that people enjoy, apparently.

Maanu Alexander is 13 years old, autistic and a Nga Tahu tribe descendant of the Moriori People of New Zealand. He is also a deep feeling poet. Maanu sings Italian Opera and plays piano. Maanu studies Japanese at school. Maanu's best friend is Aboriginal. Maanu's father is Maori. Maanu's step-father is Maltese. Maanu's mother is 8th generation white Australian.

M.D. is a thirtysomething mixed/NDN autistic who has had more of a life than was predicted by many overpaid professional doom crows. Despite having attained a college degree and maintaining various interpersonal relationships, M. D. wonders if they have truly achieved whatever is necessary to be considered a Real Person (TM), or if any of it was worth it considering the additional hurdles that came afterward. You can probably find them somewhere in the Northeast, writing furiously under a blanket covered in cats.

Melis Leflef (Melissa Murphy). Born in 1977, to an Irish mother and Turkish father, Mel has been confused for much of her life. She is the autistic mother of at least one autistic child.

Mikael Lee is a mixed race neurodivergent queer person—an disability justice activist artist & practitioner of magic. They are currently working on a book series for neuroqueer youth and adults as well as Disability Access Community Funds. They live in Seattle with their cat Philippe Glitter.

Nathaniel Hagemaster (Agony Myers) grew up as a white boy in El Paso, Texas and had to be reminded that he was a Chicano man when he moved to Central Texas for college because his identity as a biracial queer with Asperger's has been confusing to everybody with himself included. He has been a Spanish and Neurotypical Language Learner for most of his life, but has not been successful with either of those languages as of yet. His drag persona, **Agony Myers**, is a more emotive but less filtered version of him who believes that she communicates neurotypicality and sexuality fluently when in reality, she dances like a drunk baby deer. Therefore, Agony is not a stage queen. The world of a stage performer expects Agony to be talented in that regard, and the nightlife expects her to like highly social environments. Agony, as something that sounds beautiful on the surface but means something terrible, is often repressed and only emerges during situations that call for a shallow and regimented performance on the face of something that is actually terrible—special occasions, Halloween, and in Nathaniel's creative work.

N.I. Nicholson is the founder and editor-in-chief of Barking Sycamores, a literary journal publishing art, poetry, creative nonfiction, and short fiction by neurodivergent creatives. He has also co-edited Autonomous Press' 2015 Spoon Knife Anthology and co-edited the Summer 2014 Issue of Red Wolf Journal. His work has appeared in NeuroQueer, GTK Creative Journal, Alphanumeric, and qarrtsiluni. While pursuing an MFA in Creative Writing from Ashland University, he also blogs at The Digital Hyperlexic (https://thedigitalhyperlexic.wordpress.com/). He lives in Central Ohio with his fiance, and is in the process of regenerating.

Nicole S. Xurd (Shalese Nicole Heard) is an African American Woman on the Autism Spectrum. Aside from advocacy interests, she also is a travel host, lifestyle coach, and public speaker for anything Autism and travel related- as an owner and founder of the website: AutisticTravelGoddess.com. In Shalese's spare time, she enjoys water activities, shopping, amusement parks, and more traveling.

Ondrea Marisa Robinson is a young African-American autistic woman who is a serious advocate for autistic rights and loves to learn about different ethnicities and backgrounds.

Pharaoh Inkabuss (Timotheus "T.J." Gordon) is an autistic self-advocate, poet/writer, and event photographer in the Chicagoland area. Pharaoh advocates for equal, fair access to special education, public & accessible housing for all, and fighting against police brutality among people of color with disabilities. He is also the creator of "The Black Autist" a blog where he discusses autism and disability acceptance among people of color, along with sharing his special interests (e.g., American football and My Little Pony: Friendship is Magic).

Pretty Eyes Ellis is a multiracial person of color who identifies as having Native heritage, living in the Pacific Northwest. Besides being a writer, they are an artist and social justice organizer/activist who is proud to serve the poc, black, trans and autistic communities. Their writing ranges from personal stories/memoir to sci-fi, speculative fiction and horror, and they enjoy being prolific with their pieces. They are a member of Lions Main Art Collective.

Rhonda G. is former academic, and current president and lead clinician at her agency that empowers people on the spectrum and those with other disabilities to lead lives they find meaningful. Like other Autistic parents, she self-diagnosed during her daughter's diagnostic process. She currently resides in the Midwest with her husband, two daughters, and grandson. Although not fully public with her autism diagnosis, she does find it incredibly helpful in her clinical work, and often divulges her status to many of the young people with whom she works. She is compelled by the work of neurodiversity activists, which has inspired her to create clinical practices that embrace neurodiversity and are based on the presumption of competence. She is developing empowerment-based methodologies of clinical practice that will directly challenge the medical-model of disability and the deficit-focused imperative that epitomizes the vast majority of therapeutic approaches for disabled populations. Her most meaningful professional moments are when families who have been demoralized by the medical and educational establishment about their child's potential, and who have little hope for or connection with their disabled child, are transformed into engaged parents who advocate for their child's right to inclusion into society.

Rikki Katherine Lee Moses, a resident of Washington, DC, is a 15 year old young lady on the autism spectrum. Rikki expressive and cognitive skills are delayed; however she expresses them in her love of singing and art. Her artistic talents are being supported by Art Works Now, Mt. Rainer MD. Rikki art allows people to see her talent without labels.

S. Henderson is a multiracial woman in Southern California, writing has been essential to her peace of mind. She is inspired by both of her grandmothers, who were outspoken women of color and were really the only family she had who loved her unconditionally.

Shane Bentley, known online mostly as **shaneisadragon**, is a biracial agender asexual and recent college graduate. These days, they spend most of their time drawing dragons, creating pride designs, and searching for and reading diverse queer literature. They also enjoy sewing (they get that from their Native grandma), baking, and lavishing attention on their cat, Ombra. They're just a bit annoyed that they can't pace while doing most of those things.

Shondolyn Gibson is a nerdy black woman who is obsessed with music, spiders and justice. She is also bisexual and autistic. She will lecture you about the cuteness of spiders and why you shouldn't be afraid of them.

Stephan B. is a dark-skinned Puerto-Rican male, he was diagnosed with Asperger's when he was young. He just submitted a couple things he had written before, because he really wants to help break down barriers for people with autism. He really loved the idea of anthologies and wanted to contribute.

Taiyo Brown lives in Minneapolis, Minnesota. His racial/ethnic heritage has African, European, and Indigenous (Métis) roots and his name is "sun" in Japanese.

Vivie Bella Papaleo is a young spectrum princess who started writing short stories like "K O O K Y M A K A" at age 3 and now at age 5 can read at a 5th grade level. She is a Pacific Islander and Sicilian New Yorker who lives part-time in Maui. She lives, laughs and loves aloha spirit. Her enlightened viewpoint in writing allows neurotypicals to step into her world and see it through her eyes. Autism make her wonderfully different. She is charismatic, creative, and witty. She enjoys playing piano and being in show business as well. She collects vintage dolls and drives an ATV jeep.

Yasmin Khoshnood is a junior at UIC, an aspiring disability rights activist and future language interpreter. She was born in Chicago, Illinois to immigrant parents. She is of bi-ethnic heritage, Iranian and Venezuelan. She loves to read, write, learn languages, and travel. She is president of the Neurodiversity Club at UIC. She's double majoring in Spanish and French with a minor in International Studies. She wants to become a language interpreter to help immigrants and people with disabilities.

Ylanne So is a geeky Asian disabled queer, policy wonk, and text-based roleplayer who is sometimes a disability rights advocate and sometimes a disability justice organizer. She speaks at least four languages somewhat passably, and sometimes manages to cook things without setting anything on fire. As both a roleplayer and solo fiction writer, Ylanne likes subverting the kinds of characters and stories considered "normal" or "default" by developing compelling non-normative characters in complex narratives. She prefers modern/realistic settings steeped in socio-political and historical context as well as darker, often grittier, storylines that emphasize the impact of both individual choices and systems of structural oppression on characters' relationships with each other.

Yvonne Christian (Uncommon Bostonian). After growing up in the suburban Maryland area just outside of Washington, DC, Yvonne went to Emerson College in Boston in 1982. After graduating in 1986, she decided to stay in Boston because she endured intense bullying when she was going to school in Maryland and her family did not understand why she was so different which led to a lot of arguments with her parents and older siblings. She struggled with pursuing a career in Mass Communications and ended doing jobs she did not like at all and were very stressful. In 2002, she found out why she was having problems with career and personal issues when she was diagnosed with Asperger's Syndrome and Non-Verbal Learning Disorder. Since then, she writes her two blogs, Outside In and Uncommon Bostonian, to help people realize that Autistic people are talented workers. She uses her pen name **Uncommon Bostonian** when she writes on her blogs. Yvonne is also an artist as well as a published author.

Project Team

Lydia X. Z. Brown (Autistic Hoya) is a gender/queer and transracially/transnationally adopted east asian autistic activist, writer, and speaker whose work has largely focused on violence against multiply-marginalized disabled people, especially institutionalization, incarceration, and policing. They have worked to advance transformative change through organizing in the streets, writing legislation, conducting anti-ableism workshops, testifying at regulatory and policy hearings, and disrupting institutional complacency everywhere from the academy to state agencies and the nonprofit-industrial complex. At present, Lydia serves as Chairperson of the Massachusetts Developmental Disabilities Council, board member of the Autism Women's Network, and founding board member of the Alliance for Citizen-Directed Services.

Most recently, Lydia designed and taught a course on critical disability theory, public policy, and intersectional social movements as a Visiting Lecturer at Tufts University's Experimental College, where they will be returning in 2017. Lydia is a past Patricia Morrissey Disability Policy Fellow at the Institute for Educational Leadership, where they focused on employment opportunities for people with significant disabilities, and past Holley Law Fellow at the National LGBTQ Task Force, where they focused on reproductive justice and disability rights policy issues. Additionally, Lydia worked for the Autistic Self Advocacy Network for several years as part of the national public policy team, where Lydia worked on various issues relating to criminal justice and disability, healthcare disparities and service delivery models, and research and employment disparities.

Lydia has been honored by the White House, the Washington Peace Center, the National Council on Independent Living, and the Disability Policy Consortium of Massachusetts. In 2015, Pacific Standard named Lydia a Top 30 Thinker under 30, and Mic named Lydia to its inaugural list of 50 impactful leaders, cultural influencers, and breakthrough innovators. Their work has been featured in various places, including *Religion, Disability, and Interpersonal Violence, Barriers & Belonging: Personal Narratives of Disability, The Asian American Literary Review, Feminist Perspectives on Orange is the New Black, Criptiques, Torture in Healthcare Settings, QDA: A Queer Disability Anthology, Films for the Feminist Classroom, Tikkun, Disability Intersections, Black Girl Dangerous, hardboiled magazine, POOR Magazine, The Washington Post; Sojourners, The Establishment,* Al Jazeera America, NBC News Asian America, HerCampus, AfterEllen, and Vice Broadly. Lydia is now a Public Interest Law Scholar at Northeastern University School of Law, where they co-founded the Disability Justice Caucus.

E. **Ashkenazy** (Project Manager & Editor) is passionate about Disability Rights and self-advocacy. She seeks to promote widespread understanding of the needs and rights of autistic individuals, especially females.

E.A. is the Community Council Chair for Academic Autistic Spectrum Partnership in Research and Education (AASPIRE). She is highly involved in Community Based Participatory Research (CBPR), and served on the Community Advisory Board for the Partnering with People with Developmental Disabilities to Address Violence Project via the University of Montana Rural Institute. E.A. has also served on community advisory boards addressing disability and healthcare, as well as disability and pregnancy.

E.A. worked as the Chapter & Outreach Coordinator and Project Manager for the Autistic Self Advocacy Network (ASAN) for several years and is also a former board member. She also served as a member of the Screening Identification and Assessment Committee for the Oregon Commission on Autism Spectrum Disorder.

E.A. has traveled to several states for public speaking events in order to deliver narrative-based presentations that focus on life on the autism spectrum. She has also attended multiple symposiums and conferences in order to facilitate focus groups. E.A. is fluent in American Sign Language (ASL) and is also a cochlear implant recipient. She lives in Portland, Oregon with her husband and three children and also happens to be the mother of an autistic son.

Morénike Giwa Onaiwu (Assistant Project Manager & Editor) often thinks in song lyrics; the one that felt most befitting to include in this publication was: "Say it loud...I'm Black and I'm proud!" from the late James Brown. Morénike is a community advocate, writer,

Christian, mom, and educator. American-born to immigrant parents, she feels that her role as a Black Autistic woman in a multicultural, multinational, neurodiverse, serodifferent family fuels her human rights advocacy.

Morénike has several years of program management experience and is involved in a myriad of social justice activism endeavors including HIV-related advocacy, disability rights, learning via technology, research, gender and racial justice, and promoting inclusion. She has also written for and/or been featured in numerous blogs, magazines, and other platforms.

Morénike's executive experience includes the Board of Directors for Autism Women's Network; AIDS Alliance for Women, Infants, Children & Youth; Families for Justice; and the Autistic Self-Advocacy Network; two consecutive terms as Co-Chair of the Global Community Advisory Board for the NIH Division of AIDS (DAIDS) funded AIDS Clinical Trials Group (which is the world's oldest and largest international community HIV clinical trials program); former Chair of the Houston Ryan White Planning Council and several leadership roles with NIH, HRSA and CDC funded entities as well as external programs.

Morénike, who has a Master's degree in Education (with a concentration in Special Education/Autism and Developmental Delays) and an undergraduate degree in International Relations, founded a national project advocating for family-centered HIV care and services. She was also one of the organizers of the national "Million Moms March" protesting police violence and racial profiling. Additionally, Morénike is the founder of Advocacy Without Borders (a grassroots education, community advocacy and self-empowerment initiative); an affiliate editor and contributing writer for the Intersected project; a regional representative for the Arc of Texas Developmental Disabilities/Public Policy's advisory council; and a contributing writer and editor for the "Respectfully Connected" global collaborative neurodiversity parenting blog.

Extremely active in online and social media advocacy and activism, Morénike has created several social justice projects, including the #JusticeForKayleb movement; the #SaveRyanWhitePartD Initiative; the No HIV+ Women & Children Left Behind Flashblog; the #EndVAWHIV (End Violence Against Women with HIV) Flashblog; and the #NotYourInfection: Mina's Law campaign (against HIV stigma). She was awarded the "Advocating for Another: Health Activist of the Year" 2014 WEGO Health Award and the "Service to the Self-Advocacy Movement" 2015 ASAN Award.

When not online, she maintains involvement in various groups, volunteers, writes, and presents at state, national, and international conferences.

Morénike loves travel, music, books, and Thai food. She considers herself a "life-long learner" who is constantly growing and changing, hopefully for the better! She considers her wonderful children, both biological and adopted, to be her greatest accomplishment.

What does
self advocacy
look like to
you?

ASAN is proud to support *All the Weight of Our Dreams: On Living Racialized Autism.*

Visit AutisticAdvocacy.org and tell us what self advocacy means to you.

ASAN
AUTISTIC SELF ADVOCACY NETWORK